ABOUT
THE
HOUSE

WITH HENRI DE MARNE

ABOUT
THE
HOUSE

WITH HENRI DE MARNE

How To Maintain, Repair, Upgrade,

and Enjoy Your Home

Upper Access, Inc., Book Publishers

Hinesburg, Vermont

www.upperaccess.com

Published by Upper Access, Inc., Book Publishers
87 Upper Access Road, Hinesburg, VT 05461
802-482-2988 • www.upperaccess.com

Book design and interior layout by Kitty Werner
Cover design by Johnson Design, Inc.

Photographs and other illustrations, unless otherwise identified, are by Henri de Marne, Kitty Werner, and Peter Werner. Copyrights are maintained by each photographer. For information, contact the publisher.

The copyright for the name of Mr. de Marne's newspaper column, *First Aid for the Ailing House*, is held by United Feature Syndicate. Trade names and brand names of products and services referred to throughout this book are the property of their respective owners.

ISBN: 978-0-942679-30-4
(ISBN 10: 0-942679-30-X)

Library of Congress Cataloging-in-Publication Data

De Marne, Henri.
  About the house with Henri de Marne : how to maintain, repair, upgrade, and enjoy your home.
    p. cm.
  Selections from the author's newspaper column First aid for the ailing house.
  Includes bibliographical references and index.
  ISBN 0-942679-30-X (alk. paper)
  1. Dwellings–Maintenance and repair–Miscellanea. 2. Dwellings–Remodeling–Miscellanea. I. Title.
  TH4817.3.D387 2007
  643.7–dc22   2006026646

Printed on acid-free paper in the United States of America
07   1 2 3 4 5 6 7 8 9 10

Acknowledgments

My deepest gratitude goes to my daughter, Kitty de Marne Werner, herself author of *The Savvy Woman's Guide™ to Owning a Home*, for putting this book together. It would not have happened without her dedication and hard work, and her skills as an editor, writer and computer whiz. Her experience as an editor of several books for Random House in the past, and her on-going work in the design, typesetting and packaging of a number of books for other publishers, including several in *The Savvy Woman's Guide™* series, have made her eminently qualified for the monumental work this has been.

My thanks also to my publisher, Steve Carlson, for his encouragement and belief in this work, and the tremendous amount of energy he put into it.

My gratitude to United Media in New York, and the several editors who have worked with me for 27 years, for a most pleasant association and their permission to put my columns in book form.

My thanks also to the many expert friends I have made over the 33 years I have been writing my columns, friends who have helped me answer the myriad questions I have received from readers that even my 50 years in the construction industry were not enough to answer as they should be. They are too many to name them all, but I certainly appreciate every one of them more than I can say.

My deepest gratitude goes to my wife, Susan, whose advice, unfailing support and encouragement have been invaluable.

Dedication

This book is dedicated to my mother and father who, each in her and his own way, have taught me many valuable lessons: the value of hard work, education, honesty and integrity, and the respect of others.

It is also dedicated to Muriel, the mother of our three accomplished children, who has taught me much about writing, editing and, most importantly, about the daily courage of doing what needs to be done.

And to my wife, Susan, who has shared my life for the last 11 years, guided me and encouraged me through this work, and, in the past year, own incredible courage under very difficult and unplanned circumstances.

To all four of them, my enduring love, respect and appreciation for what they have meant, and still mean, to me.

Contents

Introduction

This book is the result of 32 years of conversations with readers throughout the U.S. and Canada, in more than 4,500 newspaper columns. Some of the readers are competent do-it-yourselfers, while many others seek to generally understand a problem in order to hire the best contractor to fix it—or to determine whether it's even worth fixing.

Some of the questions are extremely serious and come up again and again—covering important issues such as the damage caused by improper grading around a foundation, inadequate vapor barriers, incorrect venting, or termites and other pests. Some readers have asked for general advice, such as the best choices for heating and cooling or the longest-lasting siding materials. Others have specific questions, such as how to remove mirror tiles that are glued to a wall or how to get rid of moss or mold on the north side of a roof.

It sometimes seems like every possible issue involving houses has been covered from every angle, yet readers continue to provide me with fresh material to write about every week. Houses are complex systems, so there are always new issues and new angles to discuss. That's what makes my job as a columnist enjoyable and challenging.

But a book has one significant advantage over a newspaper column—it can combine a lot of information that is readily available at the time it's needed. When your plaster ceiling suddenly starts sagging, or your radiator mysteriously stops heating up, or you find specks all over your aluminum siding that you can't wash off, you may not remember the information from the last time you read about it in the newspaper. Now, you can easily look up the answers whenever you need them.

Regardless of whether you have been a regular reader of my column, I hope you'll enjoy browsing through the book to learn more about the house you live in, and that you'll keep it handy as a reference for repairs, maintenance, and improvements.

1 Foundations, Basements, Crawl Spaces

Foundations take many forms, including full basements, piers, slabs, and crawl spaces. They need to be strong enough to hold up the structure, built on solid ground to avoid sinking or shifting, and protected from frost, soil and water pressure. They should be constructed in ways that help keep the house comfortable, and, when possible, provide extra space for living and for storage.

Much can go wrong with a foundation. But as you read through this chapter, you'll see that similar problems keep repeating themselves: the foundation backfill is improperly done; the soil around a foundation is not properly graded or drained; the concrete is not properly cured; incorrect methods and materials are used for insulating, painting, and other finish work. Repetition is necessary because these problems manifest themselves in many ways.

Foundations for New Houses and Additions

The best time to avoid problems with foundations is while they are built. It's much easier and less expensive to avoid moisture problems, in particular, with proper design than it is to fix them later. And if mistakes are made, it's probably easiest to fix them (and perhaps to hold the contractor accountable) when the house is new. The most common serious mistakes are improper backfilling of the excavation, including provisions for a working and long-lasting drainage system and grading of the soil—which should always slope away from the house. There are also unique problems with new foundations. They include taking precautions for proper curing of poured concrete walls or choosing the right size concrete blocks for the depth of the excavation (too often, 8-inch blocks are used for foundation walls deeper than 5 feet). Once built, other problems are related to moisture in the concrete walls and floor of a basement, which may take as much as two years to dry and can cause considerable moisture problems in the living quarters.

Design of a walk-out basement

Q. I am building a house this summer. It will have a walk-out basement, which will be finished with living space. Do both sides of the concrete foundation need to be insulated? Should footing drains be on the inside and outside of the footings? What is the sequence of materials for the drain: Does the fabric go down, then the stones, the drain pipe and sand? What kind of fill do I need to backfill with to make sure my concrete walls don't crack? What is the ideal distance from the top of the concrete wall to grade? Do I need at least 4 feet of concrete below grade?

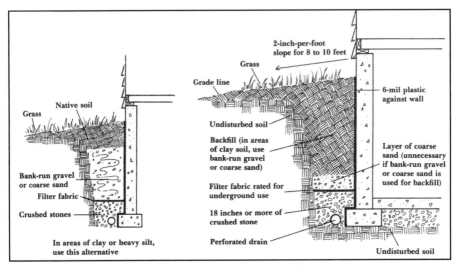

Cross section of a correctly installed perimeter drain and finish grade

A. Let's start at the beginning. Frost walls should be below the frost line of the area where you are building. The recommended practice in your climate (Northeastern U.S.) is to have frost walls a minimum of 4 feet deep below grade. It is best to have about 1 foot of the foundation above final grade but you must plan for the final grade to slope away from the house by 2 inches per horizontal foot. Concrete walls can be insulated from the outside or the inside; there is no need to do both.

Drain pipe should be installed next to the footings and not on top of them. The best procedure is to lay a 4-foot-wide band of geotextile (filter) fabric against the excavation wall (pin it with 16-penny nails) and place 2 inches of egg-size stones in the bottom of the trench. (If stones are expensive or hard to get in your area and recycled rubber tire chunks are available, they are a better alternative anyway.)

Now lay perforated pipe, holes down, over the stones; place at least another foot (preferably 18" or more) of stones over the pipe; fold the fabric over the stones bringing it up against the foundation walls and tape it to them to hold it in place until further backfilling.

Complete the backfilling with coarse sand or bank-run gravel to within a foot of what has been determined as the finish grade to ensure good drainage and protection against frost pressure. Complete the grading with topsoil. The only time it is advisable to install footing drains inside the foundation as well is if there is a seasonal high water table or very heavy soil.

Poured concrete *vs.* blocks

Q. I am going to have a house built this summer and would like to know which type of foundation is best—poured concrete or blocks?

A. Either type is fine as long as it is properly sized. For instance, if a foundation is going to be deeper than 5 feet into the ground, 12-inch blocks should be used. You may have to insist on it, as many masons simply use 8-inch blocks.

Poured concrete foundation walls are generally 8 inches thick unless special conditions dictate that they be thicker. Steel reinforcement depends on the depth of the foundation, the soil pressure it has to bear, and other local conditions.

The most important thing is the backfill of the excavation against the foundation. It should never be done with heavy soils. A perimeter drain should be installed next to the footings; the crushed stones surrounding the drain pipe should be protected from silt with a geotextile fabric and the trench filled with coarse material. Heavy native soil should only be used to top it off and should slope away from the foundation.

Preparing a slab

Q. We plan on building our raised-ranch house in the near future and would like to know the proper method of preparing for the pour of the lower-level concrete slab. Should sand be used as a base and be tamped before the slab is poured? Should a 6-mil plastic sheet be placed over the sand? How thick should the slab be? Should an interior perimeter drain be used?

A. Egg-sized crushed stones (or if available in your area, chopped tires) should be used instead of sand in order to promote lateral drainage and prevent capillary attraction, two features that sand does not provide. The stone bed should be a minimum of 4 inches and preferably thicker; it should be at least flush with the top of the footings, which are usually 8 inches thick.

The thickness of the stone bed will then be determined by the method of preparing for the footings which may be dug into the bottom of the excavation or formed on top of it (4 inches of stones are okay in the former but 8 inches should be used in the latter case). A 6-mil plastic vapor retarder should be placed over the stone bed and an inch of crusher-run (a by-product of stone crushing) spread over the plastic to promote proper drainage of the concrete as it cures. Failure to do this may result in dusting of the concrete later. The slab need not be thicker than 4 inches. In lieu of crusher run, 1-inch extruded polystyrene can be used, providing slab insulation as well.

Whether you need an interior perimeter drain, in addition to an exterior one, is determined by the wetness of the site, such as a seasonal high water table.

Basement *vs.* crawl space

Q. Would we be better off having a basement built under our eventual modular home or a crawl space at a much lower cost?

A. Basements are always useful and a lot more convenient for access to mechanical systems that are often relegated to crawl spaces, where they are harder to ser-

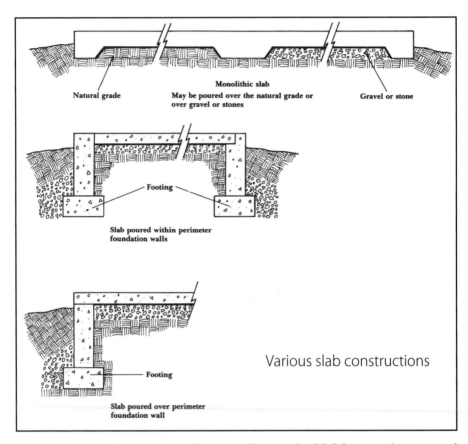

Natural grade

Monolithic slab
May be poured over the natural grade or
over gravel or stones

Gravel or stone

Footing

Slab poured within perimeter
foundation walls

Various slab constructions

Footing

Slab poured over perimeter
foundation wall

vice or maintain. Basements are also generally more healthful, as crawl spaces tend to become damp unless they are properly built.

Basements can also be used for storage or workshops and can be finished as living quarters if the family expands, as long as windows meet the emergency exit code. You will pay more now but will probably find the house more saleable, and may recover more than the difference in cost between a basement and a crawl space.

Blocks *vs.* wood for exposed basement wall

Q. We will be building a ranch house with an exposed basement. We plan on finishing the basement later and having a sliding patio door and a window installed.

Would the exposed basement walls be better built of blocks or wood? Will the weight of the house cause the wood wall to settle? What about cost differences?

A. Any walls out of the ground are better built of standard framing construction because it allows for better insulation. In your case, it will also make it easier to install the patio door and window later on. Their rough openings should be framed in now to make it even easier and cheaper to do later.

The weight of the house should not cause the wood wall to settle if the foundation supporting it is adequate. There is likely to be minimum shrinkage of the wood members as they dry. You should use 6-inch studs anyway to provide better insulation.

Adding to an existing slab

Q. I plan to add another room to double the size of our cabin up north. It is built on a 4-inch floating concrete slab. Should we first pour a footing and then pour the floor? Or should we simply pour another 4-inch floating slab to match the existing one? And, should the two be tied together?

A. It's usually best to use the same construction technique as exists, if it has proved successful. Be sure that you also match what's below the slab, *i.e.*, the same thickness of crushed stones or whatever was used.

Yes, the two should be tied together by drilling holes 2 feet on center half way down in the edge of the existing slab where the two will join and tapping ½-inch reinforcing rods at least 6 inches in and sticking out 6 inches also. When the new slab is poured, the two will be bonded.

Another way is to undercut 6 inches of the existing slab and fill it with concrete as the new slab is poured.

Planter next to foundation

Q. Can a planter made with pressure-treated logs be used around the foundation for raising the grade, a procedure you have recommended often as necessary to keep a basement dry?

A. No way! I recommend sloping the ground *away* from the foundation. All you would be doing by building a planter would be creating a higher flat flower bed. The only time a raised planter is recommended is if the footings are not deep enough and subject to frost heave. This adds protection, but the planter should be under a broad overhang to keep it from getting wet.

Plastic on top of soil

Q. I have removed flower beds against the house and plan to replace them with decorative chips after raising the grade so it slopes away from the foundation. What's the best soil to use, how steep should the grade be, and can plastic be laid on top of the soil and be covered with the chips to prevent weeds from growing?

A. I usually recommend a 2-inch slope per foot extending a minimum of 4 to 6 feet away from the foundation to prevent water pockets on grade, then the slope can flatten out. The best ground cover is grass. The type of soil, in your case, doesn't matter since it will be covered with plastic. Plastic will not just prevent weeds, but also prevent percolation.

Checking the grade

Q. I remember reading in your column about using a 2×4 to check the grade around the house for proper drainage. That is all I remember. Could you please fill in the blanks?

A. Try to use a full-length, 8-foot 2×4. If you place it on the ground perpendicularly to the foundation, it will tell you instantly if the grade is negative (leans toward the house), flat (also undesirable), or positive (slopes away from the house). Place a level on the board, if you're in doubt.

It is quite difficult to eyeball for proper grade with mulch, plantings, and even grass against and near the foundation. Obviously, any flat or negative grade is best corrected to encourage water to flow away from the foundation.

Foundation Repair

Foundations are under constant pressure from the earth that surrounds them, which can change with the seasons. Sometimes, even tough materials and structures wear out. Failure to notice and address these issues early on can result in serious damage to a house.

Basement walls bowing inward

Q. Our 30-year-old home was built on a cinderblock foundation. Three years ago, while we were adding two rooms to the house, one of the severely bowed walls was completely straightened out. Of the three remaining block walls, two have a slight bowing involving only about five blocks in the middle of the wall while the third one has a more severe problem involving about 15 blocks in the middle of the wall, beginning at about four blocks up from the cellar floor.

I feel if it took 30 years for the wall to move this far and it hasn't caused any apparent damage inside to the plaster or the outside of the house, it may not be worth undertaking the major task of digging out and trying to get the blocks back into place. Any suggestions?

A. Walls bowing inward do so because of frost or fluid pressure against them. The severity of the bowing and its location have a lot to do with whether or not remedial action should be taken.

A slight bowing may be ignored but should be watched carefully. However, if the wall is bowing significantly, *i.e.*, it shows horizontal separations between the block of ¼ inch or more, or vertical displacement exceeding 1 inch or so, something should be done about it, particularly if it happens to be supporting the weight of the floor joists and the roof.

Gable walls, for instance, are often self-supporting whereas the front and back walls of a house usually support the floors and roof. The fact that it took 30 years to get to that point is no assurance that the walls won't jackknife suddenly and bring about the collapse of the building.

There are several ways to proceed to repair the problem:

- As a precaution, support the first-floor joists near the damaged bearing wall sufficiently to carry the weight of the house bearing on that wall. Excavate carefully outside and attempt to bring the walls back into line (or replace them). Install a perimeter drain built of a perforated plastic pipe buried in an egg-sized crushed stone (1½-inch diameter) bed covered with a geotextile fabric filter. Backfill with coarse sand or bank-run gravel to near original grade. Finish the grade with native soil sloping away from the house no less than 2 inches per foot for as far away as possible. Plant grass and avoid flower beds against the foundation. The perforated pipe should be connected to a solid pipe that should come out to daylight down a bank or connect to a sump pump inside the basement.
- Reshape the grade around the house, including all appurtenances, such as walks, patios, stoops, etc., so that water drains away as indicated in the paragraph above, and build a new concrete-block wall against the severely bowed walls in the basement. This is done by drilling holes in the concrete slab every foot to insert ½-inch reinforcing steel rods in it, followed by setting 12-inch blocks over the rods, and filling the spaces between the existing wall and the new wall as well as the cores within the blocks, with pea-gravel concrete as the wall is going up. Where the existing wall is a bearing wall, the new wall must also be bearing and must be locked in at its top with a steel angle iron fastened to the underside of the floor joist with lag screws to prevent it from being pushed out. This is cheaper than doing the job from the outside, particularly if the old walls must be rebuilt. A competent masonry contractor can easily handle it.
- Have a house mover support the house, remove all the damaged walls and replace them with reinforced concrete walls. The same instructions regarding footing drains, backfilling and final grading apply.
- Call in a specialist in this type of repair who will place a steel plate against the bowed wall. In the center of this plate, there is a steel rod that goes through the wall and is anchored below grade outside to a "dead man" some distance away. A nut on the rod is tightened until the bowed wall is straightened out. The Grip-Tite wall anchor system is available nationally.

Fluid pressure, from a wet clay or silt soil, caused this foundation wall to crack and bow inward. Not only has it cracked vertically, but the lines of block have shifted as well.

Sinking of slab outside of foundation wall

Q. Years ago, I poured a 2×6-foot concrete slab against a part of the foundation wall of my 50-some-year-old house to direct water away from it. At that time, it was sloping away from the foundation but, now, it has dropped about 3 inches and water leaks down the side of the basement wall finished as part of a rec room. Does this indicate damage to the basement wall? Should I take down the rec room wall?

A. The first thing you should do is to raise this slab back so it slopes away from the foundation again. A contractor should have little trouble doing that. The hollow beneath it should be packed solid with dirt tamped down. If you prefer, you can form and pour another slab over this one to reinstate the slope.

However, if your sketch is correct, I think that the original slab dropped because the dirt beneath it was puddled and compacted by the water from the downspout you show there. If this is correct, you should raise the grade to slope away, put a concrete splashblock under the downspout shoe, and make sure that the water is directed away or you may get a repeat.

Unless the rec room wall is insulated with mineral fiber, there should be little, if any, damage; it will dry in time. And even if there is fiberglass insulation, since it is not absorbent, the water should run down the fibers to the bottom of the wall. Just look for signs of progressive deterioration before you tear down the rec room wall. You may not need to do anything with the wall.

A long crack on a block wall

Q. One of our basement block walls developed a horizontal crack and a slight bow along its full length. The soil around here is heavy clay, so we had it removed and replaced top to bottom with pea stones to relieve the pressure.

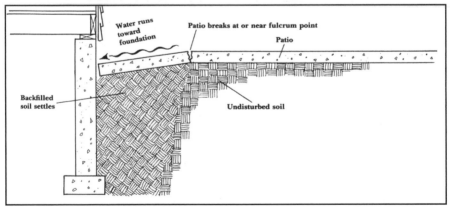

Backfill against a foundation wall can settle, causing problems. In this case, the patio slab has cracked, and water runs toward the foundation where it can cause substantial damage.

The wall is no longer bowed but the crack comes and goes, disappearing in summer and reappearing in winter. Our contractor wants to install seven steel beams but the insurance inspector says they are not needed.

A. Unless there is a way for water that may build up in the pea-stone backfill to drain away, it can freeze and put pressure on the wall. It is also possible that the clay is still pushing against the stones as it expands in winter. Try covering the pea stones with a geotextile fabric topped with a minimum of 1 inch of coarse sand. Add topsoil sloping away from the house for several feet if there is room to add it between the present grade and the siding, respecting the local building code requirements for clearance.

Depending on how you can accomplish that, you may be able to keep the clay drier and reduce the pressure it exerts on the block wall.

The beams do not appear to be necessary and would probably not help. Soil and frost pressures are irresistible; the blocks are likely to bow between the beams.

Reinforcing a block wall

Q. The blocks of the basement walls of my 30-year-old house are starting to be pushed in. I was told that I could use steel rods and concrete in the hollow of the blocks about every 4 feet to reinforce the walls. Is this safe? Or will it put a lot of pressure on the footings?

A. Whoever told you that has little practical and technical knowledge. How do you insert the rods and pour the concrete without tearing the walls apart? If the buckling is minor, it may not need any repairs but it should be watched and the size of the cracks measured several times a year to see if there is further movement.

But what you must do is correct any grade problems around the house foundation that may hold or trap water and allow it to percolate in the soil and freeze,

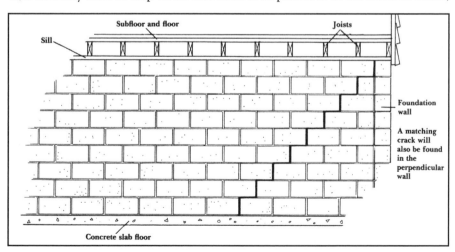

Cracks may run directly through masonry units.

exercising pressure on the walls and causing them to crack and buckle. That goes not only for the soil but also for any structure such as patio, walk, stoop, driveway, etc., that does not shed water away from the house.

One problem area I see so often in my inspections is sunken ground under decks and porches that trap water. These hollows should be filled, however difficult it may be. Correcting all these problems so water flows away instead of soaking the soil should relieve the pressure exercised on the walls by wet soil freezing and expanding.

However, if the buckling is severe enough to warrant corrective action in order to prevent collapse of the affected walls, the least expensive way to achieve this is to build another wall in front of each of them.

Holes are drilled in the concrete slab every foot to receive ½-inch re-rods, 12-inch hollow blocks are threaded over the rods, concrete is poured in the block cavities and between the old and the new walls as the walls go up and the new walls are pinned to the floor framing at the top with steel lintels. A competent mason should know how to do it. Don't worry about the pressure on the footings.

Repairing a long crack in the wall

Q. Our house was built 45 years ago. About 20 years ago, a horizontal crack appeared on the 10-inch-thick concrete block basement walls. It runs for about 35 feet, six courses from the floor, and varies seasonally from ¹⁄₁₆-inch to ⁵⁄₁₆-inch, depending on the wet and dry spells.

The basement and wall remain completely dry. I want to caulk this crack with a waterproof compound; what should I use?

A. Don't! This would prevent it from closing, if you did it when the crack is widest, and it would open right up if you did it when it is at its narrowest.

What you should do is to prevent the soil from applying so much fluid pressure on the wall. Look for low areas against the foundation and add clean dirt so the grade ends up by sloping away at the desired rate of 2 inches per horizontal foot for as far back as 6 to 8 feet, if there is enough foundation wall showing to permit it. Dirt must not contact wood, and most building codes generally require that dirt be kept 8 inches away from it.

Plant grass; do not mulch. This will move water away from the foundation and keep the deep soil drier, reducing the fluid pressure of wet earth against the wall.

Repairing cracks with epoxy

Q. I have two cracks in my basement walls through which water seeps when it rains. I have three estimates to repair the cracks. Two of them will put epoxy in the cracks from the inside. The third company said they would also put epoxy in the crack by the window next to the patio on the east side but they would excavate outside to the footing and apply silicone mastic in the crack in the front or north wall. They would also chip out that crack inside every 2 inches and inject epoxy in it.

Snow is melting down under the deck to the foundation. The slope is toward the foundation, instead of sloping away from the foundation at a rate of 2 inches per foot. This causes water to back up against the foundation and crack it.

All three prices are in the same range. I am very confused as to which one I should choose. Can you advise me?

A. You didn't say, but I will assume that your foundation is poured concrete.

Before considering spending any sizable sum on the epoxy injections, I would suggest you go over the grade outside your house. Fill any depressions, correct any areas that either collect water or direct it toward the house.

Check the gutters and downspouts to make sure they are free-flowing and that all discharge from the downspouts is collected into a splashblock or pipe extension and flows away from the foundation. Raise the grade where needed so it slopes away from the house but keep soil at least 8 inches from any wood.

If your patio slopes toward the foundation, have it resloped so water drains away. This can be done with a new concrete topping, bricks or flagstones.

It is always best to take care of these conditions first; they are usually all responsible for basement leakage. You may find it stops the leakage and relieves pressure on the basement walls.

However, if you choose to go ahead with the crack filling, I would select the one who plans on excavating and filling the cracks outside and injecting inside. It sounds like a more thorough approach for the same price.

Bricking up door in wall

Q. There is an old well room next to the house with a small access door in the basement block wall. We want to seal the wall and fill in the well from outside.

Will bricking in the opening make the wall strong enough to resist the pressure of the fill, and what type of fill should we use?

A. There should be no problem with the bricked-up access hole if you build it the full-depth of the block wall and the opening is bricked tightly on all four sides. Let the mortar set for a few days. Fill the well hole with any coarse material available.

I presume there is a cover outside over this well room and that the fill will not be subjected to wetting.

Rebuilding an old fieldstone foundation

Q. My old two-family house is in good, sound condition except for the cellar walls, which are constructed of fieldstones. These walls have deteriorated and are crumbling badly both inside and out. A contractor fixed them two years ago but they have cracked again. He has patched them up but says they were too pulverized for further repairs.

Large chunks fell out last winter and many cracks developed. I don't want to face the expense of another contractor and have the same thing happen again. Can you advise?

A. A house represents a considerable investment; its roof and foundation are the most important systems ensuring its longevity. From what you describe, I would recommend that you have the foundation redone. This can be done in one of several ways:

- The house can be jacked up and supported on large timbers and cribbing while the old foundation is removed and a new one put in. Properly done, this can give you a dry concrete basement with more headroom and add considerable value to the house.
- Another method is to replace the old walls piecemeal in sections. This does not require jacking up the house but it must be done by someone experienced in this process.
- A third option is to build new block walls against the old foundation from inside. A competent contractor can advise you which is best in your circumstances.

Sealing the sill

Q. My city home has a poured-concrete basement. There is a plastic vapor barrier between the top of the concrete and the sill.

My cottage basement was built of concrete blocks and the builder did not put a vapor barrier on the top of the block wall. Should there be one? If so, can I use Styrofoam boards instead of plastic when I raise the cottage? I feel this would seal some gaps between the blocks and the sill.

A. Sill sealers are used to stop air infiltration between the masonry foundation and the wood sill of the house, which is known as the mud sill because it used to be embedded in a mortar bed to level out irregularities in the top of the foundation. The energy crisis of the early '70s made us aware of the amount of air infiltration, and we began to use sill sealers made of cellulose between two thin plastic strips or fiberglass rolls. Later, better materials were developed that did not absorb water as the previous ones did.

You certainly could install one when your cottage is raised, but I hope you are not raising it just for that. If the cottage is for summer use and not heated in the winter, air infiltration at the sill should not be a problem. In any case, the appropriate product to use is one of the synthetic plastic sill sealers now on the market. Do not use rigid insulation board, as it would be crushed by the weight of the building.

A shifting slab

Q. Our house is built on a concrete slab. It keeps shifting, which causes cracks in the wall and ceiling gypsum board. It also affects the functioning of doors and windows. The cracks have been repaired but they come back. What can we do to correct this problem permanently?

A. A shifting house with the problems you describe indicates that the foundation is on unstable ground, or is not deep enough to be unaffected by seasonal temperature and moisture changes.

A permanent solution may be expensive, depending on what is causing the problem, and would probably require building a deeper foundation under the perimeter of the slab.

Judging from the temperature tables of your area (Oklahoma), the frost line may require footings approximately 2 feet deep. If the slab was poured monolithically with integral footings, they may not be deep enough. The moisture content and type of the soil under and around the house also have some bearing on the situation.

Talk to a structural engineer who is familiar with local conditions to determine whether deeper footings are called for or whether simply installing vertical extruded polystyrene rigid insulation around the perimeter of the slab and buried a foot or two below grade would be sufficient. The insulation exposed above grade will have to be covered with an approved protective coating and flashed to the siding.

An alternative used successfully is to bury a 4-foot-wide strip of 2-inch-thick extruded polystyrene rigid insulation on a slant, starting at the base of the slab's edge (which should be insulated as described above). Cover the insulation with soil and plant shallow-rooted plants, or spread shredded tire rubber mulch. This will stop frost penetration and keep the ground below the insulation frost-free.

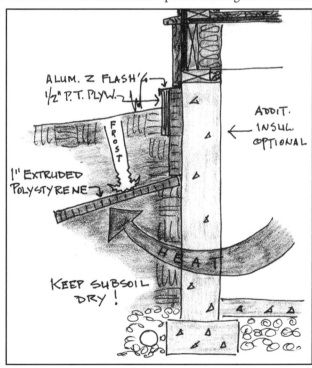

Retrofitting a frost wall with polystyrene.

Cracks in the corner of this foundation are caused by a frost-wall that isn't deep enough to prevent the frost from shifting the foundation.

Determining whether cracks are a serious problem

Q. Our one-story, three-bedroom home is about 42 years old. It has a poured foundation. There are two cracks in the foundation, one on the east wall and the other on the north wall. Are they serious? What can we do about them?

A. Foundation cracks can be serious, but most are not. Since I cannot determine whether or not your cracks are serious at this distance and with the amount of information I have, you should have an experienced and competent home inspector or a structural engineer look at it.

The size and shape of the cracks, the composition of the soil, and the grade around the house, etc., are all factors that determine whether the cracks can simply be ignored, should be filled with cement or caulked, or if more drastic measures must be taken.

Foundation cracks can also admit radon gas, if you are in an area that is prone to this type of radiation from the soil and rocks. It's a serious human health hazard. Your state health department may offer testing kits.

Deteriorating lally columns

Q. The two lally columns in our cellar, supporting the main beam, are 35 years old. In the last few years, rusty water seems to come out of several holes that have developed in the columns. Is this what is known as rising damp? Does this present a hazard? Should I have them replaced?

A. Dampness is finding its way inside the columns. It may be that they are in contact with wet soil or that water has gotten into them from a repeatedly wet cellar. Whatever the cause of the rusting, the fact that the columns have holes, and rusty water is coming out of them, tells you that they have weakened considerably. You should not wait to take corrective action before they start crumbling and the structure above them starts to sag.

You haven't mentioned whether there is a concrete floor, and whether the columns are encased in it. This makes a difference in the solution I will suggest. If there is a concrete floor, the simplest thing to do is to place a 4×4-inch pressure-treated post next to each column. Measure and cut the post exactly, jack (lift) the beam up about ⅛-inch, set the post in place, and lower the beam to put pressure on the new post.

Or, you can encase the columns with four pieces of 2×6-inch pressure-treated lumber, also installed with some pressure as detailed above.

If there is no slab, or the lally columns are sitting on it, and the columns are easy to remove, you may choose to support the beam while replacing the original columns with new ones.

Pressure-treated posts as a foundation

Q. I'm considering buying a camp on a lake shore and turning it into a year-round retirement residence but I am concerned about the construction. It's built on pressure-treated posts which the present owner says are at least 5 feet in the ground and resting on large stones.

The building itself is only 6 inches above the ground so there is no space to crawl under. Is there a problem with this type of foundation? Will it last a long time?

A. If properly set in the ground as deeply as you were told and on stones large enough to offer adequate bearing on the soil on which the stones are resting, you should be all right. Probably, if on a natural lake shore, the ground is gravely, which should offer good bearing and drainage.

Try to find out if the posts were treated to a retention of 0.40 pound per cubic foot of CCA (chromated copper arsenate). If the owner can tell you where they were purchased, the supplier should be able to tell you if they stock only pressure treated lumber marked AWPB LP-22, which is for wood in contact with ground or water. If they only meet AWPB LP-2 standard, or 0.23 lb./cubic foot of CCA, that's not good enough for in-ground installation.

Check inside the camp for settlement by looking at doors and windows: do they all open and close easily; is there sizeable variation in the reveal between doors and jamb when doors are closed; are the floors even?

Also look under the camp with a strong flashlight and check for the condition of the floor joists: Do they look healthy, or has the wood darkened substantially, and is there mold growing on it? In any event, the earth under the cottage should be covered with plastic to reduce moisture unless there is no skirting to prevent total ventilation.

Wooden basements

Q. We are looking into purchasing our first home and have found one we like, but it has a wooden basement. How durable are they? What should we check for and how safe is breathing the vapors?

The house is approximately 10 years old and the basement is unfinished with no windows. We'd like to turn it into a recreation area.

A. Pressure-treated foundations have been in use for many years in the U.S. and Canada. Properly built, they should be fine.

Since the house is 10 years old, you can easily determine whether the walls are straight horizontally and vertically (not showing signs of bowing).

There should be no vapors to worry about. Fiberglass insulation can be used to fill the stud spaces, a plastic vapor retarder installed over it, and gypsum board applied over the studs. Windows can easily be cut in the sections of foundation that are above grade.

Mortar deteriorating in a brick foundation

Q. Some of the mortar of the foundation of our 91-year-old house is soft and sifting out. The foundation is not cracked nor is it buckling or leaning, but some of the bricks were loose before I tuckpointed them. How can we decide if the foundation needs to be replaced?

A. I doubt very much if the entire foundation needs to be replaced since you have not noticed any problem; it probably needs only to be repointed, and that may need to be done in sections so as not to weaken it. Your safest bet is to call in an experienced mason to investigate and advise. Do it soon, before any more serious damage occurs.

Concrete layer crumbling from block foundation

Q. My home is 25 to 30 years old. The foundation is built with cinder blocks with a layer of concrete over the outside. This layer is coming off. What would be the best method of repairing it to avoid future problems?

A. All loose cement parging covering the blocks should be removed. You can purchase a mix of cement and sand in bags in hardware or building supply houses and mix it with water according to directions on the bag. It would also be wise to add to the mix a vinyl additive that increases the bonding to the substrate. You will have to wet the surfaces to be treated and trowel the mix on.

Unless you are pretty good at these repairs, you may be wiser to hire a mason. A poor job would devalue your house as it is very visible and it might not last long.

Repairing and finishing an older stone foundation

Q. The foundation stones of our circa 1900 house were cemented in, but the cement has turned to sand and dust and is sifting down to the basement floor. Is it possible to replace the cement and seal the rock walls?

I would like to finish off the basement to enhance the space and save energy, but I've heard conflicting arguments about sealing off rock foundations from the heat of the house. Foam panels on the outside of the foundation walls are a future goal but not for several years.

A. Yes, the old mortar can be removed by scratching it out with an old screwdriver or masonry chisel. But be careful not to remove too much of it, as this might cause the stones to shift. Clean the joints with a soft brush, make a stiff mix with a pre-mixed mortar such as Sakrete, wet the joints and stones to be re-cemented according to directions on the bag, and point them up.

Then coat the stones and mortar joints with Masonry Lusta to seal them. You may want to hire a mason to do this as it sounds as though you have a major job on your hands, and it would help to hire someone experienced in this work. It's often cheaper than correcting mistakes later.

It is not safe to insulate a foundation any deeper than 2 feet below grade if the soil against it is clay, if you're not sure there's a footing drain that's working, and if the grade and all appurtenances to the house are not sloping away from the foundation to shed water away from it and not toward it.

Crumbling concrete blocks

Q. The cement blocks in one wall of our foundation are deteriorating and crumbling away little by little. This is the wall common with the attached garage and it seems the deterioration is caused by salt that has seeped into the wall over time. The house is 30 years old. We have been unable to locate anyone who has seen this problem before or has any idea how to fix it. Any suggestions?

A. Your diagnosis is correct; salt brought in by the cars and running off toward the affected wall is responsible. I have seen this problem in houses where the garage slab was not properly pitched to the doorway but tilted toward the house wall. The area of the slab near the affected wall, and the bottom of the wall, should be thoroughly cleaned with a solution of TSP-PF or equivalent strong detergent, rinsed, and allowed to dry completely.

Have a mason build a cove along the joint of the slab and the wall with Portland cement mixed with an additive that promotes bonding. The cove should be sealed

Crumbling block damaged by moisture.

to protect it from salt damage. The purpose of this cove is to keep salt water from reaching the wall and causing further deterioration. This is less expensive than pouring a concrete cap over the slab to establish the desired drainage.

The mason should also clean and wire-brush the damaged blocks in the basement, and coat them with the same mixture to repair them.

Q. Our 22-year-old one-story house sits on a concrete-block foundation. The faces of several of the blocks have crumbled and fallen off in places. How should they be repaired?

A. The spalling is probably due to the blocks absorbing water, which then freezes and causes the blocks' faces to pop off.

Dig down a foot or so and see how the blocks look. If they are wet, that probably is the source of the problem. Dig down deeper, approximately 2 feet.

Wire-brush the exposed blocks to remove loose materials, and coat them with waterproof cement or Thoroseal Foundation Coating. This parging should be applied in two coats. Lay black plastic against the foundation, and then backfill. This should break capillary attraction in the most vulnerable area.

Maintenance problems with cinder-mix walls

Q. I need help with a problem that has plagued me for some time and requires repairs every summer. Our foundation is not made of blocks but of a poured cement cinder mix.

Every winter, the surface of the foundation chips off and I have to patch it, waterproof it and paint it. I'd like to cover the existing foundation with anything that would not need repeated repairs. Any suggestions?

A. Cinder blocks or cinder mix are not as resistant to moisture absorption as concrete blocks or poured concrete with stone aggregate, but they were widely used some years back. You have two options that should solve your yearly maintenance problem.

One is to have a competent mason remove all loose material from the surface of the foundation and fasten galvanized metal mesh to it. This is followed by the application of parging the way it used to be done prior to the "dumbing" of the trades as a friend refers to the taking of short cuts so common nowadays. A scratch coat is troweled on, followed by two coats of Portland cement.

This should be done not only on the part of the foundation above grade but at least 2 to 3 feet below grade at which point the bottom should be tapered so as not to be "caught" by heaving ground. A sheet of 6-mil black plastic should be applied from grade down past the termination of the parging to act as a slip sheet and further protect the foundation from moisture absorption.

The other solution is to have a carpenter install ½-inch-thick pressure-treated plywood over the exposed foundation and at least 2 to 3 feet below grade. The buried part should also be covered with plastic. The top of either system should be properly flashed to the siding to prevent water from getting behind.

Whitish dust from concrete blocks

Q. There is a whitish dust on the bottom cement blocks of my basement. What causes this and what can I do about it? I would like to paint the cellar walls.

A. The efflorescence is due to salts in the blocks and mortar that were dissolved by moisture and left on the surface when it evaporated. It can be removed with a stiff brush used dry or with water. It indicates moisture penetration, but causes no harm. You should remove the source of moisture which is likely to be coming from poor grading around the foundation or the problem will continue.

The only coating likely to stick is one with a cement base. But you should not waterproof block foundations from inside. Water would build up inside the cores and cause serious problems in the living floors as it evaporates.

Sandstone foundation is crumbling

Q. The foundation of our 45-year-old house is built of sandstone blocks and is starting to crumble. What can we do to stop this disintegration?

A. Have a small area, approximately 1 square foot, of the foundation washed with the most powerful jet you can achieve from your garden hose. Rub your hand on it once it is dry to make sure all loose material is gone. Apply a mixture of equal parts of Thoroseal or Thoroseal Foundation Coating and Acryl 60, and partially embed in it a piece of fiberglass tape such as the type used to tape drywall joints, leaving 6 inches of it sticking out. Wait a week and yank the tape out.

If only the tape comes out, the substrate is probably strong enough to receive a coat of the mixture after a thorough washing of the entire areas to be treated. If you use a pressure-washer, use the gentlest setting to avoid damage to the foundation.

Your choice now is between Thoroseal, a decorative and pigmented coating that comes in a variety of colors, or Thoroseal Foundation Coating, which is pure cement without pigments and not as attractive or even-colored. Otherwise, the two products have the same basic formulation.

However, if the entire patch comes off with the tape, the substrate is not sound enough to apply the cement mixture successfully. In a couple of years, it will fall off in chunks. In that case, you have two choices.

You can coat the sandstone blocks with Thorosilane, a clear silicone water repellent that will preserve the appearance of the blocks while preventing the absorption of water, the cause of your present predicament. This should be repeated every three to five years. Or you can coat the blocks with Thorocoat, a non-cementitious coating that will hide the blocks as it comes in pigmented form only.

You may need the services of a competent mason.

Water and Moisture Problems in Foundations

There are several sources of water in basements and other foundations, some of which are unavoidable. The most common serious water problems by far are from surface water seeping through because the soil is not properly graded away from the foundation. Less common but also serious problems occur from underground water supplies. Crawl spaces with dirt floors cause moisture damage to a house if the soil is not completely covered with plastic sheeting. But even a well-designed basement may have moisture from sweating pipes and condensation from humid summer air.

Helping new concrete to dry

Q. We moved into our new 1,450-square-foot ranch in November. We were told by our builder that it would take the winter for the concrete to properly dry out. We've kept a window slightly open in the unfinished basement as well as windows in the kitchen and the bathroom at night. We have two dehumidifiers going all the time since the weather got cold (one in the basement and another upstairs) and also keep the main bathroom fan going all night.

In spite of all of this, I have to dry all the windows of the main floor every morning. The lower, unused level is okay. Shouldn't this problem be clearing up by now? If not, how many winters is it going to take?

A. Sometimes it takes two heating seasons for a new house to dry completely. Much depends on the temperature at which you keep your house during the winter and the amount of moisture your family generates.

For instance, if you are a family of four, a 1,450-square-foot ranch house is not very large and the family daily activities—such as bathing (especially if you take long showers) and cooking—generate a lot of moisture in the house. If you add water-loving plants, pets, and, perhaps, improperly-vented dryers or bathroom and kitchen fans, you have a problem.

Bathroom and kitchen fans should be vented to the outside through walls—not through the roof, into the soffits or the attic, or into a ridge or gable vents. You should check that this has been done correctly as too many builders just terminate the vents in the attic or other wrong places—a serious mistake particularly for kitchen fans that can throw grease in the attic where it can ignite if a fire starts on the stove.

The fact that you do not have moisture in the basement is most likely due to your having several windows open. The open basement window lets in colder and drier air to replace the warm, moist air escaping through the upstairs windows and bathroom fan.

But the fact that you still have the problem upstairs also tells me you may generate too much moisture.

Dehumidifiers are not very effective in the winter, particularly in a cold basement, and cost a lot to run.

Remember also that houses collect a lot of moisture during the humid days of summer and it takes several months of the heating seasons to reduce the level to the point where you no longer get condensation on windows.

If you still have the problem next winter, you may need a whole-house air-to-air heat exchanger.

Water flowing over frozen ground

Q. Each winter for the last several years, there is water in the southeast corner of my basement. This happens only when the ground is frozen and we experience sudden mild temperatures with significant rain.

I have not experienced any water problems except under these weather conditions. I removed the gutters last year (they were very old) and the problem still exists. The grade around the east side of the foundation is level and the south side has a cement walk 2 feet wide and flush to the foundation. What do you believe is causing the problem and what are your recommendations?

A. What you describe is typical of what happens when water is not allowed to flow away from a foundation. With the ground frozen, the only way for water to go is down along the foundation until it comes into your basement. During the rest of the year, it seems that your soil is able to absorb the water and no leakage occurs.

The solution is to slope the flat grade gently (I recommend 2 inches per foot) and plant grass on it. Check the slope on the concrete walk; if it is not sloping away from the house and you still experience leakage after correcting the grade next to it, you may have to top it with bricks, flagstones or another layer of concrete to achieve the proper slope.

The fact that you removed the gutters makes it even more essential that rain and roof drainage be moved from the foundation as quickly as possible. Roof drainage can cut grooves in the grass, so you may want to insert patio blocks or similar masonry in the sloping grade and flush with the grade at the drip line of the roof to prevent erosion.

Raising the grade around basement windows

Q. We live in a six-year-old house. The grading has sunk around the basement windows and puddles form, causing leaks, not through the windows but just below them, at a joint in the masonry. A friend tells me that he feels the tar is not high enough on the outside walls and that the grading needs to be raised where it has sunk. Can you tell me what needs to be done?

A. Your friend is partially right—the grade should be raised in all the low spots but there is no need to raise the line of the foundation coating, as it is of dubious value. Instead, tape 6-mil black plastic to the walls from where the new grade line will be and down to a few inches overlap of the existing foundation coating. And now all you need is good dirt, a wheelbarrow, and to pin down your friend to an afternoon of work.

Bricks stood upright around a window well, set inside a 4-inch trench.

Snow-melt coming in through window wells

Q. The foundation of our 25-year-old house is low, and the window wells are recessed into the ground. As a result, we have a frequent problem with snow melt running into the window wells and into the basement.

We have tried to build up the area close to the foundation, but it hasn't been very successful. What can we do to take care of this problem?

A. Assuming that enough of your foundation is out of the ground, you should aim to raise the grade so it slopes about 2 inches per horizontal foot for as far away as possible without having soil in contact with any wood.

I often see grade around foundations where people added dirt but still left it flat at the top. The object is to have a positive slope from the foundation on out, and it is best to plant grass on it and avoid flower beds close to the walls.

If the window wells, as is often the case, are lower than where the top of the grade should be, you should extend them but not lift them, as you want the bottom to stay where it is.

The easiest way to extend them is to dig a narrow trench, 4 inches deep, around the outside. Stand bricks upright in the trench, so their flat surface is against the well. Since bricks are 8 inches long, they will stick out of the ground 4 inches.

Pack the dirt back against them and add more to follow the rest of the grade line.

Sill sealer needed on slab

Q. Three years ago, we moved into an end unit of a semi-attached ground-floor ranch-type condominium built on a concrete slab.

A year ago, we began to notice that the wall-to-wall carpeting was developing a dirty stripe along the outside walls and now, mold is beginning to grow also.

Cleaning the carpeting has not helped for long; the dirty stripe and mold return.

The rug people tell us that the reason for this is that our building does not have a vapor seal on the concrete slab whereas later units in our development have it because the building code was changed to require it.

The siding is aluminum. Is this condition due to moisture coming in at the bottom of the walls? What can be done to eliminate this problem?

A. It does, indeed, appear that there is no sill sealer under the outside wall plates. Cold air and moisture are infiltrating at these points and the carpeting gets damp and collects dirt; it becomes a perfect breeding ground for mold.

At this point, the only practical solution is to remove the bottom aluminum siding panel and thoroughly caulk the joint of the wall plate with the concrete slab before replacing the panel. The carpeting should also be pulled up along the edges of the outside walls and the same joint caulked as well. This should stop air infiltration and resolve your problem.

If it does not, the exterior edge of the concrete slab should be insulated with 1-inch rigid extruded polystyrene. The insulation should be covered with ½-inch pressure-treated plywood and both the top of the plywood and the insulation will have to be flashed to the siding.

Sill over crawl space stays wet

Q. The wood sill on top of my crawl space foundation is soaking wet. Yet a similar sill in the basement is dry. A year ago we installed 9-inch fiberglass insulation with the vapor barrier facing the heated side between the crawl space joists. The ground in the crawl space is hard and dry. Yet even with the dry summer last year, the sill remained so wet I can run my finger over it and push water ahead of it.

A. Obviously, even though the ground is hard and feels dry, there is still considerable moisture exuding from the soil. With the conditions you describe, you risk rot on the sill and floor joists, particularly now that they are covered with insulation, which reduces their drying potential. A bare dirt crawl space needs a great deal of ventilation, which you don't mention having.

The simplest thing to do in your case is to remove any debris or sharp objects from the crawl space floor. Lay 6-mil plastic all over the floor. Weigh it down at the perimeter with stones or bricks. Do the same around the piers. Where you need to overlap plastic, do so by at least 2 feet.

This sill rotted away from too much moisture, allowing mice inside the house.

After the plastic has been down for a week or so, check to see if moisture is beading on its underside. That's your clue that you have found the source of the moisture on the sill. But if there are no water beads, pull down a piece of the insulation between the floor joists and see if the area is dry. If not, you have another problem and I'll need more information about the set-up to be able to help. For instance, are there vents in the crawl space foundation, and are they always open? If so, close them permanently once the dirt floor is fully covered with plastic—they are not needed and cause problems.

You may want to place a dehumidifier as near the center of the crawl space as you can with the air intake facing the access door to the crawl space and the discharge away. Connect a garden hose to the discharge tube and have it empty into a large container in the basement for ease of handling, and run it for as long as necessary to dry the crawl space.

Grading when back yard slopes toward house

Q. My back yard slopes down toward the house and, when it rains or the snow melts, water runs down my basement. I would like to install drain tiles on the back and side lot line and lead them past the house. Which kind are recommended and should they be covered?

A. You don't need drain tiles if you are only dealing with surface water. And it is best to handle the water closer to the house than the back lot line; otherwise you still will have the problem from water coming between it and the house. Have a contractor with a small machine like a Bobcat create a gentle swale a few feet from the rear of the house and continuing as needed to the side where it can lead water past the house.

The grade should slope from the house to the swale. This will require making the grade from the swale to the rear lot line steeper unless you opt for a retaining wall on the outside of the swale. You could, then, use the extra dirt to flatten the back yard in back of the wall, making it more useful. Access to it can be created with steps and a flower bed can be made at the base and the top of the wall.

Grading when a house is between two hills

Q. Our 1863 house is situated between two hills, both steep. Water drains into the basement like crazy, and about a year ago the ancient mortar breached in one place, and the water gushed in like an open faucet. We have a sump pump but, because the floor is level, we have to push the water toward the pump with a snow shovel.

My mother had the side of the house dug up and preventive measures taken twice (I'm not sure what was done, as I lived elsewhere at that time), but that was maybe 20 years ago. A neighbor solved her problem by having an inner wall built up against the old fieldstone wall. It cants up, being wider at the bottom. It seemed to solve her problem in that area, although it's damp in other areas.

My handyman seems to think it would be better to dig yet again on the outside rather than to build the interior retaining wall, as he feels the water pressure would

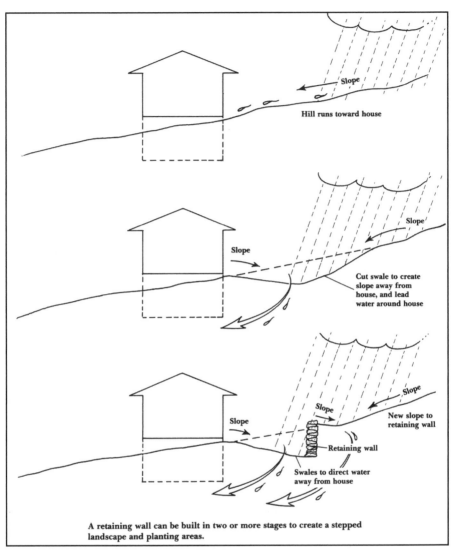

A swale or retaining wall diverting water away from the house.

breech the second wall as well. I really hate to get into digging! What is your excellent advice?

A. As proven over time, the digging and whatever else was done (twice) 20 years ago has not solved the problem. With the type of fieldstone foundation you have, it may be possible—but difficult—to waterproof it from outside. You would do this using plastic sheeting and backfilling with coarse material that would allow water to percolate to an outside perimeter drain, but the drain needs to be able to discharge water to daylight somewhere to be useful. If this is not possible, the work would be in vain.

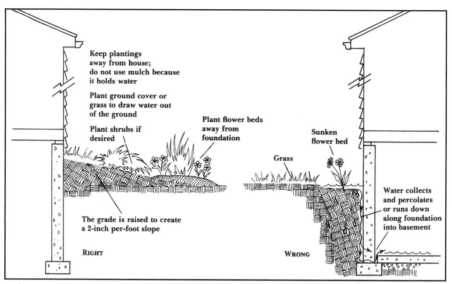

Keep plantings away from house; do not use mulch because it holds water

Plant ground cover or grass to draw water out of the ground

Plant shrubs if desired

Plant flower beds away from foundation

Sunken flower bed

Grass

Water collects and percolates or runs down along foundation into basement

The grade is raised to create a 2-inch per-foot slope

RIGHT

WRONG

This cross section shows common problems (right) and the correct way to prevent them (left).

The simplest way to deal with the problem, if it is at all possible, is to raise the grade against the foundation so it slopes away at least 2 inches per horizontal foot for as far away as possible (4 to 6 feet is ideal). This would prevent water from the two hills from reaching the foundation. Plant a healthy stand of grass on the raised grade.

If this solution is not possible, creating swales a few feet from the house to direct water to a natural outflow can also work. Or, a French drain can be built at the base of the two hills. It would consist of a trench a few feet deep with a perforated pipe at the bottom and the rest of the trench filled with stones to capture the water as it runs down from the two hills. That will also require a daylight outlet. The house side of the trench should be lined with plastic to keep the water that fills the trench from percolating toward the house.

These are all suggestions that may or may not be practical; it's difficult for me to say without seeing the lay of the land. An expensive alternative would be to have a waterproofing contractor install a fiberglass gutter at the base of the walls leading to the sump pump, which, I assume, discharges outside to an area where the water can flow downhill and not be re-circulated into the basement.

Raising the grade when siding is close to the ground

Q. The earth against our two-year-old foundation has settled. As a result, water is running against the house and the basement leaks. Unfortunately, I can't raise the grade too much as the wood siding is too close to the ground. The only solution I can see is to cover the bottom siding board with aluminum flashing and raise the grade against it. Is this a sound solution?

A. No, it isn't. Although there are no termites in your area (Northern New England), there are carpenter ants, which may delight in the damp environment you will be providing them with. Soil dampness is bound to permeate the area behind the flashing. There are other ways to solve the grading problem.

If there is enough of an overhang to discharge roof water safely away, you can set pressure-treated 6×6-inch logs about 3 inches away from the siding so as to leave an air pocket; you'll have to constantly remove all debris and leaves that will accumulate in it. Raise the grade against the logs.

Or, remove the bottom siding boards, treat the sheathing with Cuprenol Wood Preserver Green or equivalent wood preservative, and apply an ice and water guard membrane to a height of about 8 inches above the final grade. Install a Z-flashing under the last siding boards and cover the membrane with pressure-treated plywood set under the flashing.

Or create a swale a few feet away from the house, sloping the grade from the foundation to the low point of the swale. If you can lead the swale to lower ground, so much the better but, if not, at least the water is kept away from the house.

Protection from an underground stream

Q. The house I am buying is under construction. The basement is built of 8-inch-thick blocks coated with cement and black bitumen.

There is a small underground stream about 4 feet below grade. The contractor has had to use a pump to keep water out of the trench so construction could proceed.

A. The builder needs to lay a crushed stone bed at least a foot thick at the outside base of the foundation and bury a 4-inch perforated drain pipe in it. The stones must be covered with geotextile fabric and coarse material used to backfill up to a foot from the final grade. Native soil completes the backfill.

The drain pipe must either run to daylight at a spot downhill from the house, be connected to a sump (low spot) equipped with a submersible pump inside the basement, or be connected to the local storm sewer if the local authorities allow it.

Water in the vegetable cellar

Q. When we built our house four years ago, we had a vegetable cellar built under the front stoop. It has a cement floor, block walls, cement roof and two round holes on each side for ventilation. When it rains, big water drops form on the ceiling and drip down, and the block walls are also wet. We applied a sealer on the cement stoop, and the ceiling and walls of the cellar.

After the first rain, the sealer started to come off, and we are back to where we started. In winter, big drops also form on the ceiling from condensation. What can we do to make the cellar usable?

A. You did not mention what kind of sealer you put on the concrete stoop; the right kind should have worked and made it waterproof. Trouble is, what you put on may prevent the adhesion of a more effective product; it may have to be removed.

Clean the stoop floor and apply Thompson's Water Seal or a mixture of equal parts of boiled linseed oil and mineral spirits every year to repel most of the rain water. Paint the exterior walls of the stoop with two coats of a waterproofing product such as Thoroseal and do the same to the interior walls and the ceiling of the cellar. This should keep the water out. For Thoroseal to bond properly, you'll have to remove whatever you put on the surfaces first; they must be clean.

To prevent winter condensation on the ceiling, apply extruded polystyrene such as Styrofoam or FoamulaR to the ceiling with a compatible adhesive such as Styrobond. If condensation is also a problem on the walls, do the same. You'll have enough cold air coming through the four ventilation holes to keep the cellar cool.

Testing a sump pump

Q. We've recently moved into a new house equipped with a sump pump. Since I've never had any experience with these, I wonder how reliable they are. Do I have to wait until the basement floods to find out if it works?

A. First, let's hope that your builder installed it as a precaution and that you won't need it. But it's easy to check if it functions properly. Pour water in the sump until the float of the pump kicks it in, and watch it remove the water.

Why have a sump?

Q. I have read your comments dealing with the best ways to prevent basement leakage from the outside. However, if this does not seem to be working, what else could I do?

Some companies guarantee to correct basement leakage from inside with a sump pump. Is this something you would recommend? Are they expensive? How do they work? Or should I have the outside dug up and something done to correct the problem?

A. If you have done all the things I have mentioned to correct the leakage from outside and the basement still leaks, you may be dealing with an underground water source.

If there is a layer of crushed stones several inches thick under the basement slab, the installation of a sump pump may solve your problem, as the sump should pick up the water before it gets above the slab. Install it near a wall in the best place to dispose of the water outside.

The best sump, in my opinion, is made by cutting a hole in the concrete slab 30 inches square. Dig down 30 inches and place 6 inches of crushed stones on the bottom of the excavation.

Next, put an 18×18-inch flue liner on the stone bed and fill the space between the liner and the excavation with crushed stones to the bottom of the existing slab. Mix concrete and fill the area around the liner with it.

Install a submersible pump in the sump hole; connect a plastic pipe of the proper diameter to it with a check valve where it connects to the pump. Go as high as you can with it and connect a horizontal pipe to it with a slight slant to the outside.

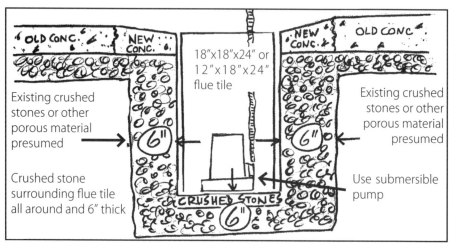

A cross-section of a submersible sump pump installed in a basement.

The pipe should discharge onto a splash block, and the grade should slope away so the water will not be recirculated down to the pump from outside.

A good-quality pump should run around $100. They work automatically when the water level in the sump hole triggers the float. Digging outside is expensive and disruptive and generally unnecessary.

Life-span of a sump pump

Q. The pedestal sump pump located in my basement is 15 years old. It looks it but it is working well. It is needed only when there are heavy rains or snow melts in the spring when it may run for ten consecutive days until the ground dries.

I am concerned that the pump will stop working during one of these extreme weather conditions. This would cause my basement to flood and perhaps put me in a situation where the stores are out of stock due to high demand or I can't get it repaired.

What is the normal life expectancy of a ⅓-horsepower pedestal sump pump? Are there ways to assess its condition? Should I adhere to the credo that "If it ain't broke, don't fix it" or to the one that says "It is better to be safe than sorry"?

A. Electric motors that are properly maintained (lubricated if need be; check the instructions or look for oil cups) should last for a very long time. In the case of your sump pump, it is only working intermittently, which is a light load on the motor.

The more likely problem with a pedestal sump pump is that the blades in the foot of the pump may become frozen from the scum and scale in the water if the pump is idle for extended periods and the water is of poor quality. Your best insurance is to operate the pump once a month or so to keep it limber.

Sump pump comes on too often

Q. We live in a house in a nine-year-old subdivision. Our sump pump comes on every 15 to 20 minutes all day and night long regardless of the weather conditions. Is this normal? Should the pump be left on all the time year around? Our neighbors don't have that problem.

A. You obviously have an underground water problem such as a high water table or a spring near or under the house. It's the only explanation I can think of for a sump pump to run as yours does. The fact that your neighbors' pumps don't run as often may be because their houses are on a higher soil stratum (if a high water table is the problem), or it may indicate that a spring is more likely to be the cause of your particular situation.

If you stop the pump, one of two things may happen, depending on the cause: If you're dealing with a high water table, the water level may not rise any higher than it is now and your basement may not flood, as I doubt that the pump can be instrumental in lowering the water table to the extent that it keeps your basement dry, but you won't be sure until you try. In the case of a spring, it may be different, and the sump pump may prevent basement flooding that would occur if you stopped it, unless there is an outlet for the spring water equivalent to its volume.

As you can see, the answer is pretty muddy. Try shutting off the pump to see what happens. Stand by and watch to see if the water level rises significantly.

Relocating the discharge from a sump pump

Q. I have a sump pump in the basement of our circa-1900 farmhouse. The 1½-inch hose from the pump leads outside underneath a porch (which has about 8- to 10-inch ground clearance, so I can't get under it) and empties onto the lawn. In the winter, the water in the hose freezes, making the pump nonfunctional until the next significant thaw. This is a problem I need to resolve. Any suggestions?

A. The best solution seems to be to relocate the discharge hose to another area of the wall, not under the porch, since you can't get under there to slope the hose downward so that it drains completely each time the pump activates.

Channeling water to the sump

Q. There is water seepage along one of my basement walls at the floor line. It is about 15 feet from a sump. I know they make a product that can be laid at the joint of the floor and wall to channel the water. Where can I purchase it?

Also, I ran the 1½-inch pipe from the sump pump 150 feet away to a ditch. The pipe is buried at least 3 feet and covered with blueboard rigid insulation but the outlet is only 1½ feet from the bottom of the ditch. There is a good pitch to the pipe. What can I do to prevent freezing?

A. I don't know where you can find such channels in small quantities and at a reasonable price but you can easily make up your own. Buy a piece of vinyl gutter that is shaped like a broad "U"; cut it in half lengthwise and place it upside down with the cut edge against the wall and its flat top edge against the floor.

Clean the floor area on which you will glue the gutter. Mark the outer line on the floor and remove the gutter section. Run a bead of flexible caulking such as polyurethane or use a waterproof construction adhesive inside the line you have drawn. Place the gutter back and press its flat top edge down into the adhesive.

If you prefer, you can accomplish the same thing with a piece of 2×4-inch pressure-treated lumber fastened to the floor in the same manner.

It is unlikely that the discharge pipe will freeze considering the precautions you took. The steep pitch will cause the water to discharge quickly and running water generates its own heat. But if you are concerned, why don't you get a hay bale from a farmer or garden supply house and place it over the discharge outlet to insulate it for the winter. Remove it and store it safely until next winter.

Stopping seepage through block walls

Q. There is a small amount of seepage through the foundation block walls in the front and rear of the house, which get the roof run-off. I think the concrete blocks were not coated underground. Once the walls dry up this summer, I plan on painting the inside walls with a waterproofing paint.

Would you suggest this or something else, and must I treat the exterior walls below grade first? The soil is very sandy.

How can I remove the white dust particles from the inside surfaces of the block walls? The block walls are now cracking. Are rain gutters a must?

A. I would advise you not to waterproof the inside of block walls. I have seen houses where this had been done in which the blocks were filled with water with very serious ill effects on the living quarters.

The fact that the walls have some cracks tells you that rain is allowed to percolate and freeze against the foundation, pushing the walls in. You need to top the sandy soil with loam with some clay in it, sloping away from the house and plant grass on it. This will move water away and may prevent further leakage. There should be no need to excavate and coat the walls; it's a huge undertaking with questionable success.

Remove the efflorescence by brushing it off with a stiff bristle brush.

I am not in favor of gutters in cold climates where ice may build up in them and cause damage.

Interior perimeter drains

Q. You have on several occasions mentioned an interior perimeter drain to solve basement water problems. We have such a problem and haven't found a solution to date. Is this the solution for us? And what is it?

A. Most basement and crawl space water problems are caused by improper grading of the soil around the foundation and negative slopes on attached structures such as walks, patios, driveways, and stoops. A negative grade means that water is

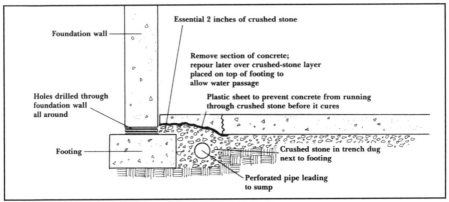

A subslab interior drain

directed toward the foundation instead of away from it. Downspouts discharging roof water directly on the ground against the foundation instead of onto a splash block or an extension pipe or those connected to an underground drain pipe that has a break are also responsible for foundation leakage.

However, if all the conditions responsible for surface water problems have been corrected and there still is leakage, an underground water source is suspected. That is where an interior perimeter drain may be the answer.

This is often easier to provide and less expensive than excavating along the foundation to install or replace an outside footing drain. This, of course, depends on how extensive the landscaping is.

To build an interior drain, the concrete slab along the basement walls is removed in a band approximately a foot wide and the gravel and dirt excavated to the bottom of the footings. A couple of inches of new crushed stones are spread on the bottom of the excavation, a perforated drain pipe laid on top and more stones put over to the level of the bottom of the slab.

The stones are covered with plastic to keep the concrete from infiltrating them, a spacer in the form of an asphalt strip or pressure-treated board is placed against the wall, and the concrete is patched. The spacer allows water that may come through the walls to flow down to the perimeter drain.

The drain should terminate into a sump equipped with a good quality submersible pump discharging to the outside onto a splash block sloping away from the foundation so the water will not be recirculated.

Protection from underground water

Q. You have dealt with ways to handle wet basements caused by surface water. Would you now deal with underground water problems?

A. Although far less frequent than problems caused by surface water, there are nevertheless cases of foundation water problems caused by underground water sources.

These can be a high seasonal water table (*e.g.*, when snow melts in the spring or during very wet periods) or, for instance, water following an underground ledge.

First and foremost, houses with basements or crawl spaces should not be built under these conditions unless foolproof precautions are taken to handle the water.

In new construction this involves laying 8 to 12 inches of crushed stones, properly compacted, on the excavated area before pouring the footings, the foundation walls, and the basement slab. Depending on the amount of water, a network of perforated pipes around the inside of the footings and perhaps underneath the floor slab itself may be advisable in addition to the standard exterior perimeter drain.

The stones covering the exterior perimeter drain should be protected with one of the geotextile fabrics available today, and the drains should discharge to daylight downslope or, in the case of a flat lot, to a sump equipped with a pump inside the basement or crawl space. The sump should have a tight cover to reduce the chance of radon entering the house.

Curtain or French drains can also be very effective in intercepting water following earth strata down a hill. However, these trenches must be at least as deep as the footings of the buildings and have slightly sloping bottoms toward the discharge point or points.

A sheet of plastic is laid on the trench side closest to the building, 2 inches of egg-size crushed stones placed on the bottom, then a perforated pipe leading to daylight and more stones. Geotextile fabric is placed over the stones before backfilling with a layer of coarse sand and natural soil.

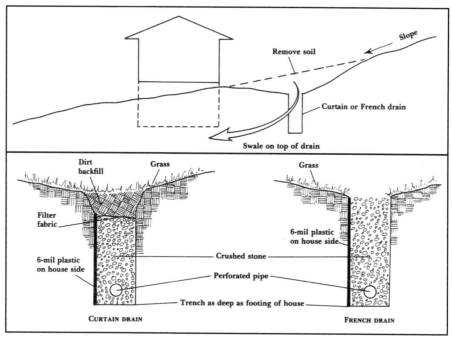

Curtain drains and French drains can be used to divert both surface and underground sources of water.

The difference between a curtain and a French drain is that a curtain drain is not filled with stones to the top whereas a French drain is, thus having the ability to catch surface water as well.

Mold, Mildew, and Musty Smells

Mold can be, at best, an annoyance and, at worst, a dangerous allergen and a sign of rot that can cause severe damage. Even the relatively normal dampness that can occur in a basement can cause problems, particularly if the basement is used as living space or storage.

Use of a dehumidifier

Q. Our basement is built of poured concrete walls and floor. It is dry. Will painting the walls cut down on the use of our dehumidifier? Should we use a concrete sealer on the floor?

A. You need a dehumidifier in a basement in the summer to remove excessive vapor in the air that causes musty odors and could lead to mildew formation on all surfaces. This is because the warmer exterior air already contains a high level of humidity and, when it is cooled by the concrete surfaces that reflect the temperature of the soil in contact with them, its relative humidity is considerably increased to the point where condensation occurs on these surfaces. Only dehumidification can control this problem.

This situation, prevalent throughout the warm and humid summer days, is the reason why I do not recommend leaving windows and vents open in basements and crawl spaces until we get dry, breezy and cooler days.

There should be no need to apply a sealer on the concrete floor unless there is a considerable amount of dusting taking place. But that is a different subject.

Cleaning off mildew

Q. The basement walls of the house I recently bought were covered with black mildew. I have used a wire brush, sulfuric acid, and white paint, but the mildew is coming through.

I don't know what else to use; I hope you can help.

A. You should have used sodium hypochlorite, not sulfuric acid. Mold and mildew spores, unless killed, will come through new paint coats.

Wash the walls with a solution made of equal parts of water and fresh Clorox bleach. Wear skin protection and old clothes and, very important, ventilate well by setting a fan blowing out in a basement window; open an opposite window. Rent a respirator labeled effective for chlorine.

Do not rinse; let the solution do its job and evaporate, but close the door to the basement and keep the ventilation going until all odor of chlorine is gone.

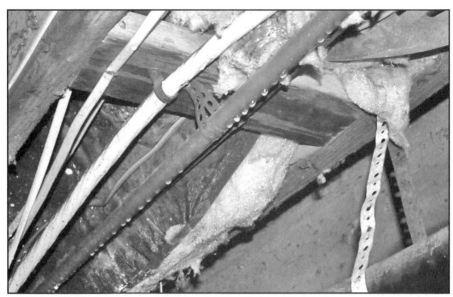

Summer humidity creates condensation on cold basement pipes, causing them to drip.

You haven't mentioned it so I assume that your basement is not leaking but if the walls are built with cinder or concrete blocks, I would not recommend painting them with a waterproof coating.

Odors when house is closed for winter

Q. We own a house on a lake in New York State. It is approximately 60 years old and on an unmaintained road so it can be used only from May to October. Originally it was a one-story, two-bedroom house with a 6½-foot high basement.

We added a second story about six years ago. Our problem is an odor that comes from the basement and permeates the house once it is closed up. I have to bring all the linens, pillows, curtains, etc., back to New Jersey and store them until springtime.

The basement is built with cinder blocks. It is unfinished and it has a drain to get rid of water that enters the basement in the spring. There are two regular windows facing the lake and two doors to bring in furniture and other items for storage.

Our next-door neighbors' house is situated the same as ours but their basement ceiling is higher and they do not experience the same damp smell as we do.

Would painting the cinder blocks help? Is there a kind of desiccant that we could use? We do run a dehumidifier during the months the house is used.

A. Do not paint the cinder blocks; it would not help and it may cause other problems.

You haven't mentioned the basement floor. Is it bare dirt or concrete? If bare dirt, it should be covered to prevent moisture from the soil from evaporating into the basement and permeating throughout the house.

The problem is what to cover it with since you use the space for storage. The simplest way to cover bare soil is with 6-mil plastic, but it will not last if there is much foot traffic and moving of stuff around.

Concrete would be the answer but, since concrete is somewhat porous, it should be poured over a gravel base covered with 6-mil plastic. This would reduce the headroom unless the soil were dug out several inches.

If the basement floor is already covered with a concrete slab, unless it was poured as mentioned above, moisture can get through it. The only way to stop it is to paint the slab with epoxy paint after a thorough cleaning.

To reduce moisture infiltration, check the grade around the house and correct any deficiencies so water is directed away from the house and not toward it or allowed to stagnate on flat grade.

Use a desiccant such as MDG Mildew Control Bags and hang the bags in the basement and the house. You can buy it in RV and marine stores. Buy enough bags to take care of the cubic footage of the areas to be protected. The product lasts up to four to five months.

Mold spores and other allergens

Q. I live in a 20-year-old townhouse with a dry basement. A few years ago, I noticed a yellowish stain about 5 inches in diameter on the basement ceiling, near a window directly below a warm air register in the kitchen above it. I forgot all about it until yesterday. Although the stain has not enlarged, half of it had turned quite black, and I suspect that it could be mold or mildew.

My husband and I have been suffering from allergies to a number of things including molds. How can I get rid of mold spores and other allergens in our house? We currently use a 3M Micro Particle and Airborne Allergen Reduction Filter, which we replace every month. If there are professionals who can remove allergens inside our house, I am willing to spend money on it. We are really feeling very miserable.

A. There are such people and you can find them in your Yellow Pages under "Laboratories–Testing," "Engineers–Environmental" and "Environmental & Ecological Products & Services."

The stain you mention does appear to be caused by molds. Its change from a yellowish stain to a black one indicates it is active. There must be some moisture getting into the ceiling. The source should be found and eliminated.

It may be from some condensation in the duct (for whatever reason) or, more probably, from some leak from an appliance near the duct. The culprit may be the dishwasher. If this is not corrected, you will have a continuing problem. Most people are not allergic to a minor amount of mold spores but molds are always worth checking out.

Cellars with Dirt Floors

Relatively few newer houses have cellars with dirt floors, but they're a common feature in older ones, including fine historic homes. They can pose some maintenance issues that differ, at least slightly, from those of other foundation types.

Moisture from the dirt floor

Q. Our house was built in the mid 1800s. It has a stone foundation. About 12 years ago, the north wall of the foundation had so deteriorated that it was replaced with a poured concrete wall. Eight inches of small stones were laid over the dirt floor.

Although I haven't noticed any water on the stones there is moisture from the dirt floor. I am planning on laying plastic down but I am concerned that holes would gradually appear in it due to contact with the stones. What would you suggest?

I am also thinking of covering the plastic with linoleum loosely laid down to make walking easier.

A. Either get some waste plastic from a construction site (builders have tons to get rid of) and place several layers on the stones before laying a clean sheet over them or put down several layers of new plastic. Instead of linoleum, use old synthetic carpeting. You may be able to get some from a carpet installer who has removed it from a job and has to dispose of it.

Why use pea stones?

Q. We have purchased an old house with an artesian well in our dirt-floor cellar. We have been advised to put down heavy plastic covered with fine pea stones and flagstones. Pouring concrete would be very expensive.

There are no windows in the cellar and not enough headroom to stand upright. My father-in-law says that if we put plastic down, we will be encouraging mold, beetles and other critters. Our neighbor says that in winter, when the house was unoccupied, the windows were encased in ice, but the house plumbing was drained so I don't know where the water could be coming from.

A. The moisture from the cellar was responsible for the ice on the windows. Covering the bare soil with plastic is the way to go, but why cover the plastic with pea stones and flagstones if there is not enough headroom for the cellar to be useable?

The plastic will not encourage mold or beetles. On the contrary, by containing the moisture in the soil, it will help dry the cellar. Boards can be used for foot traffic.

Musty smells

Q. How can I get rid of a pervasive musty odor that seems to emanate from my dirt floor cellar and permeates the house? The cellar walls are built of loose stones; the ceiling is so low we have to walk in a crouch. Though we don't use it often, we do store vegetables and preserves in it, and the steam boiler, which needs periodic maintenance, is in it.

Someone suggested placing insulation between the old logs serving as floor joists and tacking plastic underneath the logs as a way to keep the moisture out of the house.

A. Cellars built with old stones and having a dirt floor offer particular challenges. Prior to our tightening up houses to save energy, the problem was not as severe because these old houses were so leaky that the frequent air changes diluted the moisture.

But, since many of these old houses have now been retrofitted, the relative humidity in them has increased to unhealthy proportions, and excessive dampness has become a problem. Mold, mildew, and fungi are also responsible for allergic reactions.

The idea of insulating the cellar's ceiling and sealing it with plastic is not sound. Since it's impossible to make the seal tight, moisture would work its way into the insulation and be retained there, hastening the rot of the old logs, which may already be suffering from some decay.

Another problem would develop, making this situation worse. In winter, moisture from the house's interior would condense on the upper side of the plastic and add to the unhealthy environment in which the logs now find themselves. The reason they lasted so long is that they were able to breathe.

Your situation is common to all old houses with stone cellars and dirt floors. I have worked with many of them and recommend a different strategy. They all leak from rain and melting snow, and because the grading around them is often very poor, the first thing to do is to change the grade as needed to shed water away from the house.

This may not solve the problem in its entirety, but it will certainly help.

Inside the cellar, first remove all the junk and old appliances that are often left there by tradesmen. Then smooth the dirt floor, removing sharp stones and anything else that would damage the vapor retarder to be applied.

Next, dig a shallow trench against the perimeter of the walls and place the dirt as a berm on the side of the trench, away from the walls. This is to catch water leaking through the walls and direct it to a sump, or let it percolate through the soil without running all over the cellar.

Now, if the cellar dirt is relatively smooth, without many sharp stones, etc., you may lay a couple of layers of waste plastic (something contractors are usually trying to get rid of) as a cushion, and cover that with new 6-mil polyethylene. Have the plastic go over the perimeter berm. If you can get more waste plastic, lay it on top of the new sheet, to protect it against damage from walking on it.

Install a sump pump in an appropriate corner, if necessary. If the cellar floor is too rough to smooth it properly so it won't damage the plastic, you can spread fine sand over it before installing the plastic. Add boards or scrap pieces of pressure-treated plywood for walking access.

Crawl Spaces

Crawl spaces are easy to forget about until problems occur. Sometimes, they're so shallow that they're almost inaccessible. But they serve the same basic needs as other foundations; they need to be solid and supportive of the main structure. They need to be protected from moisture. Without proper insulation, they can make the rest of the house uncomfortable.

Termites in crawl space

Q. I've had a large pile of old wood in my half basement for 15 years. I'm concerned about bugs or termites living in the wood. If I have the wood removed, I'm afraid whatever termites may be under it may scatter and come up into my house. Since I don't go into the basement, as it is only 3½ feet high, I have no proof that the spiders and other occasional bugs I find in the house are the result of the wood in the basement. Are my fears about insects living in the wood unwarranted? How should I approach this dilemma?

A. The wood should be moved out of the crawl space; it should not have been put there in the first place. It is definitely an attraction to wood-eating insects like termites. But you have no need to worry about them scattering and coming into your house if they are disturbed by removal of the wood, as they need contact with the soil.

However, you may want to have the crawl space checked and, if need be, treated by an independent pest management professional.

Cold floor over crawl space

Q. We live in a 130-plus-year-old house. Our bedroom is on the ground floor with only a 6-inch crawl space beneath it.

The cold air blows through the stone foundation keeping the floor and the room very cool and expensive to heat.

Is there a way to insulate this crawl space? Can anything be blown-in as it is too small an area to get into? If not, what is the best way to insulate the foundation?

A. Such a shallow crawl space in an old house is sure not to have a plastic vapor retarder on the bare soil. Moreover, your area has a lot of clay soil and, more than likely, the soil in the crawl space is damp.

I know of nothing that can be successfully blown-in under the circumstances you describe and, if I did, I would not recommend it. Air is needed to help dry the wood members forming the floor, if indeed they can be.

The air infiltration through the stone foundation is a blessing and probably the only thing keeping your floor from rotting.

When the cold weather arrives, do what the old-timers did. Get some mulch hay bales from a local farmer, stack them tight against the foundation, force loose hay between them and the stone walls to keep the wind out. Cover the whole thing with plastic tacked to the house with wood strips and tuck the plastic under the bales or weigh it down with heavy stones.

Be sure to remove everything in April to get the air to circulate in the crawl space again.

Keeping water away from crawl space

Q. We moved into our house three months ago and discovered that water is coming into the crawl space through the footing.

There is 6-mil plastic on the ground of the crawl space but it isn't in very good condition. Any suggestions?

A. You should definitely have the plastic repaired by putting a new sheet over the existing one in all areas where the ground isn't completely covered. But that doesn't solve your leakage problem; it only prevents soil moisture from evaporating and getting into the rest of the house.

You should attempt to stop the leakage from outside by repairing any negative or flat grade that allows water to run toward, or collect near, the foundation. Make sure that all downspouts discharge properly onto splashblocks and that the latter are sloped away from the house.

If there are any patios, walks, stoops, and driveways that direct water toward the house, they also need to be repaired.

If all is well with the grade and additions, you may have an underground water problem. This is more difficult to deal with, but it is also much rarer.

Protecting a shallow crawl space

Q. My small basementless house has had two additions to it. The back porch was enclosed and its crawl space has two vents. The garage was converted into two bedrooms and a new garage was built next to it.

The crawl space under the bedrooms has only one vent, which goes into the new garage. A year ago that space seemed dry. It isn't deep enough to crawl in, and there are no pipes in it. Should I fill this space with foam insulation?

A. Do you want to make the floor warmer, or are you concerned about moisture? If it is to make the floor of the bedrooms warmer, the floor should have been insulated between the floor joists before the subfloor was put on permanently. Since there isn't enough room to crawl in, you can forget that now. You would have to insulate the foundation from the outside with 1-inch extruded polystyrene rigid insulation and cover it with a compatible cement coating or half-inch pressure-treated plywood. The plywood would have to be properly flashed to the siding. But this should be done only if the ground is completely covered with 6-mil plastic. Otherwise you will be trapping moisture in the crawl space.

An alternative is a thick synthetic pad and carpet.

Since your former garage probably had a concrete slab, it is less likely to have a problem than if it were bare soil, but you are wise to keep an eye on it periodically.

Crawl space covered with layers of 6-mil plastic

I would urge you emphatically not to blow foam in to fill the crawl space. Have you checked the other crawl space? If the soil is bare, it should be covered with heavy plastic if there is access to it.

Turning crawl space into full basement

Q. The foundation of my house is half basement and half crawl space. I am in the process of digging out soil and rock from my crawl space to make it into a full basement. I am doing this with 5-gallon plastic pails, averaging about 15 pails a week. I calculated that it would take me at least two years to complete the dig. I don't want to hire a contractor; I want to do the job myself. How can I finish the job faster and simpler?

A. You are one ambitious fellow, but I guess it's time better spent than gambling or whatever. You could do what we used to do when I was doing this sort of work as a contractor: Rent (or buy) a conveyor belt and have it dump the dirt and rock into a wheelbarrow. Of course that requires a window or a removable vent, if there is one in a convenient place. If not, I can't think of any other way to speed the work and make it easier with the constraints you have put on yourself.

However, I would caution you to be very careful not to endanger the structure of your house. Usually, the foundation walls of a crawl space are shallower than those of a full basement. If, in digging the space out, you undermine the foundation, you risk some major structural problems. If you need to dig below the bottom of the footings, you have two choices:

- One choice is to leave a slope of 45° from the base of the footings to the bottom of the excavation. This would make the floor space much smaller, depending on how far below the bottom of the footings you plan to go.
- The alternative is to work in short alternating sections of no more than 4 feet, leaving 8 feet between digs. When one section is done, excavate another 4 feet and so on. Pour concrete footings, and build a 12-inch thick masonry wall no closer than 2 feet from the footings.

If you can do this yourself, more power to you, but it is work generally better left to experienced contractors.

Should floor joists be insulated?

Q. Should I use unfaced fiberglass insulation or insulation with an integral vapor barrier between the joists of my basement ceiling to keep the upstairs floor warmer? Should the insulation be tight to the subfloor above or should I leave an air space?

I have a separate crawl space that is unvented and has a gravel floor. The existing insulation is installed with the vapor barrier down. I want to redo that, too, and have the same questions as for the basement.

A. You should consider insulating the walls of the basement and crawl space instead of their respective ceilings. This is particularly sensible in the basement, as you must have water pipes and a heating plant in it. Why lose the benefit of the radiation and stand-by losses of the furnace when you could capture them and make the basement warmer? The same should be considered for the crawl space, particularly if there are any water pipes or ducts running through it. In both cases, if the soil around the house is clay or other heavy soil, you should insulate foundation walls to a depth of only two feet below grade.

The most important thing to do in the crawl space is to cover the ground with 6-mil plastic, making sure you do a thorough job.

Remove a few pieces of the existing insulation to see if it is wet and if the floor joists and plywood subfloor show signs of dampness or mold. If so, the insulation should be removed at once, laid on the plastic to dry, and a dehumidifier set in the crawl space to remove the excessive humidity. (If you don't own one, try to borrow or rent one). This will take some time.

If all is well, and you wish to properly insulate between the joists, take your time to turn the insulation over, install it tight to the subfloor, and hold it in place with nylon string stapled zigzag to the sides of the joists, or use tiger's teeth (pointed metal pieces available in building supply houses). If you decide to insulate the perimeter instead, you can re-use the insulation on the walls and band joists.

Placing plastic in inaccessible crawl space

Q. I would like to cover the bare soil in the crawl space of the addition to our house with 6-mil plastic, but I can't get in there as the floor is too low. Can I have insulation blown in, or is there some other solution?

A. Blowing insulation would only make a bad situation worse. It is generally possible, using an Army folding shovel, to dig a trench in the center of the crawl space of an addition. Place the dirt on one side and, when done trenching, push plastic in place on the side without the dirt with a soft-bristled broom so as not to damage the plastic. Make sure it's tight against the walls; better yet, have it go up them a few inches. Then, use the shovel to pick up the dirt and heave it, as best you can, over the plastic toward the walls or place the dirt as far as you can and push it with the broom. Then do the other side.

Finally, lay a piece of plastic to overlap the other two pieces generously, and cover the trench as you retreat.

Protecting water pipes in crawl space

Q. The pipes in my crawl space freeze when the temperature drops below minus 10°F. So far I have been lucky, no pipes have burst but no water comes out of them. I am considering wrapping heat cables around them as the hardware store clerk suggested, but I am concerned that it will raise my electric bill considerably.

A. The greater concern is the risk of fire. A number of fires and some deaths have been attributed to heat cables. It is much safer and cheaper, in the long run, to insulate the pipes and the top of the foundation to 2 feet below the outside grade. You can do that from inside the crawl space with either rigid extruded polystyrene (blue or pink) or fiberglass batts. You can do it from the outside with polystyrene, protected by pressure-treated plywood and proper flashing.

However, if you insist on using heat cables, be sure that the type you buy is UL listed.

Is venting necessary?

Q. There are two small vents in our crawl space that remain open year around. In the summer, we also open the screened entrance to the crawl space. The crawl space floor is dirt.

Our house has forced air heat and air conditioning, and all ductwork and plumbing pipes are in the crawl space.

Should the crawl space be vented, or should the vents be closed? We are getting conflicting advice.

A. If it is not, the crawl space floor should be thoroughly covered with a 6-mil plastic sheet to control soil moisture. It may not seem as if there is any moisture exuding from it, but there is.

The vents and the entrance door to the crawl space are best kept closed. In winter, with the vents open, your furnace is working overtime to satisfy your needs, and the plumbing pipes are at risk. In summer, huge amounts of moisture are absorbed by all the wood in the crawl space (*i.e.* floor joists, subfloor and any other wood members) and that moisture is released during the heating season adding to the moisture in the house.

If you control the soil moisture, venting a crawl space is not advised. But, to be sure, from time to time, enter the crawl space and give it the nose test. If it smells good and no musty smell is present, all is well. But if you smell mustiness, open the vents and the door during the dry and breezy times of the year in spring and fall.

Protecting ductwork and pipes

Q. My crawl space is approximately 4 feet deep. The dirt floor is covered with heavy plastic. The ductwork is very leaky, so much so that in winter, if the foundation vents are left open, a considerable amount of warm air comes out through them, and in summer cool air comes out. There are also water pipes running through.

Obviously, the ductwork needs attention, but I do not want to seal and insulate it, which could result in frozen pipes and cold floors.

A. Although building codes specify crawl-space ventilation, research done years ago by the National Association of Home Builders Research Foundation (now called the NAHB Research Center, Inc.) found that, in most cases, crawl-space ventilation was actually detrimental if the bare soil was thoroughly covered with plastic or a concrete slab. In humid southern climates, open vents actually caused extensive condensation and rot.

You should seriously consider taping the ductwork joints with special tape you can get from a heating contractor and closing the vents year around. Also, consider insulating the inside of the foundation with 1-inch-thick rigid foam insulation from the floor joists to no lower than 2 feet below grade. The reason for this, as you are inquiring in your letter, is to avoid risking cracking foundation walls from deeper frost penetration since heat loss through them is greatly reduced.

Your crawl space will be warmed sufficiently by the heat loss from the first floor, so you should not be concerned about frozen pipes even if you decide to have the ductwork insulated—not a bad idea. It should save you a considerable amount of money summer and winter alike. You do have a very wasteful system.

But before you install rigid insulation on the inside of the crawl space's exterior walls, have a pest management professional treat the soil next to the walls to prevent termite infestation that could occur undetected behind or through the insulation.

Wet sand over vapor barrier

Q. We are in the process of adding a four-season sunroom on the east side of our house. We put in a 5-foot frost wall, filling it to grade level with sand, then put a vapor barrier on the sand with another 2 to 3 inches of sand on top of the vapor barrier. The exterior wall was coated twice with waterproofing, and drainage was installed all around it. However, the natural grade of the land on one side is a slope toward the sunroom. When the excavating is done, there will be a swale away from it. The sunroom has now been framed in, and the windows and doors have been installed.

We are now experiencing very wet sand in the crawl space on top of the vapor barrier—so much so that the new nails from the floor construction have already rusted. We can make balls with the sand, but there is no standing water on the vapor barrier. We did get three heavy downpours during the construction, but we had it covered with a tarp and feel all of this wet sand cannot be from rain getting in. We have been running a fan and dehumidifier in the crawl space with very little result. The floor needs to be insulated, but the contractor will not do so with this moisture problem. The soil around our home is heavy clay.

Ten years ago, we put an addition on the west side of our house and used this same method and have never had any problems with moisture. The nails look like

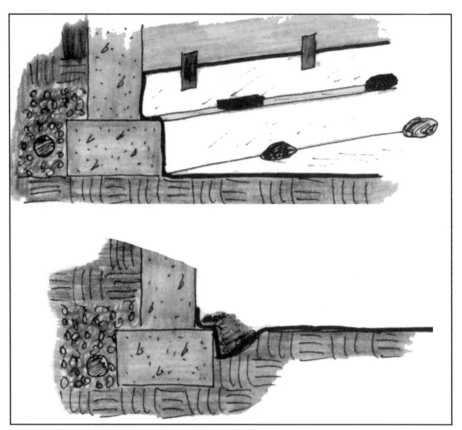

Cover the bare dirt with 6-mil plastic and cover its perimeter with a little dirt to seal moisture under it.

new under the floor, and the sand there is completely dry. We are at a loss as to what we need to do, and what could be causing this problem.

A. Check to see if there is moisture beading under the plastic vapor barrier; that may tell you if there is a lot of moisture coming up from the ground by capillary attraction or if there is leakage through the foundation. These conditions could be responsible for the problem if the plastic is not fully and properly installed. If the underside of the plastic is dry, this should reassure you that the waterproofing is working.

As for the wet sand on top of the plastic, my guess is that either the tarp did not stop all the water from the three downpours and that the sand got wet, or that the grade sloping toward the sun room (before the swale is put in) allowed surface water from the three downpours to get inside the crawl space in spite of the exterior waterproofing. It will take a long time for the sand to dry, and your builder is right in not wanting to insulate the floor until this condition is taken care of.

The best way to dry the sand is to introduce heat into the crawl space coupled with a small fan exhausting the heated and moist air to the outside. If you use a jet heater (your builder can supply one), you won't need an additional fan as it provides its own powerful thrust. But you will need an intake of exterior air to replenish the air that is exhausted out. You may have to cut openings in the floor at opposite ends of the crawl space to allow for good circulation. Be sure to keep all sunroom windows fully open. You should also stir the sand every day to bring the wet sand to the top of the bed.

Another way to handle the problem is to cut the plastic and pull it up in sections and let the wet sand mix with the other, dry sand. Then cover the entire crawl space with new 6-mil plastic, carrying it up the foundation walls a foot or so and taping it to the concrete walls. No need to put more sand on top of the plastic.

Dryer vent in crawl space

Q. My dryer vent is terminating in the crawl space. Would it be what is causing the floor boards to buckle in the center of my hallway?

A. It could indeed. A dryer vent should always terminate outdoors.

Insulating cottage floor above crawl space

Q. The kitchen floor of my cottage cannot be insulated from underneath because of the lack of clearance. Since it is used during the winter, is there a way to insulate on top of the existing floor? I can raise the floor 2 inches without any problem.

A. Use 1½-inch-thick extruded polystyrene rigid insulation (Styrofoam or FoamulaR) and cover it with ½-inch plywood. But if there are water pipes and drains running through the crawl space, it is best to insulate the perimeter of the crawl space walls from the outside.

Kitchen addition over crawl space is cold

Q. The addition to the kitchen in the house I bought last year is always 10° colder than the rest of the house and when the furnace fan comes on it feels like air-conditioned air coming out. By the time the air warms up, the fan shuts off.

There are 2 inches of Styrofoam insulation on the exterior walls of the crawl space but I don't know how deep in the ground the insulation extends; there is an outside access door. The crawl space is about 2 feet deep below the joists and the dirt is covered with plastic. How can I make this room extension warmer?

A. You haven't mentioned any insulation on the band joists (perimeter joists of the floor system). If this area is not insulated, it should be, as much heat is lost there. Use R-19 (6-inch) fiberglass batts with an integral vapor retarder. Cut the pieces needed at the ends of the joists 1 inch longer than the depth of the joists and squeeze them in over the wooden mud sill bolted onto the foundation and on which the joists rest.

Staple the insulation's side flanges to the sides of the joists and the excess inch of paper to the mud sill. Where the band joists are parallel to the other joists, cut a strip of insulation lengthwise instead of crosswise and 1 inch wider than the joists' depth. Staple the remaining flange to the floor sheathing above and the excess paper to the mud sill.

Fasten a piece of rigid foam insulation behind the access door and insulate the ducts with special duct insulation that you'll probably have to buy from a heating contractor. If there is no room to wrap insulation around the ducts, insulate the sides and bottom of the joists between which they run with regular fiberglass batts and, where they run beneath the joists, drape insulation around them as much as you can, making sure that you have slipped pieces of insulation between the joists immediately above the ducts so they are completely surrounded.

Sonotubes

Q. I have a 12×13-foot addition built on Sonotubes (poured concrete piers), and would like to close in the underside, both for aesthetics and to keep the floor warmer. The floor is insulated with 6 inches of fiberglass but is still cold. I am considering closing in the perimeter with ½-inch pressure-treated plywood. I would paint the bottom edge with black roofing cement where it comes into ground contact.

The area is fairly well drained. I know there could be some movement in winter but assume the worst it would do is buckle the plywood. Is this a good idea? Also, would I gain much by backing the plywood with 1-inch foam?

A. There is no reason why you can't do what you have in mind, but I would suggest that you make sure the soil under the addition is sloping away from the house foundation wall so no water can run back under the addition.

Common problem with sonotubes

I would also cover the soil with 6-mil plastic to keep moisture from getting into the insulated first-floor system, where it would cause eventual structural damage. There is no need to coat the bottom edge of the pressure-treated plywood with roofing cement. Not only are the plywood edges treated, but the cement will eventually degrade from contact with the soil. It would be best to bury the plywood skirt by at least 6 inches.

Considering that the underside of the floor is insulated with fiberglass, there might not be much to gain from insulating the plywood skirt with rigid insulation, but it's worth a try. You should also provide an access panel to check the underside of the addition yearly to make sure all is well.

2 Roofs and Siding

After foundations, roofs and sidings are the most important and problematic parts of the house. They are constantly exposed to the weather that they protect us from. Failure can lead to failure of other components of the house, in addition to the effects on comfort and aesthetics.

Venting

Extra roof vents

Q. We had a new roof put on last year. The old shingles were removed and new plywood, tarpaper and shingles were put on. There are two vents (one at each end of the house) and an electric fan through the roof controlled by a thermostat. The workers put four additional vents through the roof. The owner of the roofing company, while in the attic checking things out, volunteered that his workers had made a mistake by adding the four roof vents. He said that ordinarily, when an electric fan and vents are already in, additional passive vents are not added. His advice is that in summer, when the thermostat activates the fan, the four passive vents should be stuffed with plastic so they will not interfere with the airflow in the attic. Is there a problem, and, if there is, what can I do about it?

A. Not only is there no problem, but the additional passive vents should help satisfy the amount of ventilation required by the fan. Usually, the standard gable vents found in houses are not enough to provide the intake air a fan needs, so the fan draws air through all cracks, crevices and other openings between the attic and the living quarters. If you have central air conditioning, this robs conditioned air from the living quarters and costs you money to replace it with hot, moist outside air. The four extra vents should help alleviate this problem.

Expanding the venting with no overhang

Q. I am planning on having a new roof put on my house. The present one is 22 years old. The only attic ventilation is by means of two gable vents and a power roof vent.

Some roofers advocate a ridge vent. Others, a couple of low vents on the back side of the roof with a ridge vent; an additional vent at the top of the roof without a ridge vent; no additional vents. Some say use #15 felt, others #30 felt. Someone also suggested an aluminum flashing going up the roof about 6 inches and turned down

Ridge venting

over the fascia board behind the gutter. What is a person to do with all this different advice? The sun bakes on the roof all day long.

A. Your photo shows no roof overhangs and two minuscule gable vents. If there is a clear air space between the top of the insulation and the roof sheathing, I would recommend having a soffit venting system installed. I know of three products that can be used when there are no overhangs: Lamb & Ritchie makes a Vented Drip Edge, Lomanco makes the SV-10 Starter Vent; and Air Vent, Inc. makes the Drip Edge Vent.

You may be better off having a building contractor extend your roof to create a standard overhang which would allow the use of regular soffit vent strips and gutters. In that case, the suggested aluminum flashing is a very good idea to protect the house from ice penetration. Be sure you insist on Ice & Water Shield or equivalent at the eaves.

A ridge vent is also essential in combination with soffit venting, and Shingle-vent II is one of the best as it is externally baffled to direct wind over the ridge. The gable vents should be sealed up with plastic or plywood from the attic. As for the felt, #15 is okay, #30 is better.

Clogged soffit vents

Q. We recently purchased a home with ridge and soffit venting. However insulation was blown into the attic and the soffit vents are no longer working. We do have ridge venting, but it is not efficient since there is no air exchange.

Should we put in gable vents? The place for them is cut out, but they are not installed; instead, we have slits in the vinyl siding where the vents would go. Should we also put in an attic fan with a humidistat? What are your suggestions for correcting this situation? The house gets very hot during the summer months. Thanks.

A. I would not usually recommend adding gable vents, as they do not work well with ridge vents. Neither would I recommend using an attic fan under normal circumstances, as they also draw air from the living quarters of the house. This is a disadvantage if you use air conditioning in the summer and use the fan to remove excessive moisture in the winter, as it increases air infiltration into the living quarters—thereby increasing energy use—in winter and summer alike.

The best solution for you would be to pull the insulation away from the soffit vents, if it is possible, which would help both in summer and winter. If this is not possible, adding more insulation would help keep the house cooler in summer and, of course, also be of help in winter. If you prefer, a small fan can be installed in the gable opposite summer's prevailing winds and a corresponding gable vent cut in the opposite gable, but the intake gable should be sufficiently large to provide the net free ventilation area the fan requires—thus the need for a small fan. Remember that a louvered and screened gable vent only provides one-third of the free ventilation area for its size; for example, a 12-inch by 12-inch vent only provides one-third of 144 square inches of ventilation. It would be simpler to control the fan from a switch with a warning light installed on a wall in lieu of a temperature control in the attic.

Clogged ridge vent?

Q. My home near Indiana, Pa. is a single story brick veneer with an unfinished attic. The main portion of the attic is 70×30 feet. In 2000 I re-roofed with fiberglass shingles and installed a full length shingle-over ridge vent. At the same time I removed the gable vents and installed full-length vented vinyl soffit (22 inches wide by 70 feet, front and back).

During both winters since the ridge vent installation, I've noticed snow covers the ridge vent and does not melt, often for weeks and sometimes more than a month. I have a very "cold" attic with plenty of insulation and careful sealing from heated spaces. Obviously, there is no movement of air through the ridge vent at a time I believe attic ventilation is most critical. I have found no condensation in the attic during these periods of snow blocking the vents.

Due to the prevailing winds, fresh air may be entering through the front soffit and exiting on the rear side of the house. I worry that my attic ventilation is not adequate during much of the winter. What do you think?

A. It may be that the ridge vent that was installed on the roof is one of the many that does not have an external wind baffle. I have seen these types not only get clogged with blowing snow but also, if they do not have some filtering material, allow serious penetration of snow or rain to enter the attic.

The purpose of an external wind baffle is to deflect the wind over the ridge instead of letting it enter the attic through the ridge vent which, in effect, negates the purpose of a ridge vent. A ridge vent is an exhaust and not meant to become an intake.

This ridge vent was crushed by someone stepping on it while clearing snow off the roof. This type of ridge vent can also collapse under the weight of heavy, wet snow.

Unfortunately, most ridge vents offered on the market do not have an external baffle—a victim of the effort to make cheaper products in the battle for market share. That is why I always specify ShingleVent II as a shingle-over vent with an external baffle.

The most important aspects of attic health are tight seals of all perforations and joints between materials to prevent convection of warm, moist air from the living areas into the attic. High levels of insulation will help keep the attic cold. Ventilation is always helpful but since you haven't seen any problems while the ridge vent appears to remain covered, stop worrying about it and rejoice on the success of the sealing between the warm and the cold areas. Be aware also that snow is porous and sublimates constantly so it may not look like there is air movement but there may be, unless the ridge vent itself is clogged with packed snow and not just covered with loose snow.

Getting rid of attic fans

Q. Is there a compelling reason to replace an existing attic fan with a ridge vent system? I am planning to replace the shingles on my roof and this would be a good time to replace my thermostatically controlled fan and roof-mounted exhaust. The fan seems to work OK, but are there reasons to consider a ridge vent?

A. Roof and attic fans are responsible for increasing the cost of heating and air-conditioning houses because it is almost impossible to provide them with the needed amount of air intake. So conditioned air is sucked into the attic through all sorts of cracks and crannies in the ceiling and the walls of the living space and from the basement or crawl space.

A full-length ridge vent in conjunction with full-length soffit vents—which should equal or exceed the net free ventilation area of the ridge vent—is the most effective passive attic ventilation system. But there are two caveats: There must be a free air space of at least 1½ inches between the soffit and the ridge vents, and the ridge vent should be externally baffled (as Air Vent Inc.'s Shingle-Vent II and Benjamin Obdyke's Xtractor Vent X18 are) to function under windy conditions.

Soffit vents needed with ridge vent

Q. The contractor who will install a new roof on my house suggested a ridge vent. I now have two large gable louvered vents. There are no soffit vents and the contractor says the ridge vent by itself is sufficient. Is this correct?

I also have a small attic fan that goes on when the attic temperature is above 95°F. Should I have it removed? I had it installed when I replaced the central air-conditioner since I was told that it would decrease my cooling costs.

A. Oh, my! Such misinformation! A ridge vent is not effective if there are no matching soffit vents to provide an air intake. Gable louvers work reasonably well but need wind from the right direction and do not ventilate attics completely; the top center portion does not get ventilated. They are not compatible with ridge and soffit venting as they short-circuit the soffits.

The attic fan may have actually increased your cooling costs unless the two gable louvered vents could supply enough air to satisfy the cfm (cubic feet per minute) rating of the fan. If they didn't, it would draw air from inside the house through any cracks and crevices available—and the average house has plenty of them.

The best system is an externally baffled ridge vent in combination with soffit vents of equal or greater net free ventilation area (NFVA). The gable vents should be closed up with plywood from the attic and the attic fan should be removed.

Venting a single-pitched roof addition

Q. I put a 10×18-foot addition onto my home. It has a slanted roof, one end of which is attached to the side of the house. The other end has a 1-foot overhang with air vents. It is a plywood and metal roof. The rafters are 2×8 inches, 16 inches on center. I am using proper vents between the plywood and insulation. The insulation is 6½ inches thick with Kraft paper as a vapor barrier. The ceiling is 2×4-foot tiles.

There is no attic. I am getting a large amount of condensation in the ceiling. So much so that I had to take the ceiling and insulation down. They were soaked. Can you give me some advice as to how I can stop this condensation?

A. It sounds as if warm, moist air from the living quarters is convecting into the space between the ceiling and the roof through the spaces between the ceiling tiles. The Kraft vapor retarder is not very effective against this, and neither is the ventilation. Soffit venting without some form of venting at the peak of the roof is practically worthless.

I would suggest that you install a special ridge vent made for situations like yours. It is installed at the top of the roof against the house wall, but it needs to be set under the siding and whatever is used (felt, Tyvek or equivalent) over the sheathing. The vent is manufactured by Air Vent, a Gibraltar company, and it is called the Flash FilterVent. Their Web site at www.airvent.com.

After the plywood and rafters have thoroughly dried, replace the insulation and carefully staple 6-mil plastic over the entire ceiling so that the inside air will not convect into the rafter spaces.

Avoiding wide metal eaves

Q. I am planning to retire soon and am in the process of discussing the building of my retirement home with a contractor to whom I have given the plans I drew up. He suggests putting wide metal borders at the eaves of the roof to protect it from ice and snow. I don't happen to find these attractive at all but I do see many houses with them. Is there a working alternative?

A. These metal ice belts are of an age past; modern technology has made them unnecessary and you are right, they are not very attractive. They did serve the purpose before we understood that we could avoid the problems they were intended to protect the house from by effective levels of insulation and ventilation—one of the side benefits of the '70s oil crisis. You are fortunate in that, when building a

Acid rain damage on a metal border at a roof edge

new house, it is very easy to provide continuous soffit and ridge venting as well as clear air channels of at least 1½" depth in each rafter bay to keep the roof sheathing constantly washed by a current of moving, drier exterior air. In the case of a regular attic, the best way to insure the correct air space and its integrity over time is to use a specially made cardboard baffle at each rafter seat; the foam ones so commonly used with 16" on center rafter framing have several problems that, in my opinion, are reasons enough to discourage their use (foam baffles for 24" on center framing are fine). And both types are expensive. However, foam baffles do not protect the ends of the fiberglass batts from air movements at the wall plates as cardboard baffles do.

Where cathedral ceilings are planned, the best way to provide continuous air spaces between the roof sheathing and the top of the insulation is to nail 1×2 wood strips to the sides of the rafters tightly against the roof sheathing and to tack 1-inch rigid extruded polystyrene foam insulation under the wood strips. This provides an additional R-5 to the insulation of the ceiling and a 1½-inch smooth channel for air to flow from the soffit vents to the ridge vent. This is my favorite way to provide the recommended ventilation and one which I developed over 30 years ago to prevent the problems plaguing cathedral ceilings. It has the added benefit of increasing the R-factor of a roof assembly not always permitting an adequate level of insulation.

The second part of the package is to provide levels of insulation as recommended for the region and do it well.

But this subject would not be complete without mentioning another approach. Probably the best way to insulate a cathedral ceiling is to spray closed-cell polyurethane insulation directly onto the roof sheathing. Note the emphasis on closed-cell; do not use open-cell polyurethane sprayed insulation (such as Icynene) as it does absorb moisture and, under these conditions, there is no way to ventilate it out. This needs to be done by well-trained and experienced applicators familiar with this ever-evolving technology—and it is expensive—but you will have no concerns with moisture build-up, molds or any of the other problems that can develop with the use of fiberglass insulation. And be sure that a membrane such as WR Grace Ice & Water Shield is installed along the eaves and at all roof penetration.

Don't vent into soffits

Q. This winter I noticed an ice buildup approximately 8 inches thick and 36 inches wide on only one area of our shingled roof. I assume it is caused by the bathroom exhaust fan that is vented into the aluminum soffit. The builder said all bathroom exhaust fans are installed that way and that I shouldn't worry about a small buildup of ice.

Because of the fan's location, it is nearly impossible to enter the attic and check whether or not there is a buildup of ice inside the aluminum soffit or in the attic. Could there be? And would such a buildup cause damage inside? Can the ice on the roof damage the shingles? What can I do about it?

A. Your diagnosis is probably accurate and if it is the practice in your area to vent bath exhaust fans in the soffit, it's wrong. A soffit vent is an air-intake point—not an exhaust. In dumping warm, moist air into the soffit all that is accomplished is to turn the exhausted air up into the attic. Since it is warm and moist, it will do two things: cause the snow on the roof to melt and turn into ice on the shingles and, two, create condensation, which will also ice inside the attic on the roof sheathing and nearby rafters.

Inside frosting or icing eventually melts and can cause, if in large enough quantity, wetting of the insulation and damage to walls, ceilings, paint and eventually may even result in structural rot.

Roof icing caused by too warm an attic

Repeated large ice buildup on a roof can damage the shingles and tear off the mineral granules and can lead to interior leakage, as well, adding to the problems that may already be present in the attic.

You should have the fan's exhaust relocated to exit through a gable wall—not through the roof or any other vent.

Turbines

Q. A few years ago I installed two wind turbines as roof vents. I became curious about their efficiency because the attic was so hot that I tested them by leaving the trap door to the attic open and holding a match under one of the vents, spinning under a 20 mph wind outside. The flame didn't even flutter.

Which of all the devices available on the market would you recommend short of a roof vent fan?

A. Roof turbines and roof jacks are not efficient ventilators. For them to do any good you would have to have so many of them that the house would look like a porcupine.

I am not a fan (pun intended) of roof fans because they don't help to remove moisture in winter unless some fancy electronics are installed to control them safely. They also use electricity and need an adequate supply of intake air properly placed.

By far, and without question, the most efficient year round ventilating system for attics is a combination of continuous baffled ridge and soffit vents with an unobstructed air passage of a minimum of 1½ inches at each rafter bay.

Asphalt and Fiberglass Shingles

Best colors for roof

Q. Many homeowners in our area are putting black roofs on their houses and garages. Is there an advantage?

A. They show dirt and mildew a lot less. In cold climates dark roofs, properly ventilated and with well insulated attic floors, should not create discomfort in summer. When there is no snow on the roof and the sun shines it may increase the attic's temperature measurably, thus reducing the energy load on the house.

White or light-colored roofs do reflect the sun's heat and are helpful in Florida and on the Gulf Coast. However, these roofs soon turn gray and black from pollution and molds.

More and more replacements in those regions are also made with black shingles for that reason. And again, if the roofs are well ventilated and levels of insulation equal those recommended for cold regions, there should be no additional stress on air conditioning systems unless they are installed in the attic.

Is underlayment necessary?

Q. Please help settle a friendly dispute in the neighborhood. Recently my contractor installed a new roof on my house without using roofing paper. Many of my neighbors noticed it and suggested that I insist on the use of roofing paper prior to nailing the shingles. The contractor informed me that research has proven that roofing paper served no real purpose in preventing leaks and making the roof last longer. What are the pros and cons?

A. The following quote from the Residential Asphalt Roofing Manual of the Asphalt Roofing Manufacturers Assoc. should settle the debate:

"An asphalt saturated felt underlayment should always be used in new construction (the exposed deck of an existing house whose shingles have been removed is the same thing) because it provides two vital functions: It keeps the deck dry until shingles are applied thereby precluding any problems that may result if shingles were placed on wet or very moist deck lumber or if the plywood delaminated from moisture absorption.

If shingles should be lifted, damaged or torn by wind after their application, it provides secondary protection by shielding the deck from wind-driven rain and preventing water from reaching the structure."

Can new shingles be placed over old ones?

Q. Our 25-year-old house needs a new roof. Should the old asphalt shingles be replaced and new tar paper and shingles be put on or can new tar paper and shingles be applied over the old ones to save money?

A. If there is only one layer of shingles on the roof now, new ones can generally be applied over the old, although it's often not a good idea.

If there are two layers of shingles on now or the contractor is leery of the capacity of the rafters to take on the extra dead load because of their length, depth, condition, or spacing, then the existing shingles and felt should be removed and new ones put on. In snow country, most roofers will insist on removing the old shingles.

If new shingles can be applied over the old, be sure this is done in a proper manner. They should not just be nailed over the old in the same pattern as this causes ripples where too many layers build up. The first two courses should be cut and fitted to build a flat platform at the eaves. Subsequent courses are butted against the old shingle row immediately above and so on. This creates a smooth roof. Directions are generally printed on the shingle packages.

Concerns about weight of roofing materials

Q. I have a question nobody has really answered for me. Our house was built in 1863. In 1976, my dad put on a "cold roof," which consists of lots of plywood over an air space, with a vented ridge, topped by shingles. The shingles need replacing and we have talked to a number of roofers about the best way to re-roof. Tearing off all the shingles and replacing them would be terribly expensive.

We have also looked at the idea of just putting on a metal roof without removing the shingles, but I am getting concerned about the weight of the roof. I realize that a metal roof would shed the snow so efficiently that during the winter the weight would be less than it is now in the winters, but I am wondering if there is a "finite" weight that one should consider when re-roofing. Any words of wisdom?

A. There is a finite weight to consider. You would need to have a structural engineer calculate what is known as the "dead" weight of all materials on the rafters now. The steeper the roof, the better, as the rafters are stronger than on a shallower roof. But keep in mind that metal roofs do not always shed snow, so this cannot be counted on to relieve the live load on the roof.

If you are considering a standing seam metal roof, you will have to remove the shingles; otherwise, they will "telegraph" the shape of the shingles underneath; this type of roof is also quite expensive. That would not be the case with sheets of metal that are screwed on, but they are not as attractive and might affect the value of your house. With all this in mind, it makes more sense to remove the shingles.

Flashing when re-roofing

Q. We plan to reroof over existing original shingles. Is it okay to put the new shingles over the existing chimney flashing to avoid having to remove the old one?

Also, must the first row of shingles be reversed since the old ones will still be under the new ones?

A. There is no need to remove the old step flashing, but you should install a new piece under each row of shingles and a new apron. Simply lift up the counter flashing while you install the new base flashing and then put it back down again. Failure to provide a new base flashing will encourage leakage.

There's no need to reverse the first course of shingles but to get a smooth job you must first run metal drip edge over the old shingles around the entire perimeter of the roof, then cut 6-inch strips off the top of enough shingles to run the

A "cricket" used to direct water away from the base of the chimney to prevent leaks.

length of the eaves and set those 6-inch wide strips on top of the bottom course of the old shingles so they butt against the second course and fully cover the metal drip edge.

Then cut 1-inch strips off the top of enough shingles to run the length of the eaves and throw the strips away. Place the shortened shingles over the first and second courses and butting against the third course. From now on continue with full shingles as you have built, and are continuing to build, a flat platform for the shingles to be on as you go up the roof

However, most experienced roofers and other authorities don't recommend adding a new asphalt shingle roof over an old one where winter snowfalls are heavy because of the additional weight on the roof rafters.

Selecting a roofing contractor

Q. My wife and I own a home in a beautiful rural town in Sussex County, New Jersey. We purchased our home from the original owners, who had the house built in the late 1960s. I do not know when the roof was last replaced (there are two layers of shingles on the roof now), but a large number of shingles have started to peel and shingle material is starting to collect in the gutters.

I suspect this is a telltale sign that it is time to replace the roof. What are the basics of selecting a roofing contractor? I have started to research roofing contractors in my area. To my surprise, the vast majority of them have an unfavorable rating with the NJ Better Business Bureau. The BBB Web site does not give specific details behind the rating other than saying there is at least one case/dispute unsolved.

I would also appreciate any suggestions you have regarding roofing material. Are there shingles I should avoid? Are there any installation practices I should insist on?

A. Two layers of shingles are maximum. In fact, in heavy snow areas, quality roofers will not put new shingles over existing shingles. Mineral granules in your gutters are a normal wear process and do not generally indicate that the roof needs replacing unless there are other signs of age and deterioration such as the peeling you have noticed.

I would think that there are good, reputable roofers in New Jersey. The best way to find one is probably to ask friends and neighbors who have had roofs redone in the last few years.

Ask how the company dealt with them initially in providing the estimate. Then, once it was awarded the job, was the company prompt in meeting its promises to them? Was the job done on time, by workers who were clean in appearance and manner? Was the job site kept clean as the work progressed and left very clean when it was done without nails and other junk left for the homeowners to take care of? Were the dealings handled professionally throughout? Was any complaint handled promptly and efficiently without excuses and the homeowners having to call repeatedly? Were phone calls and messages answered promptly?

These are all hallmarks of a reliable company to work with. Be sure you are presented with a contract specifying all the materials and labor to be used and for a firm price without all kinds of escape clauses. You may be asked to pay part of the price in advance but be sure it is not more than 10 percent of the contract until the work has started. Do not make the final payment until you are absolutely satisfied that all work has been done as contracted. Make sure the work is warrantied in writing for at least one year and get the shingle manufacturer's warranty in writing as well.

As for types of shingles, they are all pretty much the same. The problems with fiberglass shingles of a few years back is apparently fixed. Although the practice is considered acceptable, I personally would not allow a shingle roof to be put on with staples. I have seen too many problems with them after a few years, caused by careless application by mechanics. The tendency is to go fast, without following proper techniques. Insist on #15 felt (preferably #30) being used on the sheathing.

Buying new shingles

Q. Our asphalt roof shingles are about 12 years old and beginning to curl. Since there are two layers of shingles, we know that we will have to have them all removed. This will give us a chance to check the roof boards. What else should the contractor check? Could you comment on different weights of shingles as some advertise 15- or 30-year life.

A. There is really nothing else to check and, unless the first roof was allowed to leak for a long time before the second one was applied, there is little reason to believe the roof sheathing should be damaged.

As to the weight of shingles to use, the choice is yours. The most frequently used shingles have a 20-year life expectancy.

But the fact that your 12-year shingles are beginning to curl doesn't necessarily mean they are ready to be replaced; they may have several more years of life left. However, it may indicate a moisture problem in the attic. Check that out and correct it, if necessary, by installing a continuous, externally baffled, ridge vent at the time the new roof is put on. Continuous soffit vents are essential in combination with the ridge vent to provide ventilation and, of course, there must be free air channels between soffit and ridge vents.

Fiberglass or asphalt

Q. We need a new roof. We are receiving confusing information from different contractors. One says we should use fiberglass shingles because they are lighter and more-fire resistant, while another says he uses only asphalt shingles because there has been so much trouble with fiberglass. What do you suggest?

A. Fiberglass shingles often failed in years past, because the manufacturers skimped on the asphalt needed to impregnate the fiberglass matts. The problem has been solved, I am told, but I personally still feel more comfortable using asphalt.

Why is the weight a consideration? Does the one contractor pushing the fiberglass plan on putting the new shingles over the existing ones? Although this is an accepted practice and there are specific instructions to follow to avoid problems, particularly on shallow-to-medium pitch roofs, one must make sure that the rafters or trusses can take the additional weight. This depends on their size and spacing, the dead load they already carry (sheathing and roof covering) and the live load (snow loads) expected for the area.

In snow country, it is usually recommended, and practiced, to remove the old shingles.

It is also preferable to have the shingles fastened with nails as staples are not that easy to shoot properly and, if not, may eventually work through the covering shingles.

Flying shingles

Q. The asphalt roof shingles on our condominium building keep flying off whenever we have strong winds. We've had this problem from day one and the building is only five years old. We've had the roof repaired at least a dozen times and the cost is getting out of hand. How can we correct this situation?

A. The shingles are probably fiberglass and may have been installed with staples, perhaps even skimping on that as well. If they were installed in cold weather, the seal may not have taken hold before the wind blew the first shingles off, but that would only apply to the first spring or summer.

The shingles may be defective in that there isn't enough sealant on the tabs; poor runs do happen. You would have a claim against the manufacturer. Have an experienced roofer look at the roof, you may need a replacement, in which case consider using asphalt and not fiberglass shingles and using a heavier grade.

Shingle curl

Q. My house is a small ranch with a simple hip roof that has three roof vents and numerous vents in the overhangs all around the house. There is no sign of condensation in the attic, which has 12 inches of loose insulation in the floor. I had a new shingle roof put on over the original one three years ago. Now, in the winter, I notice the edges of the shingles curling slightly. When the temperature rises in the spring, they flatten out.

I have been told it could be a ventilation problem. What is your opinion?

A. The winter curling is caused by contractional forces brought about by cold temperatures. There is a different amount of asphalt coating on the top of the shingles in comparison to their backs. Warm temperatures make them more pliable and they flatten out. It's a common problem and nothing to worry about.

Wavy roof shingles probably won't cause problems if they flatten out in summer.

Wavy shingles

Q. What causes fiberglass shingles to become wavy looking in the cold months? Some of the bottom edges of the shingles even pop up as if the adhesive under the edges has been released. It happens every winter and, when warm weather arrives, they flatten nicely. This did not happen with the old asphalt shingles, which were replaced with the fiberglass five years ago.

A. Check the previous answer to see if it applies in your case. You didn't describe how the waviness looks. For instance, does it show a horizontal pattern every 4 feet up the roof, or is it at every course of shingles?

If it shows every 4 feet horizontally up the roof, it could be caused by plywood sheets under the shingles absorbing moisture and buckling. This can happen when an attic suffers from convection of warm, moist air from the living quarters of the house, especially if the attic has inadequate or no ventilation. (Even well-ventilated attics can suffer from this phenomenon, as convection can overcome any ventilation system.)

If the pattern is at every course of shingles, it may be that the roof sheathing of your house is made of boards instead of plywood, and the boards are absorbing moisture (as described above) and cupping. This is signaled by the pattern in the shingles. As the weather warms up, the sheathing dries up and straightens out, something plywood seldom does.

The shingles themselves also shrink in winter and expand in warm weather, accentuating the patterns you see.

Just for your information, fiberglass shingles are also manufactured with asphalt. The shingles often referred to as asphalt are made with organic felts and are thicker than fiberglass, but are not rated as class A (fire retardant) like fiberglass shingles are.

Removing paint spatters from shingles

Q. While painting the second story of our house, my husband splattered latex paint onto the brown asphalt shingles over the garage. We tried Oops and paint thinner to get it off without success. The roof looks terrible from the road. What can we do about it?

A. You should not have used petroleum-based products on an asphalt shingle roof as they soften the asphalt binder. Try Savogran's TSP-PF; it is a phosphate-free substitute for TSP. Make a strong solution and daub it on the splatters until they soften, then hose it off. You may end up having to replace the affected shingles.

Removing rust stains from roof

Q. A year ago we purchased our house; the owners had the roof replaced the year before, but didn't replace the flashing around the chimney, which, according to the roofer, is what resulted in the nasty rust streak down the front of this new roof.

We subsequently had the flashing replaced and are now wondering how to rid the roof of the rust mark. I have a product called CLR (calcium, lime and rust remover), which I thought I'd try spraying through the garden hose, but I am concerned about the effect of that much pressure on the shingles and whether or not it would result in water getting underneath the shingles. Any advice? Do we face having to replace the shingles?

A. I hope, for your sake, that the old flashing was really the problem. Most chimney flashings are made of two parts: a step flashing—usually aluminum, and a counter flashing—usually lead. Neither would cause rust stains.

The only way that the flashing could cause rust stains is if it were galvanized metal, which was used on very old houses. Or perhaps there is a galvanized metal cap on top of your chimney. If so, it should be painted or removed.

Another possibility is that a wood stove was connected to this chimney. In that case, the stains may have been caused by creosote. Spraying the roof with a product that removes rust should not damage the shingles as long as the product is water-based. No product containing petroleum or its derivatives should be used on asphalt shingles, however; it would seriously damage them and void your shingle warranty if it is transferable to new owners. Water should not get under the shingles if you spray with your garden hose attachment, using a fine spray and spraying as if it were rain falling on the roof.

Be sure to read the instructions on the CLR container before using it. If CLR is not appropriate, you can make a solution to remove rust with oxalic acid crystals. Buy oxalic acid in janitorial supply stores, and mix the crystals in warm water to the saturation point (proportions are 1 pound of crystals to 1 gallon of water—that should be enough to do quite a bit of roofing). Be careful handling oxalic acid; it is a very potent chemical. Wear rubber gloves and skin protection, and use a glass or plastic container—do not use metal. That goes for the sprayer, too!

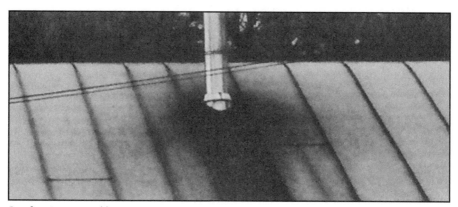

Roof stains caused by creosote

Algae-stained shingles

Q. The off-white asphalt shingles on my roof have developed a blackish stain in the area where a maple tree hangs partially over it. Can this be caused by sap dripping from the branches? If it is, is there any way to remove the discoloration?

A. The staining is more likely due to an algae that has developed because the tree shades the roof and it remains damp for extended periods of time.

You can remove this algae but it is likely to come back. It may also help to trim the tree branches so some air can circulate more freely.

Soak all plantings under the roof and cover them with plastic. If you have metal gutters, be sure water from a garden hose is run through them during the entire treatment and any following dripping.

Mix 3 parts fresh Clorox bleach and 1 part water in a plastic pail. On a windless day, working from a ladder and using a plastic garden sprayer, apply the solution at the rate of 1 gallon per 50 square feet of shingles so they get wet but not to the extent that there will be excessive dripping.

When done, rinse the plastic off and soak the vegetation again. Do not rinse the roof. It will take several weeks for the stains to disappear.

Better to replace shingles than to coat them

Q. Is there a product that can be sprayed, brushed or rolled on an aging shingle roof to extend its life? And, if available, are there any contractors who do this process? The shingles are not wood.

A. Assuming that the shingles are asphalt or fiberglass, coatings can be applied, but they are expensive and the overall look is not attractive. A new coating would not change the basic brittleness of aged shingles so, as any shingles break, the coating goes with them. You would be better off having the shingles replaced with your choice of roofing when the time to retire them has come. This will be less expensive and longer lasting in the long run.

Cedar Shingles and Shakes

Preserving cedar roofs

Q. It was with concerned interest that we read about the care of a cedar-shake roof in your column. Our roof is five years old and we weren't aware that we should give it special care. Now we'd like to start and would like to know where to purchase the necessary material and how to apply it.

A. Years ago, the cedar people had us believing that a cedar roof was a long-lasting investment that did not need attention other than removing tree debris, etc. They have now changed their minds and recommend treatment. Another victory for consumerism. My own personal experience, dating back 35 years, is that the average cedar roof generally does not last more than 12 to 15 years.

Cedar shakes, splitting, with various lichen and algae growths

Lichen growth on shingles

There are exceptions, of course, but they depend on the climate and location. Even the weather-resistant species of wood exposed to sun and water begin to deteriorate, as they lose their natural oils. It is important to preserve these roofs or to replenish them, which is why an oil-borne preservative is preferable. Otherwise, wood will desiccate, curl, check and split.

A five-year-old cedar roof is ready for treatment and one of the most complete treatments available is provided by Amteco's TWP Roof and Deck Sealant. It will replenish the oil the wood needs and has lost while also providing water repellency and protection against decay. It will need to be re-applied every three to five years.

Your roof may need to be power-washed to remove the dead wood fibers and any other pollution. Let it dry thoroughly. TWP can be applied with a garden sprayer, using as fine a mist as you can get, and wetting the wood uniformly. Wait 30 to 60 minutes minimum or overnight, and apply a uniform second coat without runs. It is best not to apply TWP in cold weather.

Breathing space for cedar shingles

Q. My 15-year-old cedar shingles are rotting and I need to have them replaced. The contractor I talked to told me that the reason why they rotted is that they were nailed over plywood sheathing instead of over boards with space in between so they could breathe.

Is this correct and, if so, how can the breathing space be provided without tearing the plywood off as he suggests?

A. In regions where heavy snow is customary, you have to weigh the advantages and disadvantages of one system over the other. Spaced sheathing obtained by strapping across the rafters does provide breathing for wood shakes or shingles but it can also result in incursion of snow in the attic unless other measures are taken to prevent it.

Both the Red Cedar Shingle & Handsplit Shake Bureau in the U.S. and the Council of Forest Industries of British Columbia indicate that either spaced or solid sheathing is acceptable anywhere, but recommend the use of solid sheathing in areas subject to wind-driven snow.

However, you can now have the protection of solid sheathing and provide breathing space for wood shingles or shakes with the Cedar Breather—a three-dimensional nylon mesh that is applied over #30 felt covering the solid decking. Ridge venting is highly recommended in combination with the mesh to allow unimpeded air circulation. This product is approved by many authoritive sources and meets U.S. and Canadian building codes, according to the manufacturer.

Roof Vegetation

Over the years, some of the most frequently recurring questions have had to do with growths and discoloration of roofs. There are a wide variety of culprits, but the most common culprits fall into two categories: (a) moss or lichen and (b) mold, algae or mildew.

Green growth on roof

Q. There are patches of green growth on my roof that are not like moss but like that on a nearby oak tree. This growth is heaviest on the part of the roof shaded by a maple tree on the side of the house.

How can I stop this growth from spreading? Is it necessary to remove the tree?

A. The sample of growth you sent me reveals it to be lichen. It is a type of fungus and it needs moisture to grow. It is a natural fungus that grows everywhere in nature—on trees, rocks, fences and their posts, as well as roofs, walls and any other damp, shaded matter. It does not cause a serious problem on shingles. Fiberglass shingles are not immune; neither are other types of roof coverings.

To kill it, you can spray it with a water-base herbicide; it is imperative that you do not use any product containing petroleum distillates, as it would damage the shingles.

Or, an alternative is to spray a solution made of 3 parts white vinegar to 1 part water on the lichen. Use a regular garden sprayer on a windless day. It will take several weeks for it to die.

If needed, trim the lower branches of the maple tree if they are too close to the roof.

Moss on fiberglass roof

Q. My house is situated in a shady area on a lake shore. The fiberglass roof shingles are covered with moss and lichen. How can I remove it and keep it from growing again?

A. To kill the unwanted growth, spray a water-based weed killer, or a solution of 3 parts white vinegar and 1 part water, but this will not remove it. The dead and decaying material may eventually be washed away by the elements. This growth

The valley is lined with a single sheet of flashing, nailed on its sides, rather than strips no longer than 6 to 8-feet long of light-gauge roll stock aluminum flashing overlapping each other, nailed at the top of each piece, and clipped at the sides under the shingles.

does not materially affect the life of the shingles and you may cause more damage trying to remove it than if you left it alone. The dampness of the site is encouraging it and the only thing you can do about it is to take whatever steps are necessary to allow more sun to shine on the roof.

Moss on shake roof

Q. You have recommended using a 3-parts Clorox bleach to 1-part water solution to remove mold from roofs. We have a lot of moss and mildew on ours. Would this mixture be safe to use on a redwood shake roof that is 12 to 14 years old?

A. This solution is very successful in killing several forms of algae responsible for discoloring asphalt shingle roofs in moist climates. It is not as successful in killing moss or lichen. Although you can try spraying a solution of 3 parts white vinegar to 1 part water, your best bet is to have the roof power-washed by an experienced contractor and then treated with a water repellent, wood preservative oil-based treatment that will rejuvenate the shakes and increase their longevity. Extensive research in the Gulf Coast of Texas, which has probably the worst conditions a roof can encounter, has shown Amteco's TWP Roof and Deck Sealants to be superior to other products in accomplishing that.

For more information, check Amteco's Web site at www.twp-amteco.com or call toll-free 800-969-4811.

An inadvertent zinc treatment from the metal vents on this barn roof. The light colored part of the roof is actually green with growth. The barn's roof is black.

Zinc treatment

Q. I recently read in your column that zinc would keep mold from growing on roofs. It also gave information about ventilation. Unfortunately, I had already had my roof reshingled; the old one was 23 years old and had rotted away from lichens and moss growing on it.

What can I do now to keep this from happening again?

A. A strip of zinc or a zinc-coated ridge vent applied to the ridge of a roof will prevent the growth of certain molds and algae that thrive on asphalt, fiberglass, asbestos cement, and certain other types of roof coverings. It may not prevent lichen and moss from developing on cedar roofs.

The small amount of zinc that would be slowly leached out from the zinc strips should not affect the vegetation below. Copper will also prevent the growth of moss, lichen and algae. (Algae is responsible for the ugly dark streaks we see on so many roofs.)

Z-Stop zinc strips, made by Wespac, are available in 50-foot rolls, 2½ inches wide. A similar product, Shingle Shield, is made by Chicago Metallic. Another choice is to have strips of zinc or copper cut out of any galvanized or copper sheet by a metal shop. Have the strips cut wide enough (8 inches would be fine) and bent in the middle to the same pitch as the roof. They can then be applied directly over the ridge vent or, if it is covered with capping shingles, over them. These methods work best on a new roof.

Black stains

Q. I moved into a new house in Florida about five years ago. Last year I noticed a black fungus, mold or mildew on the north side of my roof, which appears to be asphalt shingles.

Professional cleaners I called upon quoted me from $250 to $400 to clean the roof with only a two-year guarantee which, to me, is no guarantee at all. I'd like to clean my own roof, if you'll tell me how.

A. The prices you were quoted are not bad considering the investment in equipment, the time involved, insurance, and various other costs a contractor has to pay. Contractors can't give you a longer warranty than two years because there is no way they can stop natural processes which cause the mold to develop. You live in a hot, damp climate that is conducive to the growth of fungi, molds and mildew.

You can clean your own roof with a mixture of 3 quarts of fresh Clorox bleach to 1 quart of water per 50 square feet of roof. Apply the solution on a windless day using a plastic garden sprayer. Cover the ground under the roof, if you have no gutters, and soak the plants and the grass thoroughly with clean water before and after treatment of the roof. If you have metal gutters and downspouts, you should have someone run a garden hose in them as you spray the roof to dilute this very corrosive bleach solution.

Try to do the job from a ladder. Don't walk on the roof unless you absolutely have to and, if you do, use tennis-type shoes and walk on dry shingles in the cool of the morning. Do not walk on asphalt shingles when they are hot, or in freezing weather.

Do not rinse off the solution. Be patient; it will take a while for the mold to die.

White stains

Q. My shingled roof has a white stain caused by water, which dripped from the evaporative cooler. Is there a safe way to remove it? I have been told to use a solution containing bleach, vinegar and water.

A. You don't say what kind of shingles so I'll assume they are asphalt or fiberglass.

The stain is due to an accumulation of the chemicals such as calcium in the water. Use full-strength white vinegar. If the stain is small, use an eye dropper to put the vinegar on it or, if large, pour it on slowly. Use an old toothbrush and gently soften the calcium while the vinegar acts on it. Bleach is used to remove algae—which is not your problem.

Have a garden hose handy to flush the treated area quickly, if you notice a problem, and when the job is done.

Tar stains

Q. How can I remove tar that has bled out onto my asphalt shingles as a result of a petroleum-based insect spray that was applied to them? The roof is gray-white.

A. You have found out painfully that petroleum-based products dissolve the asphalt binder in roof shingles. Unfortunately, I have bad news for you: they can't be brought back to their original shape and the stains cannot be removed. But you could try to paint them with a latex paint mixed to match the shingles as closely as possible. You may have to redo this periodically.

Stained shingles

Q. Two years ago I reroofed my 100-year-old farm house with fiberglass shingles. The elm tree that overhangs part of the roof has caused black streak stains running down the roof where the closest branches are. How can I clean the roof without damaging it?

A. You must not use any petroleum-based material or scrub the shingles. The former would attack the asphalt binder, the latter dislodge the protective mineral granules. So you are limited in what you can do. Try the remedy for removal of mildew stains from asphalt and fiberglass shingles.

It may work in dissolving and bleaching out the sap streaks which, by the way, may also be caused by mold and mildew.

After pruning the tree, as you plan to do, mix 3 quarts of fresh Clorox bleach with 1 quart of water for each 50 square feet of area to be treated. Use a plastic garden sprayer to apply it to the shingles on a windless day after covering all shrubs with plastic. While spraying, have someone run water from a garden hose in metal gutters and downpouts that would collect the roof run-off as the solution is very corrosive. Dilute the solution that collects on the plastic and the ground with plenty of water when you're done. Allow time to judge whether the treatment works. If it doesn't, I have no other suggestion at this time.

Rust and creosote stains

Q. The asphalt shingles of our roof are stained with rust from the TV antenna and creosote from our wood stove. I was told to scrub them with naval jelly. Will it work?

A. Don't do it. The mineral granules on asphalt shingles would be dislodged by any scrubbing, thereby exposing the felt layers beneath to the action of the sun which would destroy them. Unfortunately, there is nothing you can do.

A saturated solution of oxalic acid would remove rust but, being an acid, would change the color of the pigments that are bound to the mineral granules and have an alkali base unless you have a roof color with natural rock granules, usually sea green.

But if you want to try it on a very small area to determine which gives you the least objectionable appearance, the rust or the discolored shingles, buy a small quantity of oxalic acid crystals in a drug store and mix it in hot water until some crystals remain in the bottom of the glass or plastic container (do not use metal). Apply it with an eye dropper to a very small area of the rust stains. If you find the cure tolerable in that small spot, try a larger one. And if that's still your choice, treat all the stains. For larger quantities, buy oxalic acid in paint or janitorial supply stores.

Remember, you are dealing with strong chemicals. Use heavy rubber gloves, protect your eyes and wear old clothing.

Can old slate roof be refinished?

Q. The slate roof on my 80-year-old house has rust and other stains. The rest of the house looks nice but the roof makes it look older. Is there some way to paint it or put some kind of finish on it?

A. What do you expect from an 80-year-old roof? It has served the house well, as all good-quality slates do.

There is nothing you can do to clean or coat the slates that would be an improvement on their natural aging. Can any 80-year-old avoid wrinkles? Learn to appreciate them as they are.

Metal Roofing

Metal *vs* asphalt roofing in snow country

Q. My question is about the best new roof for our home. Would you recommend standing-seam metal roofing or shingles? We're in a northern climate and get a lot of wind, so we need a strong roof.

A. The choice between a standing-seam roof and asphalt shingles depends on a number of things.

A standing-seam metal roof is considered longer lasting, especially the ones today with factory finishes (as opposed to plain galvanized metal). However, you must consider what will happen to the snow that slides off the roof—a side effect that's considered a benefit by many. I know of cases where the snow fell on decks and walks and had to be removed with great effort, because it packs itself hard as it hits those surfaces. In some instances, it had blocked doors and windows and, in one case, even broke a window pane. Snow can be prevented from sliding off a metal roof with snow guards, but I have also seen conditions where there is so much snow that it takes the snow guards off the roof.

Asphalt shingles, on the other hand, keep the snow on the roof. If the roof has been properly designed for the live load (snow, ice, etc.) of the area where the house

A hazard of winter: snow sliding off a metal roof

is built, it should not be a concern. Contrary to some local practices, it is not a good idea to have snow removed from a roof as it can, and does, cause damage to the shingles.

If you decide to use a standing-seam metal roof, be sure to specify 24-gauge metal and double-lock seams, and choose a well-established installer. Lighter 26-gauge metal has a tendency to "oilcan" (a term used to describe the noise made by metal undulating) in strong winds. If you decide to use asphalt shingles, it is best to hire a roofing contractor who hand-nails shingles with ringed stainless-steel nails as opposed to using staples or any pneumatic applicator.

Regardless of your choice, it is a good idea to have an ice and water protective membrane applied at the eaves (it should go up the roof a minimum of 3 feet beyond the intersecting line of the walls below and more than 3 feet on a shallow-pitch roof), and around skylights, chimneys, valleys and any other roof perforations.

Metal wrong for low pitch

Q. Seven months ago, I had a contractor replace the 22-year-old damaged roll roofing on our house. The contractor recommended a metal roof, which he said should last 50 years. The roof has a 3 in 12 pitch.

This winter, the roof started leaking so severely that it caused over $3,000 in damages to the inside of the house. I called the contractor and he said it wasn't his fault and that I should get on the roof and remove the snow and ice.

At my age, I don't want to get on the roof every time a few inches of ice build up on the edge of it.

Do you have any ideas as to what might be the problem? Can I fix it myself or do I need a contractor to fix it?

A. You're right. No one should have to climb on a roof and remove snow and ice all winter long. This is a preposterous answer from your contractor.

I can't tell from the photo you sent me if the new metal roof is standing-seam or of the corrugated screw-on type, but my guess is that it is the latter because of the extent of the damage you have suffered inside.

An ice dam forms at the eaves because snow is melting from heat loss in the house. This is hard to avoid in older construction with a low-pitch roof. Water backs up behind the ice dam and sneaks through the joints in the metal panels where they overlap. It is virtually impossible to seal these joints on that type of roofing. Even if you have a standing-seam roof, all seams should have been caulked before final crimping or leakage would also occur.

Nails popping on metal roof

Q. I am retired and living on a fixed income. The only answer I can get to my roof problem is a new roof for $8,000, which I can't afford. There are some leaks in heavy rains in the standing-seam roof due to loose nails that were mistakenly added to eliminate vibration noises. As you can see from the enclosed photographs, the nails were covered with roofing cement. This hasn't been satisfactory; it is unsightly and paint doesn't stick to the patches.

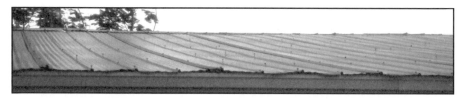

This metal roofing is becoming loose as the nails pop out.

I want to have a good aluminum paint applied by brush once I have solved the leaks. The metal roof is basically in good condition.

A. The nails are loosened when the sun causes the metal to expand and tear them off. Replace them with Woodtite screws which are equipped with neoprene washers and should never pull out. They are the answer to metal roof fastening. This should stop the leakage. Scrape off the unsightly tar. You should no longer need it.

Copper roof turning black

Q. I had a copper roof installed on my house because I love the green tarnished color it turns into over time. Unfortunately, the roof has turned black, not green. What's happened and how can I get it to turn green?

A. Copper oxidizes and the eventual green color, called verdigris, is the result of this oxidization that is a crust of copper carbonate. It takes a long time and black is the interim color. Patience! It'll "green-up" one day.

Painting a rusty metal roof

Q. The galvanized corrugated roofing over a storage building is rusting. I have previously wire-brushed the rust off and coated the panels with aluminum roof coating but it now needs redoing. Can you suggest the best procedure and material to use?

A. You have two choices:
1. The rust should be removed as much as possible with a wire brush. Prime the metal with the primer recommended by the manufacturer of the finish paint you choose and apply the finish coat. Rust-Oleum is a well-known brand; there are others.
2. Hammerite Rust Cap can be applied directly to rusty surfaces without the need of a primer. First, remove all loose rust particles. Hammerite is a product of Masterchem Industries, but at $74 a gallon, it's pretty pricey. It comes in smooth and hammered finishes. However, if it is guaranteed to last much longer than other finishes, it may be worthwhile considering that painting a roof is not the most fun thing to do.

Seams and clips popping open on a standing seam metal roof

New paint peels from older aluminum paint

Q. The metal roofs over my 165-year-old house and barn were put on about 20 years ago, and later painted with asphaltic paint—black on the barn and aluminum on the house.

The barn roof was repainted red over the black two years ago and is doing fine. The house roof was repainted with the same paint but by a different contractor last June.

By September, the paint began to peel from the front part of the house roof and continued to do so throughout the winter. The back roof, which is shaded much of the day, is not peeling.

How can the red paint be made to adhere to the aluminum asphaltic paint?

A. It is difficult to make paint adhere to aluminum paint because aluminum paint chalks off. The roof should have been thoroughly washed and even sanded to insure proper adhesion. It is possible that the painter did not do this as well as it should have been done, if at all.

The rear roof fared better as it is less stressed since it is shaded most of the time. But it's only a question of time.

The only assurance you will have of proper adhesion is to have all the new red paint removed and the remaining aluminum properly prepared—a tedious and expensive task. Painting over what is there now is only going to add to the stress by dint of the additional weight.

An oil-base paint must be used to get penetration through the remaining chalk, unless all the aluminum paint is removed.

Cleaning metal before painting

Q. What type of paint should I apply to a galvanized tin roof on my cupola? I have used a primer for galvanized metal and oil-based finish coat but they both peeled off over a year's time. I then applied a latex paint but it also peeled.

A. It sounds as if the cupola was not thoroughly washed with white vinegar to remove the factory's preservative grease. I would suggest you remove all paint, wash the bare metal with white vinegar, and paint it with Rust-Oleum or other good quality metal paint.

Touch-up painting of baked-enamel roofing

Q. My almost-new baked-enamel metal roofing is scratched down to the base metal. Can you suggest a touch-up paint that can be purchased locally in small amounts and that doesn't require heated storage over winter?

A. It would be best to get in touch with the manufacturer of the roofing and to ask it to send you some of the matching paint and instructions on how best to apply it.

How did the roof get scratched? During installation by the installers or in shipment? If during installation, the installers should repair it. If in shipment, the manufacturer may want to send you some paint free as a goodwill gesture.

If the paint is oil-based, it can be left in an unheated space; latex paints, however, must be protected from freezing. If you close your house down for the winter and head south, could you ask a neighbor who sticks it out through the winter to store it for you?

Leaky mobile home roofs

Q. Mobile home roofs eventually leak. In your opinion, which of the following methods is best to solve the problem: a complete roof-over or single-ply rubber membrane—considering cost, warranty and longevity?

A. It depends on the region. In your climate (Florida) white rubber membrane is probably the best way to go considering the cost and the need to reflect the sun's heat. You may have to wash it every year or so to keep it clean and white in order to preserve its reflective properties.

In cold climates there are definite advantages to roofing over as it permits the addition of insulation and ventilation above the metal roof. This not only reduces fuel consumption and increases comfort but it also prevents the common problem of condensation on the underside of the metal roof, the bane of mobile home owners. This leads to wet insulation and ceilings, stains, mold and increased fuel bills.

Flat Roof Coverings

Sealing against leaks

Q. An addition to our house has a flat roof covered with felt and roll roofing. All the edges are sealed with roof coating. We also cover the entire roof with plastic roof coating during the spring and summer. But when the weather gets cold, the roof starts leaking when it rains.

Any solution to this problem would be appreciated.

A. The roof coating you use must not be flexible, so the joints between the layers of the roll roofing open up as the coating shrinks in cold weather.

Cover the addition's roof with one of the synthetic rubber membranes that are available. The cost will be much higher but, considering there is living space under this roof, you would save yourself a lot of trouble and aggravation as well as further damage to the room.

If you are a handy person, you may be able to do it yourself. Box stores or home centers carry some form of rubber membrane. Follow directions carefully or call a roofer.

Replacing tar and gravel

Q. My 16-year-old house has a tar and gravel roof, which I have re-coated with a mixture of lime and cement every three to five years. Three quarters of the roof is sloping and one quarter almost flat with a very slight pitch to drain water. I have been told by roofers that, if I want to replace the roof, I would need to slope the almost-flat part and remove the tar and gravel from the rest of the roof. The removal would be very expensive because of the labor involved and the cost of disposal. Is there any type of material that can be put over the existing roof without necessitating its removal?

A. A 16-year-old built-up roof has served you well and is entitled to retirement. I see no reason why the roofers told you that you had to slope the nearly flat roof. It is best to have the tar and gravel roof removed, check for any sheathing problem, and lay fiber board as a protective layer for a rubber roof membrane. The removal should not be that expensive if you contract with a roofer who has a machine for that purpose. Disposing of the debris is another story and it is, indeed, quite costly in most areas.

To save the cost of disposing of the asphalt impregnated felt, ask the roofer if he could simply scrape off the gravel and lay the fiber board and elastomeric membrane over the remaining old roof. The gravel may not be too hard to remove off a 16-year-old roof.

PVC or rubber membrane?

Q. Our 12-year-old built-up roof is leaking and we know it's time for a new one. We have talked to several reputable roofing contractors and the debate is whether to put on a glued-on rubber roof or a heat-sealed PVC roof over our existing surface.

We have heard that PVC is better for warmer climates, but we know of several in our northern climate that have shattered in the winter. Those promoting PVC say this is no longer a problem.

What would you suggest given the dramatic temperature swings of our climate?

A. PVC has had its problems in cold weather, but by all reports it has been improved. Either PVC or EPDM rubber membranes are fine.

Water ponding on a flat roof surrounding a chimney

Water pooling on rubber roofing

Q. We had a rubber roof installed on a flat roof about two years ago. Lately we have noticed water collecting in an area 4×6 feet. We are concerned that this may lead to a potential roof problem in the future. How can this be corrected?

A. There is not much to worry about with this type of roof covering. The water should evaporate quickly.

It's more of a problem with built-up roofs made of layers of asphalt and felt and covered with stones, as the felt can absorb the water and steam bubbles can develop between roof covering and sheathing.

Water pooling on built-up roof

Q. The flat roof over my garage and part of the living room of my eight-year-old house is covered with tar and gravel. There are two drain pipes on the sides of the roof. However, pools of water accumulate after a rain, especially over the living room. There are no signs of leakage so far. My neighbor has a similar type of roof but the water disappears quickly and the roof dries out. Should I be concerned about this and take some action? What type of maintenance or inspection should be performed to insure the roof is in good shape?

A. The water ponds on certain areas of your roof because the roof rafters have deflected, however slightly. Although the present thinking is that this is not desirable, there is no reason for you to incur the expense of taking corrective measures at this time. Keep in mind that, years ago, built-up roofs were designed to allow ponding of water to keep them cool, supposedly. We know better now. Your neighbor may have a different type of construction that kept the rafters from deflecting as much as yours so the water is not so deep.

A built-up roof may last from 10 to 15 years, depending on the number of plies. There is no need for any action at this time and really no maintenance worthwhile.

Just have it checked by a competent roofer every couple of years; he or she can tell whether time for replacement is near. Bubbles, known as blisters, are a sign of trouble and should not be stepped on.

Eaves

Replacing metal ice belt

Q. I will need a new roof soon. Presently, there are metal strips at the eaves which I would like very much not to have to keep on the roof as I find them unattractive.

However, I do not want to risk having water backing up in the attic and house as it used to do before these metal bands were installed many years ago. Is there an alternative, or am I stuck with these ugly things? My house is an old farm house.

A. When the present roof covering is removed, as it should be, the sheathing should be cleaned up for three feet up from the eaves and a self-adhering product such as Grace Ice and Water Shield placed over it. It comes in a roll and must be installed carefully as, once in place and the protective paper is removed, it cannot be adjusted.

Shingles are nailed through it, and a seal forms around the nails so that no water can penetrate.

What causes ice dams?

Q. Why do some houses have terrible problems with ice back-up and icicles on their roofs while houses next door may have none?

A. Ice dams that form on the eaves of certain roofs and large icicles hanging from the eaves are caused by the melting of the roof's snow pack from beneath because the air in the attic is above the freezing point.

When this melting snow hits the cold eaves, it freezes and the ice dams it forms build up, trapping water behind them. As more water runs down the roof, it seeks a way out which, if no protection was provided at the eaves, results in its backing up under the roof shingles or slates.

What follows is leakage into soffits and, worse, into the walls where it can wet the insulation—affecting its effectiveness—and even penetrate the living quarters. This is a serious situation that requires attention.

Houses with gutters in cold winter areas of northern North America fare even worse, as the gutters and downspouts fill with ice very early. The ice in the gutters forms a sort of block that directs ensuing melt water under the roof's edges and into the structure while the ice in the downspouts can pop their seams or crack them open. Ice can also deform gutters or even knock them off the house.

Houses that have no icicles or ice dams have a cold attic where its temperature is close to the outdoor temperature. That is what is known as a cold roof.

A cold roof is obtained in several ways:

- There are no convective paths from the living quarters and basement or crawl space into the walls and attic, so the warm, moist air of these areas is confined to them and does not find its way into the attic.

Metal ice belts such as this are still seen in cold climates, but a modern synthetic membrane looks better and is more effective.

- There are no other sources of heat into the attic such as bath and kitchen fans erroneously discharging into the attic. (I see this too often from builders ignorant of the problems it causes.)
- There is a high level of insulation in the floor of the attic and, certainly desirable but not always essential, depending on other factors—good attic ventilation from the soffits to the ridge.

But even in a well-built roof with a cold attic, there can be problems with ice dams because of skylights and other perforations such as chimneys. This is why I would always recommend that measures be taken to protect the eaves and other vulnerable areas. The best such measure is the installation of a membrane specially designed for the purpose, such as Grace Ice & Water Shield, the most prevalent but not the only one.

Avoid the metal ice belts at the eaves that you often see on older houses, as they encourage secondary ice dams once the ice falls off the metal. Also to be avoided is the removal of snow from the lower parts of the roof as it, too, encourages secondary ice dams. These dams may cause back-up higher up the roof over the living areas.

Roof leaks in winter

Q. Our roof is leaking in the winter when there is snow on it and we want to get it fixed before next winter. The problem is that a number of people have worked on it, tarred it, caulked it, put metal flashing on it but nothing seems to work for more than a few months.

The leaks are coming in just below the chimney and also at the skylight and at the eaves which have a lot of icicles when there is snow on the roof. We have been unable to find anyone capable of solving this problem.

A. It appears that the leakage in the areas you have indicated are all due to water from snow melting from the bottom of the roof blanket which becomes trapped by ice dams and backs up under the roof shingles. The surest way to eliminate this problem is to have a competent roofing contractor remove some shingles around the chimney, the skylight and at the eaves to a distance of 3 feet. He or she should clean the sheathing and apply over it a synthetic membrane such as Grace Ice and Water Shield according to the manufacturer's instructions. The shingles are then, re-nailed over the membrane which seals around the nails like a puncture-proof tire. Ice dams will still form unless you are able to make the necessary corrections to eliminate them, but there will no longer be any leakage.

Testing for heat loss

Q. I have had a problem with huge ice dams for years. Water would get in the house and cause some damage. I had a new roof put on two years ago with ice shields at the edges of the roof. But, last year when we had so much snow, water leaked again.

I called on an energy consultant who proposed to seal the attic from the rest of the house for $3,000. Will this solve my problem?

A. Ice dams are caused by melting snow from the roof's ice pack that freezes when it reaches the cold eaves of a roof. It is an indication that there is some heat loss from the living quarters. The greater the heat loss, the bigger the ice dams will be, although time is also a factor. Ice dams can also be the result of inadequate attic insulation and, in some cases, poor ventilation.

The solution is to find out where the heat loss is coming from and to seal it. It can be due to recessed lights in the ceiling below the attic, an attic access panel or folding stairway that is not weatherstripped and insulated, a bath or kitchen fan vented into the attic—both no-nos!—or any other paths allowing warm, moist air to convect into the attic including around pipes and wires concealed in the walls.

Sometimes it is difficult to find some of these paths and only infrared thermography coupled with a blow-door test and perhaps in combination with a fog-test can show them to us. Did the energy consultant perform these tests or was he or she able to do it by just examining the house?

I can't tell you if the price quoted is reasonable; you may want to get a second opinion and estimate.

Unexpected leaks

Q. We had leakage in our living room and through a light fixture under the eaves from ice dams forming on our roof. This house was built for us in 1954 and we have been in it ever since.

A new roof was put on the house four years ago. All shingles were removed and we asked the roofer to pay special attention to the flashings. He promised to ice-proof the first three courses of shingles by putting on the sticky ice-dam material.

This has not prevented leaks. He now says that it is guaranteed for only one year. Is he right?

A. It sounds to me as if the roofer did not put on what you aptly call "the sticky ice dam" material.

In the first place, the synthetic rubber membrane roof underlayment, such as Grace Ice & Water Shield, is 3 feet wide; it would go up 7 courses of shingles—not 3.

The warranty for this product is not stated in years but says that the product will be replaced or a refund made if it is shown to be defective in its manufacture. You should get back to the roofer and have him redo the job right, but it's too late for this year; it should be done when the temperature is moderate enough to permit the removal of the shingles without breaking them.

Ice is backing up into the shingles from the dam at the edge of the roof.

If he refuses, tell him you will file a complaint with the Consumer Protection Division of the Attorney General's office of your state, and do it.

Icicles on well-insulated roof

Q. I live in a large cape built in 1965 that I have maintained and improved. I have good insulation, but when the sun shines on a winter day and there is snow on the roof, icicles develop on the southern side.

They can become quite large as temperatures hover in the 30s. For 15 years, I have made it a practice to knock them down from both stories because I have heard that there should not be huge icicles hanging off the house.

My neighbors have the same thing but don't bother to do anything about it and it doesn't seem to hurt their houses.

Am I wasting my time removing the icicles?

A. It depends on what you mean by huge. Icicles that are a couple of feet long should probably be knocked off to avoid the stress they impose on the bottom row of shingles, and the potential danger they present to anyone walking under them as well as shrubbery and any appendages such as decks, walks, etc. if they were to fall suddenly.

A lot of small icicles on a house are usually a sign of a well insulated and ventilated roof. You will see them on unheated buildings; they are caused by external factors and not by heat loss through the roof.

The fact that yours occur only on the south side and when temperatures moderate and the sun shines indicates that your roof is, indeed, well insulated.

Are overhangs necessary?

Q. I am planning on building a house this year in an area of heavy snow. After living in a house with overhangs and huge icicles for years, I am wondering if it wouldn't be wise to omit the overhangs on my new house since I understand that icicles are caused by melting roof snow which freezes as it travels over the cold overhangs. Doesn't that make sense?

A. The best answer I can give you is to tell you that, several years ago, I saw a contemporary house built without overhangs for that very reason; however, snow melted anyway and froze on the outside walls. The result was that the front and back of the house were covered by a thick coat of ice that blocked all the windows and doors. Damage to the interior of the structure from water penetration must have also been a serious problem.

Overhangs offer needed protection to walls and should not be omitted, even on gable ends.

But there is a way to reduce the melting of snow from a roof through heat loss from the house and the resulting formation of icicles. Build the roof of the house with elevated rafter seats or trusses, thus allowing for higher levels of insulation in these crucial areas at the eaves. Be sure to provide proper baffling to protect the insulation from wind at these vulnerable points, (there are cardboard baffles made for the purpose that are much better than the popular flimsy polystyrene type so frequently used). Allow an unobstructed air space from the eaves to the peak of the roof, provide continuous soffit and ridge venting, using commercially available products, but be sure that the ridge vent is externally baffled like Shinglevent II.

Is drip edge necessary?

Q. I had a new roof put on my duplex last April and paid the contractor in full upon completion. I recently discovered that the drip edge was missing from both ends of the roof. He is willing to rectify this oversight but what is the best way to correct it? I would like to be informed before I accept his work again.

A. If, by both ends, you mean the gable ends along the slanted parts of the roof, it is difficult to retrofit a full-size drip edge as there are shingle nails close to the edge of the roof. A drip edge with a narrow top may be inserted and nailed through its face instead of its top.

It may be useful in protecting the rakes of the roof but, if the shingles overhang the rakes (the boards nailed immediately under the roof following its slope) by ½ inch or so, they are probably not essential and it may be better to leave things alone. However, if the shingles are flush, or nearly flush, with the rakes, it would be a good idea to protect them from potential water damage by adding the drip edge.

Raking roof not a great idea

Q. We are having a problem with ice dams with the recent nor'easters that dumped huge amounts of snow in the area. Our local hardware store sells roof rakes for removing snow and told us that just removing the snow from the eaves where the ice dams form should solve our problem. What is your advice?

A. Bad idea! Ice dams form when the snow cover on the roof is melting because of a heat loss from the house. As the melt water reaches cold eaves, it freezes and ice dams form. Take this one step further: If you remove several feet of snow off the roof with a snow rake, this will not stop snow from melting from the upper parts of the roof. As the melt water reaches the open parts of the roof that have been raked,

Electric roof cables do not solve the problem!

it will freeze and form what is known as a secondary ice dam. Water backing up behind this secondary dam will also find its way under the shingles, but higher up than it would if snow is not removed from the eaves. It will wet the insulation and damage interior finishes more so than if the ice dams form at the eaves.

If you want to remove the snow from the roof you should do so for the entire roof, but that is not possible with a snow rake on the average roof: the handle is simply not long enough even when working from a ladder. Snow rakes also cause damage to older and more brittle shingles and can actually break them. Walking on a snow-covered roof is risky and not good for the roof, either.

It is best to handle the problem in one of the following ways:

1. Increase the insulation in the attic to reduce the heat loss. Also increase the attic ventilation, or make sure it is functioning effectively from soffit vents to an externally baffled ridge vent.
2. If this is not possible, have a special membrane such as Grace Ice & Water Shield applied to the eaves when the roof shingles are replaced. Make sure the membrane covers the sheathing at least 2 feet up the roof above the point where the exterior house wall would intersect the roof if a line were extended up from the wall. This will not stop the formation of ice dams, but it will keep water from getting into the house. It is also a good idea to use the same membrane around valleys, skylights, chimneys and any other roof penetrations.

Stained fascia

Q. The cedar boards under the bottom edge of our metal roof get black stain streaks from the metal roof. These lines get wider and darker with time.

Last year, we had the wood sanded and re-coated with clear wood finish and Thompson's Water Seal but this is still not solving the problem. I hope you can suggest a solution.

A. The stains that are clearly visible on the photos you sent may be caused by rain water running back under the bottom edge of the metal roof protruding from the house and running down the fascia boards. If this is the case, the fix is relatively simple.

There should be a metal drip edge under the metal roof panels that overlaps the top of the fascia boards. Sometimes, the flare at the bottom of the drip edge is not sufficient to shed water clear of the wood. Or it may be that this drip edge was omitted. The solution is to increase the flare of the drip edge with a hand-held metal break such as the one made by Vise-Grip or to install another piece of metal with a greater flare under it or the roofing such as Lamb & Ritchies' Positive Rite Flow Drip Edge (available in better building supply stores).

Don't insulate eaves

Q. We have a two-story brick/frame house, with the second floor having a 2-foot overhang on both the front and rear of the house. We think there is little or possibly no insulation in this area and would like to know some information concerning this. What are the different types of products available for insulating this area? And should a DIY'er handle this project, or would it be better left to a professional? Thank you for any help you can give.

A. Eaves should not be insulated. If you insulate them and leakage from snowmelt penetrates the structure from behind ice dams, the insulation will become soaked and never dry out. Rot is not far behind in this situation. Attic insulation should stop at the outer edge of the walls below the attic space.

Heat cables?

Q. In view of the amount of ice and snow on our roof and our concern about ice dams, I was considering installing heated roof cables. What are the pros and cons of this possible solution?

A. If installed properly, they may work but I also have seen some ripped right off the roof eaves by ice. They are quite expensive to run. They are also said to present a risk of fire and need to be turned on and off as circumstances dictate.

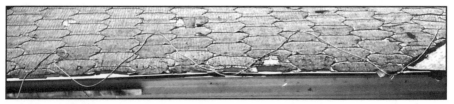

Shingles ruined by ice—note the wiring used to melt the ice dams.

A better solution is to install a waterproof membrane such as Grace Ice & Water Shield or equivalent directly to the sheathing and under the shingles at the eaves. If you will need a new roof in the near future, that will be a good time to have this done. It should also be applied at all valleys, around skylights, chimneys, and all other roof penetrations.

Replacing fascia boards

Q. I am going to replace the fascia board between the gutter and the house. Should this 1×6-inch board be white pine?

A. I assume you are replacing the fascia because it has developed some problem such as rot. Exterior trim is usually made of white pine. Be sure that you treat all sides and cuts with a wood preservative, prime them, and paint them with two coats prior to installing. Another choice is to replace the fascia with one of the synthetic pre-finished material available in building supply houses; they are supposed to be indestructible and can be painted the color of your choice.

Gutters

Avoid gutters in cold climates

Q. What's the best material for gutters to be installed on a Victorian house with a metal roof in a northern climate?

A. Seamless aluminum or vinyl are okay, but I prefer to see roof water handled on the ground, when possible, in cold climates.

If gutters are used, the downspouts should terminate over splashblocks that, if the grade slopes properly away from the foundation, dissipate the force of the water and move it away from the house.

But, in northern climates, where ice forms on roofs and where heavy snowfalls are common, gutters can get severely damaged and even knocked off the house by these conditions. They can also increase the risk of water backing into the eaves.

Under these conditions, my preference is to lay 1-inch-thick rectangular flagstones, 12 inches wide and random length, or concrete patio blocks, flush with the soil at the drip lines of the roof. The water splashes on them without causing erosion and, if the grade slopes properly away from the foundation, the water will run off and not percolate too deeply near the house, where it can cause problems.

Leaf guards

Q. Can you give me your opinion on leaf guards for gutters? I live in a heavily-wooded area and have many leaves in the fall and many seedlings in the spring that clog my gutters. Is it worthwhile investing in gutter guards, or is it better to pay someone to clean my gutters every year?

A. I think you are better off having someone come clean your gutters after the spring shedding and again when all the leaves have fallen off the trees in late fall,

These little maples are growing in a hidden gutter.

because I haven't yet seen a gutter guard that really works. The mesh-type guards collect seedlings, pine needles and spring blooms that eventually clog them so that they need to be removed. That is what I have to do every year, even though I thought I had finally found a gutter guard that should work, but didn't.

There are some solid (as opposed to mesh) gutter guards advertised under various names that are supposed to spill all leaves and debris while directing water into the gutter, but they don't mention the fact that pine needles and seedlings also follow the water into the gutters. And in heavy rainfall, the water would then simply overshoot the gutters.

Aging gutters

Q. My aging gutters and downspouts are leaking here and there. The gutters have pin holes in them. Since repairs don't seem to stick through freezing and thawing, are replacement plastic gutters a good idea? Aluminum gutters and downspouts no longer seem to be popular; in fact there are no replacement parts available.

A. Plastic gutters and spouts are fine, but so are seamless aluminum replacements. Seamless gutters have replaced the type of aluminum gutters that came in various pieces, which were put together like an erector set. It was impossible to keep those from leaking, eventually.

Cracking gutters

Q. A friend tells me that vinyl gutters are inferior because they crack and fall off the house. Is this possible? What makes them crack?

A. Leaning a ladder on them, particularly in cold weather, and ice and snow sliding off the roof. Metal gutters can also be deformed by a ladder and by ice and snow. All gutters installed in cold regions should be secured with frequent hangers to gutter boards, which should be strongly fastened to the rafter tails.

Winter problems with gutters

Q. I have a yearly problem with my gutters. Ice damages and distorts them and I have to have them repaired or replaced all too frequently. Yet I do need them and do not want to get rid of them. Is there another practical solution?

A. Ice is a serious problem in harsh winter climates when the attics are not sufficiently insulated and the roof not sufficiently ventilated. Correcting these shortcomings is not always easy to do although it is the best solution.

One way to mitigate this problem is to cover the gutters for the winter. Use standard metal drip edging, slip the top part of it under the bottom shingle starter course, and put the vertical flange inside the gutters. Cut slots in the flange as needed to accommodate the gutter fasteners. Buy metal drip edge in building supply stores.

Rain leaks behind gutter

Q. Rain is leaking between the roof's edges and the new vinyl gutters I just had installed and, in heavy rains, water overshoots the gutter in one corner of a 90-degree angle in the roof. How can this be corrected?

A. You should have the installers come back and rehang the gutters so water would fall into them or install a metal drip edge that covers their backside such as Lamb & Ritchies' Positive Rite Flow Drip Edge.

At the angle, a baffle should be installed on the inside of the outside edge of the gutters so that the water is diverted to each side of the angle formed by the L-shape of the house.

Gutter too high

Q. The plywood sheathing of my roof was not extended far enough at the eaves so the shingles curl up and this forms a trough in which water sits. What can I do to remedy this?

A. Your sketch shows a gutter onto which the ends of the shingles rest. This would indicate that the gutter has been installed too high. You should remove the gutter temporarily, insert a metal drip edge under the starter course of shingles (shingling a roof begins with a starter course applied over the felt paper covering the plywood; next the first course of shingles is applied over the starter course so as to cover the cut-outs between the tabs).

This gutter is covered in winter to protect it from ice damage.

This type of damage is all too typical when gutters are used in colder climates.

The metal drip edge will extend beyond the end of the plywood and support the shingles. Now the gutter can be re-hung just below the drip edge.

Water from two stories

Q. The people who installed the gutters on our house let the water from the second-floor roof run onto the first floor roof from where it runs into the lower gutter. This seems to me to be wrong as a lot of water washes over that section of the shingles and I fear they may wear out soon.

How should it have been handled?

A. It would have been best to extend the second-floor roof downspout to dump the water directly into the lower gutter but precautions would have to be taken so that the water does not splash over the gutter or behind it.

A shoe directing the water toward the outlet but not obstructing the flow from the high side of the gutter, together with adequate protection against side splashing, can work.

But, sometimes, letting the water run onto the roof may be the best solution.

Painting aluminum gutters

Q. I would like to change the color of our four-year-old aluminum gutters from beige to white to match our doors and new vinyl windows.

Is it possible to paint aluminum white without having to repaint it every year?

A. Yes, it is. But you must first clean it thoroughly by washing it with a strong detergent solution, the best being TSP-PF. Mix 1 cup TSP-PF in 1 gallon of water.

You may want to mix 1 part fresh Clorox bleach to 3 parts water in the cleaning solution to take care of both dirt and possible mildew in one operation.

Rinse thoroughly and be sure to cover plantings below. Also, wear old clothing, eye and skin protection.

Prime the aluminum with Zinsser's Bulls Eye 1-2-3 and paint it with a top quality exterior latex paint. If you use a 100% acrylic paint, the job should last many years, but the key to a lasting paint job is always the preparation.

Cleaning stained gutters and soffits

Q. Our vinyl gutters, fascia, and soffits have become stained with dirt and grime from highway traffic and the coal-burning furnace of one of our neighbors. We have used liquid and powdered cleaners and scrubbed the stained surfaces, but we can't completely remove the stains from the fascia. Is there a way to clean them? I hope we don't have to replace them.

We have shrubs around the house which may need to be covered.

A. Replacing the fascia would only solve the problem temporarily. You would need to remove the sources of pollution to solve it permanently. In looking at the photo you sent, I see another concern. For the stains to develop as they did onto the fascia, water had to get behind the gutter. You should check this out and correct it; it's not what should be happening. You may need to install some flashing that would fit under the roof shingles and cover the inside edge of the gutters to direct water into them, such as Lamb & Ritchies' Positive Rite Flow Drip Edge.

Indeed, cover the vegetation around the foundation with plastic after soaking it thoroughly. Try a mix of 1 cup TSP-PF (buy in hardware or paint stores) to 1 gallon water and gently wash the stained areas. Do not rub hard as it would "polish" the vinyl and give it shiny areas.

If that doesn't work, you may want to try the following in this order: 1) mineral spirits, 2) auto tar remover, 3) auto radiator cleaner, 4) xylene, or 5) lacquer thinner. Only in the case of the last two should you use vigor in rubbing or scrubbing. With the others, be gentle and use a clean cloth. Rinse thoroughly after each treatment. Flush the plastic to dilute any drippings on it and do the same to the vegetation after removing the plastic.

Gutter pitch

Q. One of the gutters on the house I recently bought is slanting in the wrong direction: the end with the downspout is higher than the other.

What can I do to correct this situation if I need to do so?

A. It depends on the type of gutters you have. Although it is desirable to have all gutters pitched properly to allow for effective drainage, prevent the rotting of vegetation and the breeding of mosquitoes, some types are more vulnerable to physical damage than others.

Standing water will encourage rust in galvanized gutters and it may not be so easy to correct the pitch if they have been installed with gutter spikes and ferrules. It will require two people to do it.

Gutters installed with couplings may get damaged and leak when standing water freezes in them and opens the joints. Seamless gutters are less vulnerable. Corrections may be made by installing a new downspout at the low end or relocating the one at the high end, if it is possible, to drain the water in that location. Some do-it-yourself gutters can be repitched by adjusting the hangers.

Look at your gutter carefully to determine which of these scenarios apply to it or simply have the gutter replaced.

Miscellaneous Roof Problems

Sheathing is rotting

Q. Our roof has some dry rot under the composition roofing. The actual roofing material should last a few more years. If we do not have the plywood sheathing replaced at this time, what would be the repercussions?

A. If no one walks on the soft spots and the roof is not subjected to heavy snow, it may be all right. It really depends on how rotten the plywood is. Meanwhile, you can support the worst spots from underneath, if you have enough working room in the attic, by toenailing 2×12s, set flat against the rotten plywood, to the rafters.

Be aware that dry rot is a misnomer. Rot starts with moisture (some people in the hot and dry Southwest may disagree, but that's a different story). When you replace the rotten plywood and the roof, be sure there is adequate attic ventilation and control of any convection of air from the living quarters into the attic.

Sagging ridgeline

Q. The roof ridge of my 28-year-old house sags slightly between supporting posts, perhaps because the old shingles were left on the roof when it was reroofed 12 years ago. I'm considering adding additional support posts but worry that jacking the ridge and then letting it back down on the new posts might cause structural damage. Should I leave well enough alone or should the problem be corrected?

A. The ridge sag may also be due to the house walls bulging out if the attic floor joists were not properly fastened. You should investigate that first. If it's part of—or the whole—problem, it may be advisable to have a contractor experienced in that kind of work (such as a house mover) bring them back in line and then stabilize the structural members as needed. But it may be necessary and preferable to accept the situation and simply prevent further movement and deterioration. This can easily be done by screwing down plywood sheets bridging the joints of the floor joists. Collar ties may have to be added or secured better.

If the sagging of the ridge is due to the additional weight of the second layer of shingles having caused undersized rafters to sag, you should have collar ties installed at each set of rafters so the weight from each side of the roof is balanced by that of the other side; collar ties reduce the rafter span.

I do not recommend jacking up the ridge. In doing this you would put great stresses on the ceiling below and may cause some damage. You can add supporting posts, if necessary (but it may not be needed after other measures detailed above are taken) by making them snug. You should first set a 2×8 flat on top of and spanning several joists before setting the posts so as to spread the weight the roof may put on them.

Getting rid of vine tentacles

Q. How can we remove dried-up vine tentacles from our overhangs? We tried brushing them off to no avail. Is there anything we can use to loosen this stuff?

A. Use a sharp putty knife. If there are a lot of them, use a broad knife (a wide blade putty knife). You may need to sand the areas after scraping. Medium sandpaper wrapped around a wood block should do or use a vibrating or orbiting electric sander.

Bulging sheathing

Q. I noticed a bulge in the shingles of my roof. Upon examining the area underneath it from the attic, I saw that, on one edge of the plywood, nails had missed the rafter. Is there a product or a method to pull this piece of plywood down to the rafter and eliminate a future problem with the shingles?

A. You should fix this problem as it can cause the shingles to break at that point, particularly if a load of heavy wet snow accumulates on them. However, if the plywood is permanently warped from moisture absorption, you are unlikely to be able to bring it back down.

But if it is simply loose from missed nailing, the best way to repair the problem is to nail or screw a 2×4 to the side of the rafter under the piece of raised plywood after nipping the protruding nails out flush with the plywood. This will give you added bearing to perform the repair from above since, obviously, there was not enough before. Once this is done, carefully go on the roof, pry the shingle tab closest to the center of the raised plywood edge with a flat bar, and screw the plywood down into the new block with galvanized drywall or deck screws. Alternately put additional screws above and below the center one, each time carefully lifting the appropriate shingle tab, until you have fastened the entire piece. Be sure that you place the screws in areas that will be well covered by the tabs you lift when they go down again.

The screw heads will have to go through the shingles and bear directly onto the plywood to be able to apply all the necessary pressure onto it. You may have to drive the screws in progressively to bring the plywood down tightly. In other words, start at the shallow edges of the bulge and work toward the center.

Snow melts near chimney

Q. My house is a 40-year-old raised ranch with a massive interior chimney containing two fireplace flues and a boiler flue. We rarely use the fireplaces. The attic has 12 inches of insulation, with good ventilation, so I have more snow on the roof than anyone in the neighborhood. I'm happy about that, but of course, near the chimney, the snow melts sooner, and we have noticed deterioration in the drywall ceiling upstairs on the downslope side of the chimney, without any conspicuous signs of leakage in the attic.

It occurs to me that a small ice dam could be forming downslope from the chimney and causing some leakage in that part of the attic. I wonder if I should wrap the chimney in the attic with insulation. Would this help? Could it cause problems? Is there another solution?

A. Your diagnosis sounds quite correct. There are two solutions. If your roof is nearing its second replacement (assuming your roof is covered with asphalt shingles with an average lifespan of 20 years), have a membrane similar to Grace Ice & Water Shield—the first and most common such product, although there are others—applied at the eaves of your roof and all the way to and around the chimney when the new roof is installed.

The other solution is what you suggest: Wrap 6-inch-thick fiberglass insulation around the chimney in the attic, holding it in place with string tied loosely so as not to compress the insulation. Choose unfaced insulation or, if you buy insulation faced with aluminum foil, install it so that the foil is facing to the outside and not against the chimney.

Roof trusses rise in winter

Q. As winter is upon us, I hear ominous sounds in our roof. Our ranch house was built in the early '70s; it has a full basement. We bought it this past summer and moved in shortly after the purchase.

The roof is not steep and is built with trusses. It sounds as if nails are being pulled out and a gap is opening at the joints between the ceilings and the interior walls in the middle of the house. It is worrisome and it startles us when it happens in the evening while we watch television or go to bed.

Is the house settling? What is happening and what can be done about it? How can we seal the crack I see opening up?

A. You are experiencing truss uplift or what is known as "the rising truss syndrome." This is a particular phenomenon to well-insulated attics. When cold weather is here and we heat our houses, the trusses begin to arc as the moisture content of the bottom chords, buried in insulation and kept warm, remains constant while the top chords, subjected to a cold attic—and thus increased relative humidity—absorb moisture in the air and stretch out. This causes the bottom chords to be pulled up in the middle by the webs, and the ceilings begin to move up.

Your house is not settling, the interior walls are not dropping, the ceiling is moving up until spring, when it will come down again as the top chords return to their normal shape.

There is nothing you can do to stop it but you can hide the cracks with a molding, which should be fastened to the ceilings only. This creates a slip joint that moves up or down with the seasons.

Siding

Wood Siding

Coating new redwood siding

Q. We just had new redwood clapboards put on the frame wing of our circa 1823 brick house. What can we coat them with that will preserve them while retaining their present natural color? The clapboards are finger-jointed and there is a good deal of variety in the overall effect of the pieces.

One person we consulted said we needn't put anything on the redwood. We're skeptical. We'd like a slightly grayer tone while preserving the essential red of the wood.

A. The clapboards should be coated with a finish as weather and sun will cause problems with any unfinished wood product in time. Many good quality stains are available, from clear to opaque.

I'd raise two concerns. The first is whether you'll be happy with any transparent stain through which the grain of the wood will show when applied over finger-jointed material with the grain variation your sample shows. The second you may want to discuss with an experienced restorer of old houses or a historic preservation group. It is whether natural redwood clapboards are in keeping with your period house. Would painting be better?

Coating new cedar siding

Q. Our new house has cedar siding with no finish on it. This spring, we would like to treat it so it keeps its original appearance. Do you have a suggestion?

A. Too bad the cedar boards were not treated on all sides before installation; it's the best way to insure a trouble-free future.

I also hope, for your sake, that the builder used the right type of nails or you may be plagued with rust and extractive bleeding stains around the nail heads. The only nails recommended by the cedar people, in order of descending preference, are stainless steel, high tensile strength aluminum, or double hot-dipped zinc coated nails—the latter meeting ASTMA-153 standards. Other galvanizing processes such as hot galvanizing, mechanical- or electro-plating are not acceptable but, unfortunately, are the most commonly available nails in most building supply stores. Very often the better nails must be specially ordered well in advance.

There are a number of good preservatives on the market but the best ones to use should also be water repellent. The most outstanding in performance and longevity tests run in the Texas Gulf Coast area—a tough environment—is Amteco's TWP. It comes in a cedar tone tint, among others, and can be applied by brush or spray.

The most important measures you can take to reduce the chances of extractive bleeding (dark tannin stains brought to the surface by water penetration into the cells of the wood), is to soak the areas around the nail heads with the preservative and caulk all joints between siding and other materials with polyurethane caulking after applying the preservative to these joints.

TWP should not need to be re-applied for about five years, but keep an eye on it as certain exposures may need more frequent application.

Treating shakes for uniform appearance

Q. I am replacing cedar shakes on my house. In removing the old shakes, I note that they have been treated with some solution which darkens them. Could you please advise what I can treat the new shakes with to make them look more uniform in color?

A. Not knowing what the existing shakes have been treated with and what shading they have makes it difficult to advise you intelligently. But you probably can't go wrong using a product I have used personally and recommended to clients and readers for years. It is Amteco TWP Shake & Shingle, a preservative, specifically made to be used with cedar but that is equally good used on other wood species. It is a wood preservative and a water-repellent coating that has UV and mildew protection. It can be applied with a garden sprayer, a roller or a brush.

Cedar siding has turned black

Q. The rough-sawn Western red cedar siding of my 25-year-old cottage has never been treated and has turned black. How can I remove these stains so I can stain the siding a more attractive color?

A. First, try reconditioning the siding by power-washing it using a solution made of equal parts of fresh Clorox bleach and water. That should remove most, if not all, of the black stuff, which is likely to be mildew. If the results are not up to your expectations, re-wash with a solution made of 1 quart fresh Clorox bleach, 1 cup TSP-PF or other strong detergent, and 3 quarts water. Rinse thoroughly. Be sure to protect all vegetation and rinse it also. Wear eye and skin protection.

Or, if you prefer, your paint store probably carries a wood renewer. It is important that you carefully follow the directions and the precautions listed on the container.

When ready to restain, use a semi-transparent stain if you want some coloring, and be prepared to reapply it every 2 to 3 years. Avoid solid color stains that are really paints under another name, unless you want to hide the wood's natural grain. In that case, you must apply a good quality oil-based primer first as you would for any other type of paint.

If you want to keep the wood natural, and cedar is a beautiful wood that should be kept natural, use Amteco's TWP.

Siding wicks water from ledge

Q. The cedar siding on my house is sitting on a brick wall capped with a concrete ledge. Snow accumulates on this ledge and is absorbed by the cedar. This has caused unsightly stains. I have caulked this joint but it did not help. What should I do now?

A. The bead of caulking is probably accentuating the problem. What should have been done was to leave a ¼-inch gap between the bottom of the siding and the metal flashing your sketch shows in contact with it. As long as there is contact, water will be absorbed by the open grain of the wood.

Since it would be impractical to provide this gap now, your best bet is to remove the caulking, bleach the water and extractive bleeding stains with a solution of equal parts water and fresh household bleach (try it first in a less conspicuous place) and let dry.

Then make a sort of small pan with aluminum having a flange that can be inserted between the siding and the existing flashing and raised sides and front approximately 1-inch high. Slip the flange under the siding until the sides are tight to the siding and slowly pour a clear water repellent wood preservative into the pan. Continue pouring as long as the wood fibers absorb the preservative and then move down to another spot.

When the bottom edges of the siding are done that way, apply the product to the siding as well to protect it. You may have to remove earlier finishes by sanding.

Power-washing cedar siding

Q. Our cedar clapboards were coated with a clear wood finish when the house was built five years ago. They have developed gray patches, drip lines and some mildew problems which we wish to remove before applying another coat of wood finish.

A siding dealer recommended cleaning the siding with a power sprayer and a solution of 1 part Clorox bleach to 3 parts water. Others have recommended the use of oxalic acid or commercial cleaners. What would you recommend to clean the siding and to apply on it afterwards?

A. Power-washing with the recommended solution is the first approach to take, but be aware that any metal and vegetation will be affected. All plants will have to be covered with plastic sheets, all metal wetted before application, and everything flushed thoroughly immediately after the treatment. Any remaining finish will have to be sanded off or removed with a semi-solid paint and varnish remover.

In my experience, the best finish for cedar siding is Amteco's TWP.

Renewing color of weathered wood

Q. The siding of our home built in 1967 is cedar in a board and batten pattern. It has weathered to a very dirty color. Can it be power-washed? I would like to get it back to its original color. Must I apply a semi-transparent stain or can it be left untreated as it has been all these years?

A. Look into using a wood renewer to get the siding back to its original color. Apply it first in a small, inconspicuous area, following the instructions on the container and heeding all safety precautions. Use synthetic rollers and brushes only. Buy it at a well-stocked paint store.

Allow the product time to do its intended job and remove the gunk with your garden hose at full strength or rent a power-washer.

The potential problem with power-washing such board-and-batten siding is the likelihood that water will get behind the siding and cause some problems of its own. It will depend on the care exercised by the operator.

If you do not protect the siding, it will weather again along the same lines.

Rusting nail heads

Q. I plan on repainting my house this summer, but the siding nails are rusting through. What can I do about it short of replacing them?

A. If the nails are flush with the siding, remove the rust from the heads by rubbing them with emery cloth, then prime them and any rust stain on the siding with a stain killer such as B-I-N. But, if the nails are counter sunk and puttied over, just sand the stained areas and seal as mentioned above before painting.

Paint doesn't hold sheen

Q. I had my house painted last year; it looked great, shiny and clean until this spring. Now the siding looks dull again. Why didn't the paint hold its good original color and sheen and what can I do to get it back?

A. You probably used an oil-base paint. These paints don't hold their luster very long in the elements. Next time, try a latex-base paint; as they have much better color retention.

Artillery fungus shoots spores from mulch

Q. I have the following problem. Some months back, I noticed a very large number of small blackish/brownish dots on the siding and windows of the front of my house. The evenness of the dot pattern makes them look like they were sprayed on. No matter what I do (razor blades) or use (bleach), I cannot get them off of my big picture window. I have not tried to work on the siding yet. Do you have any idea what this is or how to get it off of my windows and siding?

A. I have bad news. These dots are spores expelled with tremendous force from the fruiting bodies of artillery fungus. The spores come from wood-chip or tan bark mulch placed against your house's foundation. As the wood decomposes, the fungus grows, matures and expels the glebal masses, which can be shot 15 to 20 feet in the air. As the fungus explodes, it is attracted to light and attaches itself to the brightest nearby surfaces, usually the siding.

In order to mature, the fungus needs light and moisture; because it is temperature-sensitive, it is a problem in the spring and fall. Winter is too cold and summer too hot.

The spores cannot be effectively removed from the surfaces to which they have adhered without causing some damage. If you have painted-wood siding the damage can be repaired, but this is not the case with aluminum or vinyl siding. Moreover, if the spores are scraped off they will re-infect the mulch, in which they are believed to have an 11-year life span. The solutions are to remove the bark or wood-chip mulch and use some other form of mulch, such as rubber mulch, or to entirely cover the old mulch yearly with new mulch.

Treating mulch to avoid fungus?

Q. In a recent column, you responded to an inquiry about artillery fungus on the siding of a house by saying that its origin is in decomposing bark or wood-chip mulch. As an alternative to removing the mulch, is it possible to periodically apply a garden fungicide to control the fungus? If so, which fungicide would you recommend?

A. I do not have an answer to whether there is an effective fungicide for controlling artillery fungus. The drawback to using a fungicide for this purpose—if there is one and it is used as often and in the quantity as needed to be effective—is that rain will leach it into the soil, where it may eventually reach the water table. It is safer and simpler to cover the decaying mulch with new mulch every year, which is the alternative to removal of the old mulch given by the university extension service that discovered it.

Paint color has little effect on insects

Q. I am considering various shades of Sherwin-Williams Woodscapes Acrylic Solid Color Stain for the exterior of our house. Are insects (flies, carpenter bees, wasps, etc.) more attracted to lighter or darker colors? Are there any other aspects to consider?

A. There should not be any difference except in the cooler days of the fall, when cluster flies and paper wasps (polistes) congregate on sun-warmed (darker) surfaces. This should not really be a consideration in your choice of color, as it is a very temporary phenomenon.

Painting of house trim

Q. We are having the aluminum siding on our house painted this spring. We are wondering how well paint holds up on trim such as fascia, soffit, shutters and metal doors. Also which comes first, painting the siding or replacing the old gutters.

A. Is the trim you are referring to wood (except, of course, for the metal doors) or covered with aluminum as well? If the surfaces are thoroughly cleaned, any quality latex paint should hold well on either metal or wood.

However, an experienced painter should be able to determine whether or not any wood should first receive a primer coat.

It would be best to remove the old gutters, paint what is normally covered by them, and install the new ones when all else is done.

Paint chips because of poor preparation

Q. The exterior of my white-painted cedar clapboards ranch house is terribly discolored. Some areas appear as if gray paint had been brushed on. Others have a black, dust-like coating. I assume they are both mildew. When I had the house painted a few years ago, it had some staining but this time it's much worse and it appeared in a short time. The paint is also peeling and chipping. The painter washed the siding with detergent and bleach. Is it poor preparation or poor quality paint?

What should I insist the painter do? Power-wash? What concentration of bleach? Should all paint be removed? What type and brand of paint to use? Mildewcide in the paint?

A. The paint chips you sent definitely show a heavy mildew infestation in the back of the chips. It looks as if the painter didn't get it all off before painting last time. Mildew will grow through new coats of paint. The paint chipped because of poor adhesion with the older paint. The chips are also quite thick indicating too thick an application last time or that several coats applied over the years failed suddenly because the additional weight of the last coat was the last straw.

Have the siding power-washed with a strong mixture of bleach and detergent. This should remove all unsound paint. Prime with a synthetic (alkyd) oil-based primer, paint with a quality latex with mildewcide.

Investigating the reasons for paint failure

Q. Because I am having trouble keeping paint on my siding, my painting contractor has suggested putting little wedges under the clapboards so moisture will be able to get out. Is this a good idea?

A. Not in my opinion. When the wind blows against a building, it has no place to go but upwards and to one or both sides. So when the wind blows and it is raining, water is driven between the clapboards to a far greater extent than if the wedges weren't there. This is not what we want.

There are a number of reasons why paint fails and an experienced person should be consulted to determine why it is peeling. Keep in mind that most paint failures are due to external causes. The few which are caused by interior moisture should be controlled from inside by sealing all cracks, crevices, and holes that allow interior moisture to enter the outside walls and condense on the sheathing and back of the siding, pushing the paint out. Excessive interior moisture should be controlled by means of ventilation through open windows, fans exhausting to the outside, air-to-air heat exchangers, dehumidifiers where appropriate and, perhaps, some changes in living habits.

External causes of paint peeling may be mill glaze; improper preparation of surfaces left unpainted too long or contaminated by mildew, dust and other pollutants; water penetration by one or more means through exterior cladding or behind it caused by absence of caulking at joints of dissimilar materials; capillary attraction from back splashing getting behind cladding that has not been treated on all sides before installation; leaking windows; bad flashing installations; roof leaks; snow melt behind ice dams, etc.

As you can see, it takes some investigation by an experienced person to avoid going off in the wrong direction.

Preparing the surface for painting

Q. The wood siding of my house built in 1920 hasn't been painted in 10 years. The paint has blistered and peeled, exposing the wood surface. I will be scraping and wire brushing the surface to prepare it for painting next year. Do I need to prime the siding prior to repainting?

A. Yes, all bare wood should be clean and free of mildew and other pollutants. Sanding before priming is a good way to achieve a good base. Prime as soon as you can after sanding—before pollutants, water, and the sun affect the surface adversely. Use an oil-based primer, and apply it by brush. Where the existing paint is sound, sanding it lightly to remove foreign matter is all that's needed before applying the final coat, unless the paint is still chalking. You can determine this by rubbing your hand over the surface. If it does leave chalk on your hand, wash the siding with a solution made with 1 cup TSP-PF or strong detergent, 1 quart fresh household bleach, and 3 quarts water. Rinse thoroughly. Use a good-quality latex paint as a finish coat.

Installing siding over old plywood

Q. The siding on my house is plywood with grooves every 12 inches. Because it is starting to delaminate, I would like to cover it with 6-inch-wide shiplap boards installed vertically.

Is the existing wood adequate to anchor the vertical boards with nails or should brass screws be used, the objective being to keep the new boards from bowing or gaps from developing between them?

A. The existing plywood is not adequate to nail new siding to it. The pulling power of wood subjected to moisture changes requires nailing into 1½ inches of solid wood. Brass or stainless steel screws are very expensive, and it would be a horrendous job.

The best, easiest and least expensive way to accomplish what you want to do is to screw 1×2-inch furring strips horizontally, 24 inches on center, over the plywood, using 2-inch minimum galvanized deck screws going through the plywood and into the studs. Then nail the new siding with stainless steel siding nails through the furring strips and plywood.

The most important thing to do to lessen the chances of the new siding twisting or shrinking too much is to use dry wood and to coat it on all surfaces with a water repellent wood preservative prior to installation.

Re-siding over hardboard

Q. Our garage and back porch are covered with hardboard siding from which paint is peeling. I do not wish to repaint it so I am thinking of covering it with vinyl or aluminum siding and doing the job myself.

Are either of the two methods I am considering practical:

1. Using vertical strapping spaced 16-inches apart and horizontal siding over the strips or,
2. Vertical siding applied directly over the existing siding? Would the air space cause a problem?

Which type of siding would you recommend?

A. Many houses built in the 1960s with hardboard siding that was not kept painted in a timely fashion over the years are now afflicted with delamination and disintegration of this siding and the owners are faced with the need for replacement.

Either method you propose to use should be satisfactory and the decision should depend more on whether you feel the house will look better with horizontal or vertical siding.

The decision to use vinyl or aluminum depends more on the color you like (vinyl comes only in pastel colors), local availability, prices and preferences and whether there is industrial pollution in your area—vinyl withstanding chemical fumes better than aluminum.

Another consideration is whether your area is subject to hail storms—aluminum can be badly dented by hail. Vinyl, on the other hand, can break if hit hard enough when very cold. Some building codes also require aluminum siding to be grounded.

But the most important consideration is the type of sheathing there is under the existing siding as you need a sound nailing substrate. And in windy areas, the industry specifies nailing every 12 inches, which may add to your installation problems unless the sheathing is ½-inch plywood. The nails should penetrate into each of the studs and not be driven in tight to allow for movement or the panels will buckle.

Aluminum siding with a weather exposure of 8 inches needs backer boards to prevent what is known as "dishing." You may be able to find in your area backer board panels that are saw-toothed shaped and provide not only backing but also insulation behind the beveled siding. Craneboard vinyl siding has integral foam backing (www.craneboard.com).

Re-siding gives you a one-time opportunity to add insulation to your house but its feasibility depends again on the type of sheathing behind the present siding. Use ¾-inch or 1-inch rigid extruded polystyrene but take care to seal the corners well to prevent heat loss through the air spaces.

Moisture problems with vertical boards

Q. The second floor of our 25-year-old house has vertical tongue-and-groove fir siding. Because of heat and moisture, paint will not remain on the grooves. I have

Because of poor surface preparation prior to painting, the paint is failing on this clapboard siding.

removed it twice, caulked, primed, and put two coats of top-quality exterior latex paint on them, but the paint cracked nonetheless. I thought a high-quality caulking in the grooves would help; it hasn't.

Would you recommend a caulking that would work? Or should I add battens over the grooves? I can cut boards 1½ inches wide but, because of the swelling and contraction which occurs, should I nail both edges of the battens or only one? Should the battens be primed and painted on the back before installation?

I am not thrilled with the batten idea but, considering the time and effort I have put into the other approaches and the fact that I have to set up scaffolding whenever I work on the siding, it may be the best solution.

A. Vertical or diagonal siding is prone to suffer from the problem that plagues you because water is drawn inside the grooves and wets them and the tongues, causing excessive dimensional movement.

If the siding boards were not backprimed or coated with a preservative before installation, there is little hope of solving the problem without major work.

You have two feasible options (excluding covering the siding with aluminum or vinyl for the time being, although it is another option).

1. Remove all caulking. (Applying it was a mistake.) Then remove all loose and cracked paint from the tongues and grooves by chemical means, using a heavy-bodied paint and varnish remover that is water rinsable so that once its work is done you can remove the resultant sludge with a strong jet from your garden hose. You may need to use an old toothbrush to dislodge recalcitrant residue. Sand adjacent paint edges to feather them. Let the tongues and grooves dry thoroughly and coat them liberally with a water-repellent wood preservative. You want it to penetrate as deeply as it can. Then prime with a good-quality oil-base primer and paint with a good-quality latex paint, but use only one coat. Apply a second coat in a couple of years, and after that only when needed—every five to ten years.

2. As an alternative, buy ready-cut 1×2-inch boards, or rip them from wider boards. Depending on what is readily available in your area, you can use fir,

Paint peeling off poorly prepared clapboard. Also note the cross-grain cracking from too-thick or too many coasts of paint.

cedar, redwood, pine, or spruce. Lay them out outside on saw horses and wet them on all sides with your garden hose once a day for three days, letting them dry between wettings. This removes the mill glaze and opens the pores of the wood. When dry, once the water treatment is done, coat them liberally with a water-repellent wood preservative; prime them, nail them on using two nails at each point, and finish painting them with one coat of a good-quality latex paint.

Either way, you do have your work cut out.

Cautions when removing paint:

For all readers facing the type of problem described above, here are some words of caution. Do not use torches to remove paint from siding, as it can cause a delayed fire within the walls. Use care in handling all chemicals, including eye and skin protection and old clothing. Finally, do not use water-rinsable paint removers on veneers, as the rinsing process can raise the grain on the veneer.

Replacing vertical boards

Q. The front of our house is stone with vertical brown cedar siding. Elsewhere we have brown, vertical hardboard siding that is deteriorating and we plan to replace it. What is the best siding to use? To keep the house's rustic look we'd like to stay with a vertical siding. I prefer wood whereas my husband wants something maintenance-free like vinyl or aluminum as we are near retirement.

A. Since you have vertical cedar siding in front, this would be my choice for the rest of the house. It would enhance your house and perhaps increase its value.

Have the cedar coated with a clear wood preservative before installation so all sides are treated, and have any cut ends dipped in a can of the preservative. This will protect it against extractive bleeding. Amteco TWP is my favorite.

The siding should be nailed with double-hot-dipped galvanized or stainless steel nails. Don't confuse the commonly available galvanized nails with double-hot-dipped; only the latter is long lasting. Use of the wrong nails will result in unsightly, difficult-to-remove, rust stains.

Then, coat it with the same material as the front cedar. A clear finish must be redone every year, a semi-transparent stain every two or three years, a solid color stain or paint every five to seven years.

If you opt for a solid color stain or paint, prime the wood first with the primer recommended by the manufacturer of the finish product you plan to use.

Sorry, "maintenance-free" doesn't apply to wood products.

Repairing cracks in wood siding

Q. I own an 1800 colonial reproduction home near the ocean.

The front is made of wood with long horizontal strips. They have checked and cracked. I would like to patch and paint them as I cannot afford to have them replaced right now. What can I use to fill the exposed area that will withstand sea air, sun and wind?

A. Try Minwax High Performance Wood Filler. It's an epoxy putty that can be sanded, drilled, shaped and, once painted, makes the repair invisible. It does not shrink or crack.

Solid stain, paint, or transparent stain

Q. Our house is 70-plus years old and has painted cedar clapboards. Many of the boards are damaged and peeling. Our brand new addition will also have cedar clapboards and we want to stain them. I know you do not advise any finish containing linseed oil, but the brands I have checked—Cabot's, Moore, etc.—all contain a small amount of linseed oil. The sales people I have dealt with all advise a first coat of an oil-based stain on new wood, or an oil-based primer topped with an acrylic stain.

The old painted clapboards will be stripped, primed and stained with an acrylic stain. Is there an oil-based stain that has no linseed oil, and that could be applied to the entire house? Or should we go for the primer and acrylic stain?

A. If you are planning on using a primer, you will not have the natural wood showing through, since all primers are white or tinted. So you would use a solid color stain to cover the primer. Solid color stains are really thin paint, and won't last anywhere as long as a high-quality paint. Instead, if you want a solid color, you should use a 100% acrylic latex paint.

But if you want to keep the natural look of cedar, and stain it with a product that offers mildew, UV and insect protection while also being a water repellent, use Amteco's TWP. It comes in several hues.

Red stain fades in sun

Q. The four-year-old cedar siding on our house was stained with a Cabot's semi-solid red stain. Every two years, it needs to be re-stained because of sun fading.

What can we do to make it last longer? We are willing to try paint if you feel the color will last longer.

There is no sign of mildew anywhere on the siding.

A. Reds don't usually last as long as other colors, and all semi-transparent stains do have to be re-applied about every two to three years. Good quality paints will last longer but you must decide whether or not you want to obliterate the grain of the cedar.

If you decide to paint, prepare the surface properly by having it power-washed. Then, apply an oil-based primer. Cabot makes one called Problem Solver because it does just that. Apply a 100% acrylic latex paint top coat and you should be set for some years to come as latex paints hold their color longer than oil-based (alkyd) paints.

Preserving cedar without staining it

Q. We are building a house which will have cedar siding. Which sealer do you recommend to keep the cedar natural, without darkening it or turning it gray?

A. It is best to coat the siding with a water-repellent wood preservative on all surfaces prior to installation. But the smooth side has what is known as mill glaze that prevents proper adhesion of any material. To get rid of it, you can sand the boards—a huge undertaking—or you can either wet them a couple of times or let them get rained on. This raises the grain and makes penetration of any coating possible. This is why I always recommend using the rough side out.

All field cuts should be treated (dipped in a can containing the preservative) before installation. My choice is Amteco TWP, but be aware that any good quality coating is going to darken the wood. Repeat every three to five years.

Painting not recommended for cedar shakes

Q. What is the best way to clean cedar shake siding? What is the best paint to use?

A. I presume your shake siding has blackened over time and contact with water. You can coat it with Flood's Dekswood, Wolman's Deckbrite, or other similar oxidizing solutions.

I certainly would urge you not to paint cedar shakes. Instead, coat them with one of the many semi-transparent preservative stains available on the market today, Amteco being my favorite.

Removing linseed oil

Q. Every five years or so, I apply linseed oil to the natural wood shakes that form the siding of my 23-year-old house. In the last few years, they have turned black and I am told this is mildew.

I have tried different ways recommended by a local paint store to remove this blackness, including bleach. A contractor gave me an estimate of $1,400 to remove the blackness with a gray-looking substance and a high-powered water spray. How can I return the shakes to their normal light brown color so that I can apply linseed oil on them again?

A. Mildew spores simply adore linseed oil; to them, it is caviar served with champagne. Continue doing it and they will love you but you must, then, accept blackened shakes.

The most effective way to remove the mildew and airborne dirt that have discolored your shakes is to have the siding power-washed with a solution made of the following ingredients per gallon: 1 pound TSP-PF and equal amounts of fresh Clorox Bleach and water, or use Wolman's Deck & Fence Brightener, or Flood Dekswood.

The pressure to use to apply the solution and to rinse afterward should be between 1,000 psi and 1,500 psi, but it must be done by experienced personnel so as not to fray and otherwise damage the wood.

Allow 24 hours of good drying conditions and apply the finish of your choice. I recommend Amteco TWP because of its water repellency, wood preservative formulation, and longevity.

You can apply it yourself using a garden sprayer. Adjust the tip to atomize as finely as possible and apply a uniform wet coat. Allow to penetrate for 30 to 60 minutes and apply a second wet coat without runs (if need be, it's okay to wait overnight to apply the second coat). Repeat every three to five years as needed.

Staining over creosote

Q. My cedar siding was last painted with creosote 15 years ago. I have left it to weather so I could, in time, cover it with a safer coating.

The boards are now rough, unevenly gray, and have some cracks. But I have been told that no preservative will stick to them after tests were made on a small piece. Is this true, and what should I do now? I like the gray color, so this is not the problem.

A. After 15 years, the creosote stain has crystallized, and you should be able to treat the siding satisfactorily. Mix 1 cup of TSP-PF with 1 quart of fresh Clorox bleach and 3 quarts of water. Apply to the siding with a garden sprayer, starting from the bottom and working in vertical sections to obtain even results.

Next, power-wash the siding with no more than 1,500 psi pressure and with a 40/20 tip, keeping the nozzle 24 inches away from the surface and following the grain of the wood. Rinse off. Be sure to cover vegetation with plastic, after wetting it, and hose it off thoroughly afterwards. Wear eye and skin protection.

When dry, coat the siding with a mix of equal parts of Amteco's TWP Cape Cod Gray and Prairie Gray stains. This will give you a driftwood appearance that should not be affected by the remaining creosote crystals as could happen if either of these stains were used alone.

Painting over discolored clapboards

Q. Our cedar clapboard siding weathered for five years with no treatment. Paint was recommended at that time rather than stain due to uneven discoloration and black streaks. The painter claimed that he had a new primer that made the sanding and bleaching recommended by the paint store unnecessary.

After one coat of primer and one of latex finish coat, we still see discoloration through the white paint. The painter tells us now that we need to replace many of the clapboards to eliminate the dark bleeding through. What do you think of this?

A. Too bad you didn't bleach the siding then; it would have removed most, if not all, of the discoloration and you could have applied the finish I have mentioned many times which gives cedar a rich tone while keeping it natural. Now, you are stuck with painting. Instead of replacing many clapboards, which seems senseless if their only problem is bleed-through, paint the siding with Zinsser's Bulls Eye 1-2-3 and a 100% acrylic latex top coat.

Paint is "crazing"

Q. My three-story old house was insulated with blown-in cellulose some time ago. The paint on the front of the house has crazed every time the house is painted. Would it be okay to put new siding over the existing siding, or would it cause a moisture build-up between the boards? What kind of siding would be best?

A. If the paint crazing, as you refer to it, were caused by the insulation, it would more than likely occur all over the house or, at least, in a number of places. What I believe you call paint crazing is probably what is known as crossgrain cracking. This is the result of many coats of paint applied over surfaces that have not weathered enough. The paint becomes very thick, or has been applied in too thick coats, and loses all elasticity.

It develops cracks across the grain of the wood and looks like alligator skin. There may be any number of reasons why the problem occurs only on the front of the house. Perhaps it does not get as much weather as the rest of the walls, or you have it painted more often. Perhaps it's under a front porch.

If your house has historical value and fine details, it would be a shame to cover the siding with a new one of any type. It would be preferable to remove the old paint down to bare wood and start all over with a good-quality oil-base primer followed within a short period of time (two days to a week) with a coat of 100% acrylic latex.

When choosing a stripper, you must keep in mind that your paint may contain lead and must be disposed of in an accepted fashion. Peel-Away is one such stripper. It is applied with a trowel, allowed to dry for 24 hours, and peeled off like a skin. The lead paint is encapsulated within the skin and should be disposed of ecologically. It can remove as many as 30 coats of paint with one application. More information is available at www.dumondchemicals.com.

Call your municipal offices for information on proper disposal.

Even if your house has no historical value, and only the front wall needs to be stripped and repainted, it's worth doing to keep the original wood siding.

Painting should not be done too often; it's best to wash the walls with water and TSP-PF instead.

Removing mildew

Q. We stained our house two years ago with a semi-transparent gray stain over an earlier brown stain. After a year, I noticed areas that were getting darker, some close to the ground, some not. More areas developed these dark stains in the second year so that now, 75% of the house is covered. I am sure it is mildew.

Do you think it was on the brown stain prior to the application of the new stain? How can it be removed? Can a solution be mixed and applied with a pressure washer? Once removed, do we have to wait a year before restaining to make sure the mildew will not return? Can anything be added to the stain to prevent recurrence?

A. The mildew may have been on the earlier stain or may have developed recently. For it to develop, it needs spores (they are in the air at all times) and the right humidity and temperature. Yes, it can be removed by pressure washing with a solution containing a mildewcide such as household bleach. Since you have a severe infestation, you will need a strong solution made with half water and half bleach.

A problem with pressure washing is that spray may damage nearby vegetation. Doing the washing by hand and scrub brush is less risky but, of course, more tedious. You should be all right if you can cover all nearby vegetation with plastic. Rinse the ground thoroughly after you have finished but do not rinse the walls. You do not have to wait after the treatment to restain. The elements propitious to the formation of mildew are ever present and there is little you can do about it. Mildewcide can be added to the stain before application. You will need to restain every couple of years.

Mildew develops after new paint job

Q. We own a large country farmhouse that we use as a second home. The exterior is sided with clapboards and, although the house is used infrequently, it is heated through the winter. About six years ago, we had the house repainted. The painter used an oil-base solid white stain. After two years, an obvious mildew problem developed on the sides of the house most exposed to sunlight. We had never had a mildew problem before.

The painter came back and power-washed the affected sides of the house and it looked great. But over the past four years, after the power-washing, the mildew has returned worse than ever. Now the place looks terrible with large gray areas of mildew.

What can I do to get rid of the mildew forever, or at least keep it in check until the house needs repainting? I don't want to power-wash every two to three years. In fact, I am reluctant to have someone power-wash the house again as the first power-washing drove water up under the clapboards resulting in interior water stains.

A. You had no mildew problems before because the farmhouse was probably paint-ed with a gloss or semi-gloss oil-base paint that tends to shed water quickly, and was self-cleaning through a chalking process. The painter used an oil-base flat stain that retains water longer, thus encouraging the development of mildew. Any oil-base paint, whether alkyd (synthetic) or linseed (organic) oil-base, is more prone to mil-dew (especially linseed oil, which is food for mildew) than latex paints would be.

Country houses in farming areas are also most prone to mildew problems, as the spores are everywhere in the air from hay and other crops. The fact that the mildew developed on the sunny sides is probably due to the prevailing winds in the area (south and southwest).

An experienced power-washer would not get water behind clapboards. Power-washing should be done with a downward aim to prevent this from happening. The house should be power-washed by someone experienced in doing so with clap-board siding, using a strong bleach-and-detergent solution. Then it should be re-painted with a 100% acrylic latex paint as soon as the wood is dry enough to do so (latex paints can be applied to damp but not wet wood)

For periodic maintenance, have the house power-washed as needed to keep it clean. Top-quality acrylic latex paints should last many years.

White residue appears on recently painted surface

Q. My house was repainted in August. Recently, I noticed a white residue in the shape of circles on the soffits. Strangely, the residue is gone in the morning but re-appears in the afternoon. It can be rubbed off with a cloth. What is it and how can I eliminate it?

A. It's probably a surfactant from the detergents used in paints coming through because the paint was applied on a hot, humid day. It should come off with a damp cloth but it may take a couple of treatments.

Painted shakes are warping

Q. The cedar shakes on the sunny side of my house have a tendency to dry and warp, especially in the summer time. This causes them to loosen from the nails and drop off.

The shakes are 30 years old and painted, and those on the other three sides of the house are in excellent condition. Will a coat of linseed oil penetrate the paint and prevent drying? Are there other solutions?

A. The fact that the shakes warp on the sunny side of the house indicates that the paint has become porous and that they are absorbing water. The sun drives the moisture towards their back and their front becomes dry. Linseed oil would be the worst thing to use as it would encourage the development of mildew although, where the house gets a lot of sun, it may inhibit it.

The best solution, if that side of your house is not too large and since the shakes keep falling off, would be to replace them with new ones that you would treat with a wood preservative to saturation on all sides before application. Once up, they can be painted.

If the shakes are otherwise in good condition, wait until you are sure they are dry and try applying a wood preservative over the paint. If it penetrates readily, apply it all over to saturation and repaint.

A middle solution is to remove the shakes, treat them front, back and all edges and re-install. Repaint.

Staining T1-11 siding

Q. The 30-year-old Texture 1-11 plywood siding of our house was coated for several years with Cabot's Bleaching Oil to give it a weathered look. This has taken place, but spottily, with some brown patches still persisting.

No treatment was applied for about a dozen years and the plywood is drying out and cracking in some places. What would you recommend I use, how should it be applied, and how often?

A. The remaining brown patches are due to the hardness of the grain of the wood, preventing absorption of the stain, which washes away after a while.

All stains should be applied again every two to three years. At this point, use the same material you have used in the past and apply with a brush for better coverage and penetration.

Paint peeling from hardboard siding

Q. My well-insulated house is sided with 8-inch-wide hardboard beveled siding. The south side of the house peels to the bare boards within a year after painting with latex and finish coats. Should I repaint with an oil base paint, replace the siding, or cover the whole house with vinyl siding?

A. Properly prepared and painted hardboard siding should not peel that soon. Something is wrong there and you should try to find out what it is. Here are possibilities:

Nail heads should be flush with hardboard siding. Here, the nails have popped through the painted surface.

- Whether the siding was factory primed or not, it should have been painted shortly after installation. If not factory primed, it needed a coat of oil base or latex primer—depending on what the manufacturer of the selected finish coat recommended. Siding not properly painted shortly after installation would need to be cleaned (and re-primed in the case of factory-primed siding) to remove airborne dust, pollen and molds.
- Is there ice build-up on the south roof in winter? This may result in leakage in the wall behind an ice dam. The resultant wetness will cause paint failure.
- Another possibility is interior moisture migration through the walls if there is an improperly applied vapor retarder on the warm side of the insulation. A south wall is more susceptible to paint failure because it gets a lot of sun exposure through most of the year.

Replacing the siding or covering the whole house with new siding should be last options and only after any moisture problem has been solved anyway or you'll simply be hiding the problem.

Installing new siding over old

Q. My pressed-board siding is starting to deteriorate along the edges in certain spots. I am told not to put any new siding over it as it will continue to deteriorate. Is it so? What would you suggest I do?

A. It depends on the reason for the siding's deterioration. If it is because it hasn't been properly painted or maintained and it has become damaged from rain, it should be perfectly safe to add new siding over it. However, if the deterioration is due to *internal* moisture migration, the new siding may trap this moisture and deterioration may continue.

You need an expert opinion on the cause before you can safely proceed. Look in your Yellow Pages under Building Inspections for an inspector who is a member of the American Society of Home Inspectors (ASHI) for assurance of competence in a field getting crowded with people with little experience. If you can't find one, call ASHI at 800-743-2744 in Washington, D. C. for the name of a nearby member. Or visit their Web site at www.ashi.org where you can find inspectors in your area.

Treatment recommended for all exterior wood

Q. Our lakefront property has a pressure-treated deck, cedar-shake siding and redwood trim, as well as white painted panels under the windows and porch screens.

We were told that the cedar and redwood, if left natural, would eventually turn gray; is this so? Will the wood age gracefully or become stained and weatherbeaten? What would be the best way to coordinate and preserve these three woods? If we stain the shakes gray, what will happen to the redwood trim?

A. It is best not to leave cedar and redwood without a protective coating; they would lose their natural oils and become grungy-looking.

There are a number of high-quality semi-transparent stains on the market that would protect these various woods and unify them. The gray you are considering for the shakes can also be applied to the redwood. As for the deck, you need to exercise caution; most stains are not made to be walked on. You have to select one that can stand foot traffic. Pressure-treated wood should be coated with one of the specially-made products that will help reduce discoloration, checking, and warping.

These treatments will have to be repeated every few years, depending on the exposure of the various woods to the weather.

Installing vinyl siding over wood clapboards

Q. The wood siding on our house gets a lot of weather beating from wind and sun resulting in frequent painting. The siding on the east and south sides is actually pulling away from the house.

We are going to have vinyl siding put on and I want the old siding removed because I think it will give a better look and not make the house look "flat" with the windows.

My builder thinks it is unnecessary to remove the old siding and says that, if we ever want to sell the house, the buyers may like the option of removing the vinyl siding and exposing the wood again. What is your recommendation?

A. If the vinyl siding is ever removed, the wood siding beneath it will look like woodpeckers had a field day on it. And many boards may actually have been split by the nailing of the vinyl siding.

You may be able to re-nail your old siding, but I would opt for removal and, perhaps, considering using 1-inch-thick extruded polystyrene under the vinyl to improve the energy efficiency of your house. In any case, felt paper or housewrap should be applied under the vinyl siding.

Installing vinyl over wood shingles

Q. I live in a 30-plus year-old side hall colonial. Last year we had replacement windows installed and put in a new front door. At that time I got four estimates on siding the house. It has the original cedar shingles, which we painted about seven years ago.

Two contractors said they always put the siding over the existing shingles, with a layer of housewrap in between. The other two contractors said they always re-move the shingles first. Of course, that job costs more because of having to dispose of the shingles. Is there any advantage to having vinyl siding installed over the shingles? One of the contractors said that if you put siding over shingles, it will not line up and seat properly. I'd really appreciate your input on this.

A. You must have a good reason for wanting to cover cedar shingles with vinyl, so I won't try to talk you out of it. This is your last chance to improve the energy efficiency of your house. Consider having the shingles removed and 1-inch-thick rigid extruded polystyrene insulation applied over the existing sheathing. Be sure it is blue, gray or pink to ensure that you are having the right insulation installed.

I would urge you not to accept what some siding contractors may offer you: a thin, unfolding or rolled synthetic insulation that has very little value.

This will cost you more, of course, but you will begin to save on the fuel you use to heat your house and on the cost of electricity to air-condition it. If the sheathing of your house is made of boards instead of plywood or particle board, using a housewrap is a good idea regardless of whether or not you go for the added insulation I suggest. But if it is plywood or particle board, and you go for the added rigid insulation, there is no need to use a housewrap as these materials are air-tight anyway.

If you decide to skip the chance to improve the insulation on your house, removing the shingles would give you a more even job. You should use a housewrap regardless of the type of sheathing you have as the sheathing needs protection from wind-driven rain that will undoubtedly get behind the siding.

If it works, why change?

Q. You have commented on preservatives for cedar shingles and decks but not about cedar siding. We own a 30-year-old house on a lake that has wide cedar boards. Over the years, we used Cabot's Bleaching Oil which worked out beautifully. The wood continues to look good, but it is time to do it again. Should we continue to use the same product or is there a better alternative?

A. Why change horses in mid-stream? If it works, stay with it.

Vinyl Siding

Vinyl with foam backing

Q. Do you have any information about vinyl siding with foam backing? Is it much better than regular vinyl siding? Is it applied over existing wood, or must the outside wood be removed first?

A. Vinyl siding with integral foam insulation is more resistant to damage from impact, such a being struck by a ball, etc. This may be a consideration when there are children playing around the house. The back-up insulation is made of expanded polystyrene—an inferior product to extruded polystyrene—and is only about ½-inch thick at the thickest point. CraneBoard is such a product.

If you are looking for energy improvement, it is better to have 1-inch rigid extruded polystyrene insulation applied over the existing sheathing or siding, and have the vinyl siding nailed over the insulation.

If the existing wood siding is in rough shape, it may be best to remove it and apply the insulation directly to the sheathing. But if the siding is not in bad shape, the insulation and vinyl siding may be installed directly over the old siding. The important thing in this case is to make sure the insulation is tight at all joints and especially at all corners.

Fixing a hole in vinyl

Q. There is a hole about the size of a half dollar in my vinyl siding. Hornets have made a nest behind the siding, using this hole. How can I patch it?

A. The easiest way is to have a siding contractor replace the panel. But you can patch it effectively, although not aesthetically, as follows: buy a zip tool from a siding contractor and ask for a demonstration on its use; unzip the panel above the damaged one and have someone hold it up while you remove the nails of the damaged panel.

Remove the damaged panel, flip it over and clean the area to receive the patch with PVC cleaner. Apply a patch of the same siding with PVC cement.

Replace the siding panel but do not drive the nails tight; the siding must float lightly. Use the zip tool to re-snap the upper panel over the repaired one.

White vinyl is chalking

Q. My white vinyl siding is chalking when you rub your hand on it. Is it a sign of deterioration?

A. White vinyl siding is formulated to chalk so as to look clean; colors are formulated to chalk less.

How to clean vinyl

Q. My vinyl siding needs cleaning. What is the best way to do that? Should I start at the top or the bottom?

A. A long-handled car washing brush makes the job easy. Use plain water from your outside faucet; this is often sufficient.

However, if you live in an area suffering from industrial pollution and you need to use a cleaning solution, make it with a cup of powder detergent (TSP-PF is best) and 1 gallon water. If mildew is also a problem, substitute 1 quart fresh Clorox bleach for 1 quart water.

You can also get a siding cleaner from any paint, hardware, or building supply stores, or from siding contractors.

The usual recommendation is to start at the bottom and work up, to avoid having the dislodged dirt from above run onto the dry dirty surfaces below. If this happens, it creates streaks that will be difficult to clean when you get to them.

White vinyl stained by driveway sealer

Q. My white vinyl garage siding has been stained by splashing asphalt driveway emulsion. I've tried mineral spirits and gasoline with little effect. I finally used "Goof-Off" which contains xylene. It did remove the emulsion stains but left yellowish stains behind.

I've tried bleach and several household cleaners without success. I should have left the emulsion stains alone. Any suggestions?

A. Try auto tar remover and lacquer thinner. One of them should help. Use a clean white cloth and rub gently along the length of the panels. Rinse with plenty of fresh water.

Vinyl pops loose

Q. We have a five-year-old house with vinyl siding. On the south side of the house, the siding about 3 feet from the ground is not fastened securely and keeps popping loose. We go out there and slide a hand along it and it seems to pop back into place. Then, a few days later, it's loose again. What can we do to anchor it permanently into place?

A. It sounds as if the pieces that are loose have not been fastened as snugly to the adjacent pieces as they should have been when first installed. As a result, they do not lock as they should. Your best solution is to have a contractor familiar with vinyl siding remove these pieces and snug them up. This may entail the readjustment of quite a number of pieces.

Putting back shutters after re-siding

Q. We recently installed vinyl siding over the clapboards of our house. Can we put back our somewhat heavy wood shutters or would they pull out of the siding? These shutters are 16 inches wide by 35½ and 47½ inches tall.

A. If you didn't have rigid insulation put over the wood siding before having the vinyl siding installed, you should be able to use longer stainless steel screws that would go into the wood siding.

Make the holes through the vinyl siding a little wider to allow for expansion and contraction and do not fasten the shutters tightly so the siding can move.

Removing spider spots

Q. How can I remove spider spots from white vinyl siding?

A. If they are truly spider spots, rather than artillery fungus, try one or more of the following, in the order given:

1. Use Fantastik and a good scrubbing with a soft bristle brush and a lot of elbow grease.

2. Use a good cleaning fluid applied with a clean soft cloth in long strokes to minimize splotching.

3. Use lacquer thinner applied with a clean soft cloth; use long and gentle strokes but do not rub. Go easy as this chemical tends to take some of the vinyl surface off.

Removing cement splatters

Q. Cement was splashed onto my light tan vinyl siding when new sidewalks were poured along the side of an addition to my house. How can it be removed?

A. Too bad concrete workers do not take the precaution of taping plastic against surfaces adjacent to pours. A few minutes spent doing that would save untold distress, anger and work later. (If any of you readers are having concrete poured next to your house, either insist on protection or install it yourself.)

Use a putty knife to dislodge gently and carefully as much of the splatter as you can. Do not scrape; you may damage the siding. Then use one of the two following methods and observe preliminary general cautionary advice, *i.e.* wear old sacrificial clothing, heavy rubber gloves and eye protection.

1. Dilute muriatic acid (buy in hardware or paint stores) in water by a ratio of 1 to 3 respectively in a plastic bucket. Do not use metal. Apply to splatter remnants with a soft bristle, natural fiber brush (do not use nylon, as muriatic acid dissolves it), rubbing gently with the grain of the siding. When the splatters have softened, rinse with clear water.

To complete the job, if necessary, gently rub with Scotch Brite pad (it's also made of nylon so it cannot be used with the acid, only after rinsing).

2. Go talk to a Concrete Ready-Mix producer and ask them if they could let you buy, or just give you, a small amount of Remov-ox or similar product they use to remove concrete from concrete trucks. It is not supposed to affect painted surfaces so it should be safe on vinyl siding, but first try it in an inconspicuous area to make sure.

The splatters may need to be soaked for several hours by applying a rag wet with the solution (the trick is to devise a way to hold it there). Then rinse with a solution containing vinegar.

Either method should work. You may have to use both if the splatters are old.

Removing insect-repellent stains

Q. I sprayed a screen door with OFF and now there is a brownish stain on my new white vinyl siding. The spray manufacturer can't help. I have tried vinegar, Fantastic, etc. without success. Is there anything that will remove this stain?

A. Try the following, one at a time; one of them should take care of the stain. But if they don't, keep in mind that time and the elements generally do a good job, particularly on white siding, which is formulated to chalk with time for self-cleaning.

1. Use a soft white cloth and mineral spirits, rubbing gently to avoid polishing the treated area with too much pressure. Rinse with water.
2. Use same procedure as above but with auto tar remover; if still unsuccessful, use auto radiator cleaner.
3. Next, try lacquer thinner, using the same precautions as above.
4. Lastly, dampen a small section of clean white cloth with xylene and rub only the stained area vigorously. Rinse with water.

Cleaning spots left by clinging vine

Q. I recently removed Virginia Creeper from my yellow vinyl siding. I scraped the suction cups with a hard brush and a knife, washed the siding with a detergent, and finished the job with SOS pads.

From a few feet away the vinyl siding does not look too bad, but up close I can still see the brown spots left by the suction cups. How can I get rid of them?

A. It's amazing that after the harsh treatment you gave it the siding still looks good. Unfortunately, there is not much more you can do to remove the remnants of the suckers but to try the SOS pads again.

Removing paint splatters

Q. My husband used a rust-preventive primer and then an enamel paint recommended for wrought iron railings. Unfortunately, some of each coat of paint spattered on our vinyl siding. Any hints on removal without damaging the color of the siding?

A. Use a soft cloth and dry-cleaning fluid. Do not use too much pressure as it will "polish" the siding and leave a shiny spot. Be sure to wear rubber gloves, and avoid breathing the fumes.

Another option is chewing gum remover, available at janitorial supply stores. It will freeze the paint, which you should then be able to chip off with a razor blade. There are also graffiti removal sprays, such as Vandal Mark Remover, available at janitorial supply stores, but if you choose one make sure it's safe to use on vinyl siding.

Aluminum Siding

Aluminum expands and contracts

Q. My aluminum siding fits into an aluminum flange around all openings but it is not tight to these flanges. There is no caulking between the flanges and the end of the siding. The contractor says it is to allow for expansion and contraction. He says that if the pieces were tight or caulked, the siding might buckle. Is he right?

A. Yes, he is.

Cleaning aluminum siding

Q. I have a Turbo-Wash power pressure washer that attaches to my regular garden hose. What can I use with it to clean my aluminum siding safely?

A. You don't really need a power-washer to clean aluminum siding; a regular garden hose equipped with a long-handled car-washing brush is ideal. I can't assure you that the pressure washer would be safe to use; it will depend on how you use it so as not to damage the siding or allow water to seep in back of it.

Hardware stores sell siding cleaning products, but you can also make your own by mixing 1 cup of TSP-PF with 1 quart of fresh Clorox bleach and 3 quarts of water. Rinse thoroughly afterward. Be sure to cover vegetation with plastic.

Repainting aluminum siding

Q. Our 25-year-old aluminum siding, originally red or maroon, has faded to a pink color. We want to paint it ourselves next year. How should we clean it and paint it? We would like to paint it a light beige color. Will the original color bleed through?

A. Wash the siding with a mixture of 1 cup TSP-PF, 1 quart fresh household bleach and 3 quarts water. You'll need several gallons, but keep these proportions and mix 1 gallon at a time.

Apply it with a soft fiber scrub brush. Rinse with clear water. Cover all vegetation with plastic and rinse it off thoroughly afterwards. Wear eye and skin protection, including heavy rubber gloves.

Once clean and dry, paint with a good-quality 100% acrylic satin or semi-gloss latex exterior paint or choose one especially formulated for metal siding. An excellent choice is a urethane acrylic; it has long-lasting quality, great color retention and sticks to metal and vinyl better than most other paints. It is available in spray formula or in brush/roll formula. You may need two coats to hide the old red.

There is no need for a primer if the old finish still covers the metal but if, after washing, you find that there is a lot of bare metal, a compatible primer should be used.

New lacquer already peeling

Q. I had my aluminum siding lacquered and the south side has already peeled. Can I get the siding painted or do I need new siding? I am concerned about the other sides of the house peeling if I get the siding painted.

A. I wish you had mentioned what product was used on the siding. But it does sound as if the siding may not have been prepared properly before application of what you call lacquer.

It is possible to paint aluminum siding successfully but, as for all painting jobs, success depends on a thorough preparation of the surfaces. The siding should be cleaned to remove all pollutants, after which it can be painted with a good-quality paint made for metal or a 100% acrylic latex exterior house paint.

If you intend to paint the peeling lacquered surfaces, the lacquer should be completely removed and the surfaces washed with lacquer thinner before the final cleaning.

Caulking aluminum where it adjoins brick or wood

Q. The aluminum siding of our 23-year-old house is caulked at the ends of each panel and where it adjoins brick or wood.

The caulking has become dry and has separated from the siding in many areas. We are planning on repainting the siding this summer and are wondering if we should replace the caulking. If it should be replaced, what is the best way to do so and what is the best type of caulking to use?

A. Because aluminum siding is subject to considerable expansion and contraction with temperature changes, it is doubtful that any caulking you do will remain effective where siding panels overlap each other, as they should. And because they overlap—or should—there is no need to caulk them.

However, where siding adjoins wood or brick, it is a good idea to caulk those joints to keep water from getting behind and potentially affecting negatively whatever water-sensitive material is in back of the siding. The movement should be less at these joints because the panels subject to it butt against less affected materials.

Remove as much of the old caulking as you can with a plastic or wood scraper and the residue with a soft cloth and mineral spirits. My overwhelming preference is in favor of polyurethane caulking because of its longevity, resistance to drying and cracking and its flexural strength. You may not find it in retail stores; it is available in construction specialties supply houses, waterproofing material suppliers and some large concrete suppliers. My favorite brand, which I have used for over 40 years, is Sikaflex-la.

Removing rust spots from aluminum

Q. The screws from our awnings have created rust stains on the aluminum siding. How can the rust be removed?

A. The finish on aluminum siding is very fragile. First, try a household detergent or non-abrasive cleaner such as is used to wash dishes. Apply with a soft white cloth. If that doesn't work, use a mild abrasive such as Bon Ami, Comet or Ajax but apply it only on the rust spots. Remove the offending screws and replace them with stainless steel or aluminum.

Aluminum is pitted and rough

Q. The aluminum siding on my older home is approximately 15 years old. The two top panels appeared very dirty, so I attempted to power-wash them a few weeks ago only to discover the surface is not dirty but pitted and rough.

The white finish on the siding is chalking and dull and there are a few rust spots also besides the problem near the roof. Any ideas why this happened and what I can do to correct it shy of replacing the siding altogether?

A. The chalking is normal; it helps keep the siding clean. The top panels, protected by the roof overhang, were not subjected to the washing effects of rain and the pitting is most likely caused by air pollution.

If the siding is truly aluminum and not steel, and the spots are really rust and not some other type of stain, they are caused by the splashing of water contaminated with oxidizing iron.

You can sand the rough panels until they are smooth, clean the entire siding with TSP-PF and fresh Clorox bleach, rinse it and paint it with a 100% acrylic latex exterior house paint or a paint specially formulated for metal siding.

Removing old caulk and tape

Q. What can be used to remove dried silicone caulking and masking tape from white aluminum siding without damaging the siding? The siding is over 20 years old but in good condition.

A. If the caulking is indeed silicone, you can pull it off, but it might take a bit of paint with it.

Remove old masking tape with Goo Gone, Avon's Skin-So-Soft, Turtle Wax Bug & Tar Remover, or cooking oil. Apply and rub in gently.

Removing egg stains

Q. Early this spring, someone threw eggs at the aluminum siding of the house I later bought in July. I washed the entire outside of the house, using water and Ajax dishwashing soap. Some of the egg came off but some areas are stained and, in others, the aluminum appears bare.

Is there anything I can do at this late stage?

A. Too bad the then owner didn't clean the egg off right away; it would have all come off without harming the siding. All stains should be treated before they have a chance to set.

Since some of the aluminum siding finish came off and some of the egg stains are still present, your best bet is probably to repaint the affected areas with a latex paint mixed to match the color of the siding as closely as possible.

Another possibility is to have the representative of a siding dealer look at your house and see if he or she can tell which product it is. The appropriate dealer may be able to replace the damaged panels satisfactorily if they aren't too old and faded.

Removing mildew and tree sap

Q. I noticed what appeared to be patches of dirty spots mostly on the north and west sides of the aluminum siding of my house. The installer suggested I wash the siding with a mixture of TSP-PF, bleach and water. This did help a bit but did not remove the spots. He said the spots may be mildew or tree sap (I have a honey locust and oak trees near the house).

I am afraid to do too much rubbing on the siding. Is there anything else I can do? I don't want to affect the resale value of my house.

A. The bleach solution should have removed mildew if you use the right proportions the installer suggested. So the tree sap may be the culprit. Try removing it with Lestoil. You are right; don't rub too hard as it would damage the finish.

Asbestos Siding

Are asbestos shingles dangerous?

Q. Many homes have asbestos shingles as siding in our area. Is this dangerous? If they have to be removed, how is it done and how are they disposed of? Please discuss this for the benefit of the many who own houses with that type of siding.

A. Asbestos fibers in siding and roofing shingles are encapsulated in cement; they should not present any problem if in fairly good condition. Moreover, they are outdoors. (In urban areas a lot of asbestos fibers are already floating in the air from vehicle brakes and other uses and we are exposed to them daily.) Government authorities recommend that nothing be done to asbestos-containing products that are in good condition.

Where some damage is visible, the recommendation is to have it evaluated by specialists who probably will recommend encapsulation as opposed to removal. Removal is a last resort and must be done by specialists and disposed of according to federal regulations.

Finding replacements for broken shingles

Q. My 75-year-old duplex has asbestos shingle siding. A few are broken and I am having a problem finding replacements for them. Can you tell me where I can locate left-overs?

A. Have you checked with long-established siding and roofing contractors? They probably installed asbestos shingles some decades ago and may still have left-overs in their warehouses.

Another possible source is general contractors or asbestos abatement and removal specialists who may be called upon to remove asbestos shingles from buildings.

Repairing and painting asbestos siding

Q. I have asbestos siding that is flaking at the roof line over my garage. Is there a paste or something that I can use to repair the siding and then paint it? If removing the siding is the only alternative, would I remove the siding down to the roof wood?

A. First, you should wash the siding gently with warm water and a detergent such as TSP-PF or equivalent, using a soft bristle brush. This will not only clean the asbestos shingles but also prevent any loose particles from floating in the air.

Once the shingles are dry, you have several choices:
1. Coat the affected areas with a masonry conditioner such as Masonry Lusta. Buy it in building supply stores specializing in masonry products. Choose their matte finish so that the coated areas will not be as conspicuous as if you used their glossy finish. It comes in gallon cans at around $50 per gallon.

2. Apply Benjamin Moore's 024 Exterior All Purpose Oil-based Bonding Primer to the affected shingles and paint the treated areas with a latex finish paint.

3. Coat the affected areas with Zinsser's Bulls Eye 1-2-3 or Kover Stain and paint them with a latex paint.

4. Use Pittsburgh Paints 6-80 latex-base Special Primer and apply a finish coat with a latex paint. All the primers mentioned above are in the $20 to $25 per gallon range, but they do need a top coat. Any one of these products should stabilize the damaged sections without having to remove the shingles. All are recommended for use when the ambient temperature is 50°F or above, so, depending on where you live, you may have to wait until next year.

Removing moss or fungus from asbestos siding

Q. My asbestos shingle siding on the north side of the house is covered with moss or fungus. How can I get rid of it without a big expense?

A. The simplest way to remove moss from siding (not recommended for roofs) is to pull the moss off with your hands or with a putty knife.

To remove residue and other contaminants, apply the old, tried and true, cheap formula: 1 quart of fresh Clorox and 1 cup of TSP-PF mixed with 3 quarts of water and applied with a soft scrub brush.

Buy TSP-PF in hardware, paint or agricultural supply stores.

If you prefer not to pull the moss off or you also have lichen, spray them with a solution made of 3 parts white vinegar and 1 part water.

Removing rust stains

Q. The asbestos siding on my house has been stained by black metal shutters. Is there any way to lighten or remove these streaks?

A. Assuming that the streaks are caused by rust, mix oxalic acid crystals to saturation in hot water, using a glass or plastic container—not metal. Apply with a paint brush and allow the solution to do its work. Rinse thoroughly with water.

Oxalic acid is a very strong chemical; use eye and skin protection and caution in applying so as not to spill on surfaces that do not need to be treated or on vegetation.

Brick Houses

Cleaning dust from bricks

Q. We have a four-year-old clay brick house. The bricks are coated with a dust that gets on clothing and skin on contact. I'd like to wash them. What method should I use?

A. Modern hard-burned bricks with a sand finish should not be subject to dusting. If the dust is due to the construction process, you should be able to wash the bricks with your garden hose at full pressure.

If the problem is really due to a defect in the bricks, you should have the contractor look at them and get the manufacturer's representative to examine them and suggest a solution. Coating them with a siloxane-based treatment may solve the problem.

Powdery residue on bricks

Q. A white powdery residue is forming on the bricks of my garage. It seems to be eating the bricks. What is it and what can I do about it?

A. It is called efflorescence. The salts in the bricks are dissolved by moisture and brought out to their surface where they are left as deposits as the water dries up. They are not harmful and are certainly not eating the bricks. Remove them with a stiff brush. Do not attempt to seal the bricks, as it would trap moisture within them and cause spalling, *i.e.* breaking-up of the surface of the bricks as the moisture within freezes.

But try to ascertain where the moisture is coming from and whether it can be prevented from being absorbed. For instance, if the bricks are in contact with the soil around the garage foundation, dig the soil away to a shovel's depth or deeper and place heavy black plastic against the bricks. Backfill and make sure the soil slopes away from the foundation. Cut off excess black plastic 1 inch above the new soil line. Plant grass. This should break capillarity and keep the bricks dry. Gutter and downspouts should prevent splashing.

Crack in brick wall is expanding

Q. There is a crack in the brick wall of our 1968 house. It starts on the east side and runs up toward the corner of the house and continues around the south side in a zigzag fashion about 3 feet above the foundation.

This crack has been here for several years. This past May, we noticed that it expanded. It did so even further this past August.

In May, the basement was leaking and we noticed that the foundation was cracked in several places. This was repaired but, in checking it recently, we noticed that the crack has expanded. At this point, there are no cracks on the basement floor itself.

Can you give us some idea as to what the problem could be, whom we should get in touch with and tell us if this could end up being costly?

A. It sounds as if the southeast corner of your house was built on unstable ground and the weight of the house is causing the ground to pack. Masonry not being flexible, the part of the house affected is sinking slowly. The fact that the crack is continuing to expand is a bad sign.

You should contact a structural engineer or a contractor specializing in unstable foundations to come up with a repair plan. Do it soon, as this is not going to get better and you could end up with far greater problems. It is likely to be very costly.

An example of spalling bricks. These bricks have absorbed moisture, then frozen, popping pieces of brick out of the chimney. You can see the chunks on the roof in this photo. Used bricks are very prone to this problem, as they are "soft" brick.

Chunks of brick flaking off

Q. My semi-detached house is approximately 20 years old and has an outer shell of bricks. Chunks of the bricks are flaking off the front of the house that is facing north. This is primarily happening on a wall that separates my balcony from my neighbor's and underneath the concrete front porch slab.

I believe it's probably caused by water seepage. Is there a product to patch these areas and, if so, can it be color-matched to the bricks that have a yellow tinge? Obviously I do not want to replace the wall or the porch.

A. Your diagnosis is correct. Moisture has gotten in the bricks and has not evaporated before freezing temperatures cause it to pop the face of the affected bricks. I do not know of any satisfactory way of repairing the spalled bricks except to replace them. If there aren't too many affected, and if that type of brick is still available, a skilled mason should be able to replace them in a short time.

But, to prevent continuation or recurrence, the source of the moisture should be found and corrected. The same skilled mason should be able to find it and take care of it.

Securing shutters to brick

Q. What's the best way to secure exterior vinyl shutters to a brick wall? The wind keeps blowing them off. Molly bolts between the bricks haven't held up.

A. Plastic anchors should be inserted in a hole of the proper size drilled in the mortar joints with a carbide-tipped masonry bit. Choose the right size anchor for the size screw provided with the shutters and implant it a little deeper than its length.

Bricks stained by white aluminum siding

Q. Our home has white aluminum siding on the top and brick below. The white of the aluminum has run down onto the bricks. What can we use to clean the white residue off the bricks without damaging our shrubs below?

A. The finish on white aluminum siding is formulated to chalk off in order to make the siding look clean. The chalking is what is staining your bricks. Use Savogran Strypeeze and follow directions on the container. It should work fine for removing chalked aluminum siding paint.

If Savogran's products are not available in your area, you can usually get them by special order through Sherwin-Williams stores.

Or, mix 2 pounds of TSP-PF in a gallon of water and scrub the stained bricks with it. Leave it on for a short while to soften the paint pigment that is causing the staining. Then hose it off. Be sure to wet the ground and vegetation around the walls to be treated first and cover everything with plastic. Wear old clothes and eye and skin protection. Rinse profusely afterwards. When repainting the house, have it pressure washed and use 100% acrylic latex paint; it does not chalk.

Wet your shrubs and cover them with plastic. Rinse thoroughly when done.

Green stains may be vanadium salts

Q. Some sections of my brick walls have developed a green mold. What can I do to remove it?

A. If the stains are indeed caused by mold, you can probably remove them with a solution of equal parts water and fresh Clorox bleach.

However, if the stains do not disappear with the above treatment, they may be caused by vanadium salts. These salts are dissolved by water and acid and form a greenish stain on the surface of bricks. To remove them, wash or spray the affected sections with a solution of ½-pound sodium hydroxide to 1 quart water.

A readily available form of sodium hydroxide is the popular drain-cleaner, Drano. If you use this, mix a 12-oz can with a quart of water. This will leave a whitish salt residue on the bricks; after a few days, wash it off with your garden hose.

Do protect eyes and skin and wear old clothing; all acids are dangerous and require care in handling. Follow the directions on the container.

Removing ivy tentacles from brick

Q. We removed ivy that had crept up our brick walls for years but we can't seem to get rid of the little feet that stuck to the bricks. How can this be done as easily as possible?

A. Burn them off with a butane torch. Be careful of adjacent woodwork. This system is very effective but can only be used on masonry. With wood buildings, the tentacles have to be scraped off—a tedious job.

Removing old caulking from textured bricks

Q. Is there a product or technique that can safely remove old caulking from textured bricks?

A. Remove as much as you can with a knife blade, digging it out of the brick's crevices. Further removal depends on the type of caulking used. If oil-based, try soaking it for a long time with cleaning fluid, paint thinner or turpentine. The trick is to hold several layers of cloth saturated with the chemical and covered by a piece of plastic (to reduce evaporation) onto a vertical surface. These chemicals may also work on latex caulks. For silicones, the only way I know is to dig out the stuff. If the products mentioned don't work, try using MEX or Xylol. Buy in building supply stores, large paint stores, or janitorial supply stores. Wear heavy rubber gloves.

Removing specks and drips of paint

Q. How can I remove paint stains that have leached down onto the bricks under our shutters? Sandblasting?

A. Since the stains are caused by the leaching paint pigment, you should be able to remove them with a strong solution of TSP-PF at the rate of a ½ pound of crystals to 1 quart of hot water. Use a stiff bristle scrub brush and work on it for a while. Then rinse with clear water. If that doesn't do it, try a gel paint remover but test it on a small, inconspicuous area first.

Cleaning soil stains from brick

Q. Our ranch-style house is 23 years old and constructed of a creamy white brick known around here as Cream City brick. In the last three to four years we have noticed a gradual brownish yellow discoloration occurring on the lowest five to six courses of bricks where flower beds are located. We believe it's from the heavy clay soil.

We have experimented cleaning the brick with bleach and Lime-A-Way without much success. Can you suggest a remedy that will not affect the cleaned bricks to the extent that all of the bricks will have to be cleaned to match?

A. Since the staining occurs only at the flower beds, I must presume, as you do, it's caused by soil splashing up during rains. Dirt stains are difficult to remove, especially from textured bricks.

Try scrubbing with a stiff fiber brush and scouring powder. If that doesn't work, scrub with a strong solution of 1 pound oxalic acid crystals per gallon of warm water mixed in a glass or plastic container (do not use metal). Wear eye and skin protection and old clothes as this is a potent acid solution. Buy oxalic acid in this quantity from a chemical or janitorial supplier.

You may also try pressure-washing.

However, the most effective method is to have the bricks steam cleaned, particularly if they are heavily textured. Find a firm doing steam cleaning in your Yellow Pages under "Steam Cleaning Industrial" or, if you wish to rent the equipment and do it yourself, under "Steam Cleaning Equipment."

Old and new bricks don't match

Q. I had an addition put on my home this year. My original bricks are orange but the bricks on the addition are yellow. The house looks awful!

Is there a stain or paint to rectify this mistake?

A. Have you talked to the builder about it? What was his or her answer? How old are your original bricks? Could the builder have matched them or are they no longer available? You may not get a straight answer anyway if the builder wants to cover his or her tracks.

There are three ways to remedy the problem. The builder could have both the new and old bricks painted if you agree to it; he or she could replace the yellow bricks with the right ones if this is a brick veneer or, if there are so many bricks on the addition that it would make it too onerous, he or she can contact a representative of the Nawkaw Corporation. Nawkaw has a 25-year-guaranteed system of staining bricks to match any existing bricks. It's all done in a day or two depending on the size of the area to be treated. It may be a lot less expensive and disruptive for the builder to go this route than to have to replace the bricks. And it is the builder's responsibility to get the job done right.

Nawkaw is a North American company with a main office in Bartlett, Illinois and Mississauga, Ontario. Its Web site is www.nawkaw.com.

Old and new mortar don't match

Q. I own an old brick house. The mortar is very dark gray and appears to be quite dirty. I had a mason point up a number of cracks, which I was told are due to some settlement.

Unfortunately, he used a bright white mortar that sticks out like a sore thumb. Is there anything I can do to make this white mortar blend in with the old one?

A. Try mixing boiled linseed oil and lamp black until you get the right shade. Apply some to a joint with a small brush and let it dry to see if it is still the right shade after it has cured. If not, adjust by either adding more oil to lighten it or lamp black to darken it. When you are satisfied with the mix, finish the job.

Bricks near the ground are deteriorating

Q. The bricks from my 40-year-old two-story house are deteriorating from the ground to about 3 feet above grade, and there is an accumulation of white deposits in some places. What's the cause of the problem and the recommended remedy? Could it be attributable to the escape of air moisture from the basement which, in turn, is condensing out onto the exterior brick surfaces?

A. There could be several reasons, including the one you advance. If the basement is very damp, moisture can be absorbed by the foundation bricks and freeze before it has a chance to evaporate. This would cause spalling—the breaking off of the bricks' faces.

Other possible causes are rising damp—the absorption of ground moisture by capillary attraction or splashing from water falling off the roof, if the house has no gutters or downspouts.

The white deposits are efflorescence—salts leached out of the bricks by evaporating moisture; this is not serious and can be removed with a stiff brush, either used dry or with clean water. The remedy depends on the cause of the ailment.

If interior moisture transport is responsible (the least likely cause), try to reduce the amount of moisture in the basement by doing the necessary repairs or changes to keep it dry. If the inside wall surfaces are sound, an epoxy paint can be applied to provide a vapor retarder.

If rising damp is the culprit, you'll have to excavate down a foot or two, apply 6-mil black plastic against the brick walls, and backfill. The plastic should prevent capillary attraction. Slope the grade away from the house for good drainage. But, if roof water is the root of the problem, install gutters and downspouts.

Repointing bricks prior to painting

Q. We live in a 180-year-old brick house. Because of repairs in the past, there are several different types of brick used in the veneer walls. We would like to paint the house, but wondered if we would need to repoint the bricks first.

A. Absolutely. All joints should be tuck-pointed to prevent water from getting into them, freezing, and causing spalling (crumbling of the faces) of the bricks, as well as peeling paint. Then the surfaces to be painted must be thoroughly power-washed to remove all pollutants that have accumulated over the decades. When the bricks have completely dried, apply a masonry conditioner (all paint companies have their own brand) and paint them with a top-quality acrylic finish coat.

Replacing clapboard siding with bricks

Q. My house is currently sided with spruce clapboards. I am interested in re-siding it with brick, which would be beautiful and would not need regular maintenance. I have recently learned that a building in my area was sided with authentic brick panels. Can you advise me where these panels can be purchased, how they are installed and what is their durability? What would it cost and who would install such a system, a mason or a carpenter?

In the alternative, is it possible to retrofit a house currently sided with clapboards with traditional bricks? How would this be done?

A. There are several manufacturers of thin bricks. These are about ½" thick and made of real clay, as are regular full-size bricks. The installation is quite easy on a flat and clean substrate. They do not require a foundation.

Regular full-size bricks would require some kind of foundation although they can be installed on a steel lintel lag-bolted to the house if the height of the installation is not too great. A competent mason should be able to tell you which method is safest and direct you to a masonry supply store that can show you samples.

Paint peels from damp bricks

Q. We first painted the outside bricks of our basement with a concrete oil paint; it did not hold up too well. We then scraped most of it off and tried an outside latex paint. This is holding up better, but we have to touch up or repaint yearly. Can you recommend something else?

A. Although, exterior latex house paint performs well under low moisture conditions, there may be too much moisture in this case.

The peeling you are experiencing may be due to soil dampness working its way up the bricks by capillary attraction, known as rising damp, if soil is in contact with bare bricks without the protection of cement parging (a thin coating to protect it from moisture) or asphalt foundation coating.

If this is the case, raise the parging to above soil level, or remove all paint and use a cement-based coating.

Stone Houses

Replacing washed-out mortar

Q. The mortar appears to have washed out between the Lannon stones of my house. I believe these spaces should be filled. What is this process called and what type of firm should I contact to do it?

A. It's called tuck-pointing and a mason does it.

Removing vine remnants

Q. The home we are interested in purchasing is covered with a vine. How do we remove the vine from the Lannon stone, the metal gutters and the wood trim?

A. I assume you are referring to the tentacles that are stuck to all those surfaces after pulling the bulk of the vine off the house.

Try to use a propane torch on an inconspicuous part of the stone to make sure it does not get stained or discolored. If it works, it's the easiest way to remove them. Using the torch on the gutters may damage them; try scraping the tentacles off—you may need to repaint the gutter.

Obviously, don't do that on the wood trim. There, you'll have to use a scraper or sharp putty knife. Have fun!

Removing paint drippings from stone

Q. How can I remove old paint drippings from the stone of my house? These drippings were caused by the repeated painting of the gables.

A. They should come off with a gel paint remover. Apply it with a small paint brush on the drippings themselves, avoiding adjacent areas as much as possible.

You may find that the stones are of a different color where treated. Washing the stones with as strong a detergent as you can, TSP-PF is best, and rinsing, may even things out.

Log Houses

Pitch oozes from logs

Q. I have owned an 11-year-old pine log home for four years. The outside is coated with Cuprenol Semi-Transparent Nutmeg Brown Stain. However, pitch is oozing out of the wood discoloring the house on the sunny sides. The Cuprenol people gave me a formula for cleaning the pitch but it came back within two weeks.

Is there a cure for this condition other than covering with new siding?

A. Heavy pitch bleeding is impossible to stop as far as I know. Minor pitch discoloration, not oozing, can be hidden with a stain killer but that's not your problem, and anyway your log home is stained, not painted. Afraid you'll have to live with it.

Stain has worn off in places

Q. I recently purchased a log home that is about 12 years old. It looks as though it was coated with a stain that is worn off in some places. I also notice that the tops of the logs stay wet quite a while when it rains or snows. What can I do to protect the logs from future damage?

A. You did not say whether the stain is solid color or semi-transparent; that's quite important to know. If most of the old stain is still on and you don't want to change the color, you should use an exterior stain that has water repellent, wood preservative properties that matches it. But, it is very likely that the worn off areas are on the tops of the logs as they get the most wear. In that case, and if the present stain is solid color, you should first apply a wood preservative on the bare areas as a primer.

You may want to rent a power-washer to clean the logs and remove any surface pollutants before applying the new coating. This may also remove more of the original stain that may not be too well bonded to the wood.

Restoring logs to original light color

Q. I would like to restore the exterior of my log home to its original light color and apply a preservative to retain it.

Is sand blasting an alternative, and what should I use for a preservative?

A. Power-washing with a solution also containing bleach is a much better way to restore the logs. The best preservative will repel water at the same time it protects against the elements and decay, while it also resists UV degradation.

Amteco TWP is one product with such properties; re-apply every three to five years.

Varnish peels from logs

Q. The varnish on the log home I have recently bought is peeling badly and is completely gone in many areas. It has obviously been neglected for a long time and there are many logs that have turned black.

What's the best way to remove the remaining varnish and clean the logs, and how should I protect them and give them a better appearance?

A. It is best not to use varnish on log homes. You should use a penetrating, wood-preservative, water-repellent semi-transparent stain. Repeat every two to four years.

The easiest and most effective way to clean the logs and to remove all loose varnish is to have them power-washed. Any remaining sound varnish can be removed with a heavy-bodied paint and varnish remover. Savogran's Strypeeze Original or Strypeeze Biodegradable are particularly suitable, as they are water rinsable with a garden hose.

Stucco

Removing stains from stucco

Q. Our clapboard house was covered with stucco molded into brick shapes. Over the years, the gray stucco has become stained and minor cracks have developed.

Is there a method of patching and cleaning the stucco that we can do ourselves or are there paints which would allow the stucco to breathe?

A. Clean the surface by scrubbing it with a strong detergent solution or have it power-washed. You can rent the equipment or hire a power-washing contractor.

Then, coat the stucco with Thoroseal. It will seal the minor cracks and protect the underlying stucco. It comes in a variety of colors.

Trellis protects stucco

Q. Why do you need a trellis for vines to climb? Why is it bad to let them climb up the side of a house? My outside walls are stucco. Will the vines (in my case ivy) damage or cause cracks in the stucco? The stucco covers cement blocks.

A. Climbing vines hold onto surfaces with tentacles, which are often erroneously called tendrils. These tentacles adhere so tightly to whatever they grasp that they are impossible to remove without leaving permanent pieces behind or causing damage to the surfaces to which they were attached. They can also find any small cracks in the stucco and conduct water into them, which, when it freezes, may cause the stucco to break off in sections.

Water enters through porous stucco

Q. I live in a newly-constructed adult community consisting of 14 three-story buildings of concrete and metal frame construction with artificial stone and stucco exterior. My building was occupied two years ago. During a driving rain, con-

This mason is tuck pointing brick, but the same method is also used between stones.

siderable amounts of water still enter a sizeable number of the units, mostly those facing east.

We have been informed that four experts have tried to solve the problem, but no one can pinpoint where the water enters. The latest effort was made in July, when the entire building was caulked and the surfaces were sprayed with a sealant, which supposedly lasts for 20 years. One of our condo neighbors recently read or heard that this type of construction is becoming more prevalent. However, because of the porosity of this type of finish, water from rain seeping into the walls of the building is becoming a more widespread problem. I would appreciate any suggestions to solve this puzzle.

A. Do you know what the sealant applied is? It may be too late to apply a product that has had a long history of success if the sealant already applied would prevent a solid bond. The product I am referring to is Thorolastic by Thoro, a BASF Building Systems Company. Thorolastic is an elastomeric acrylic polymer coating for all types of masonry surfaces such as the ones you describe. A limited bond test would be advisable to make sure there is no problem with adhesion.

Miscellaneous Types of Siding

Vinyl-covered steel siding shows rust stains

Q. Our vinyl-covered steel siding is stained with rust from watering shrubs along the house. Is there any way to remove this?

A. Try one of the following three methods recommended by the industry:
 • Mix 1 tablespoon of oxalic acid in 1 cup of water in a glass or plastic container (do not use metal), apply it to the rust stains with a soft bristle brush, wipe with a damp cloth and, finally, flush with clean water. Wear eye and skin protection.
 • Wipe rust stains off with an auto radiator cleaner, using a clean cloth, rinse with clean water. Protect eyes and skin.

- Wipe rust stains with a strong solution of muriatic acid (mix half and half with water) and rinse with clean water. The acid changes iron oxide to iron chloride which is soluble in water. Wear eye and skin protection.

You should rinse with rust-free water, but this may not be possible for you since your water is what caused the rust stains in the first place.

Painting a mobile home

Q. I would like to re-paint the crinkle finish of my 22-year-old mobile home in a flat brown color. The present two-tone light green and light brown finish has faded. What type of paint should I use and how should I apply it?

A. Wash the existing siding with a solution made of 1 cup strong detergent per gallon of water. If mildew is present, substitute 1 quart of fresh Clorox bleach for 1 quart of water. Rinse thoroughly.

Paint the siding with a top-quality 100% acrylic latex house paint.

Painting cinder blocks

Q. I would like to paint the cinder blocks in the front of my home. They are currently unpainted and I wish to paint them to blend with the brick on my house. What is the proper way of preparing the blocks before painting, and is acrylic paint the best to use for this project?

A. The best coating to use on cinder blocks is a cementitious one. Thoro Products makes a very good coating for masonry called Thoroseal. You should be able to get it in well-stocked building and masonry supply stores and some box stores. It is applied by brush and comes in 13 colors. Mix it with Acryl 60 for greater bonding. There are other similar products.

Preparation is always of foremost importance in any coating job. For blocks, use a strong jet on your garden hose to remove all loose stuff and follow the instructions on the bag of the chosen product.

Miscellaneous Issues

Painting shutters

Q. The existing shutters on our century-old farm house are made of plastic, perhaps vinyl as well, and are in excellent condition. But we would like to change their color and are concerned about the paint running down on our new vinyl siding. Is there a special technique or type of paint we should use and should the paint be sealed to protect the siding?

A. Whether your shutters are made of vinyl or fiberglass, they can be painted but they should first be thoroughly cleaned and dried, then primed with Zinsser's Bulls Eye 1-2-3 which you should be able to buy in some paint or hardware stores. Then paint with a 100% acrylic latex paint to ensure that there will be no chalking.

3 Windows and Doors

Windows and doors are among the most conspicuous components of any house. Their performance is essential to the comfort, energy efficiency, and aesthetics of our surroundings. They are also quite expensive, so over the years, readers have frequently asked for advice on purchase, installation, maintenance, and cleaning of their windows and doors.

New and Replacement Windows and Doors

New and replacement windows and doors are expensive, so it's tempting to look for the cheapest products. But in the long run you'll save money by choosing windows and doors that will remain sturdy and functional for many years, backed by manufacturers who have good warranties and a reputation for making good on their promises.

Choosing replacement windows

Q. I am looking to replace the windows and storms on my 40-year-old home. Some of the casings and windows are in bad shape. The top of the line wood windows I am aware of are very expensive. Do you have any suggestions for a good, durable window that isn't so expensive? Also, what should I look for when deciding on purchasing windows?

A. Don't compromise on the quality of windows; they're there for a very long time. You're better off borrowing to have the best than to settle for second-string stuff. Choose windows that are custom made so there will be as little disturbance of the existing openings as possible. They should have soft coat low-E glass, and argon gas between the panes. In your cold climate, you should seriously consider triple glazing—storm windows that are independent of the primary windows to insure a thermal break between the two.

Replacement of storm windows

Q. I am thinking of replacing my 15-year-old wood storm windows. I have been told that wood is best by one, vinyl by another and aluminum by a third. I am seriously considering aluminum but was told by a salesman that this would be a quick fix. I want the replacement to improve my home, not detract from it.

A. Whichever you choose, buy a good quality product with as low an infiltration rating as you can get. Combination windows that also include a screen are best. They should not be completely sealed at the bottom; weep holes are essential to allow escape of condensation in winter and drainage of rain water when the screen is used.

Good-quality skylights

Q. We are interested in having skylights installed. How can we insure quality in the product and installation?

A. Buy an established name product. Decide whether you want skylights that are fixed or open to allow ventilation. Good names in ventilating skylights are Velux, Wasco, and Ventarama.

Choose a reputable, established general remodeling contractor. Call the local chapter of the National Association of Home Builders' Remodelors Council or ask your friends for names of contractors they have used with success.

Replacing a storm window insert

Q. I'm missing a vinyl storm window insert and would like to replace it. There is no manufacturer's name anywhere on the frame or inserts. Dealers have told me they need to know to be able to provide a replacement and, even then, the cost of replacement would be about the same as getting a new window. Is there an easy way to find a replacement insert?

A. Why don't you just get a new window, since the cost will be the same? You've exhausted other possibilities.

Plexiglas storm windows

Q. The old schoolhouse windows in my log cabin do not have storm windows and are framed so that storms cannot go on the outside. I have received information on Plexiglas interior storms that are held on by magnetic gaskets to a steel strip on a molding. Do you think a screen system could be combined with these Plexiglas storms? The windows are quite drafty. The cabin is in northwestern Arkansas.

Finally, quite some time ago you mentioned replacement windows that were put into the existing window frames. Will you please send me the sources on that?

Thank you very much. I always find value in reading your column but often don't know I need to keep the information until long after I have thrown the paper away.

A. Magnetic storm windows are very effective, but they will need to be removed and stored for the summer—an inconvenience. They must be handled carefully, as Plexiglas scratches easily. Screens may have to be custom-built to fit in the old windows.

As for replacement windows, several major manufacturers make windows to fit in existing openings. Ask your local building supply house.

Adding storms to sliding glass doors

Q. We get a lot of condensation on cold days on the glass and metal frame of the sliding door to our deck from our dining room. Sometimes, this condensation freezes and we can't open the door to add seeds to our bird feeders. Do you have any solution to offer?

A. There was a time when you could get sliding door storm doors in building supply houses, but they are no longer made. But you can have one made to order by Mon-Ray in Minneapolis. Their toll-free number is 800-544-3646. Their Web site is www.monray.com They come single-glazed and would provide you with triple glazing while isolating the metal frame of your primary door. This should stop condensation from forming.

They are very easy to install but may require some beefing up of the sill. This can be done by adding a piece of pressure-treated wood on top of the decking if the deck is flush with the house floor. If it isn't, you may be able to fasten a pressure-treated piece to the existing sill under the sliding door, using lag screws for strength.

Steel entry doors

Q. We are thinking of installing new entry doors in our home and were considering steel doors, but have been hearing such negative reports on them that we are hesitating. Some time ago, I remember reading in your column about a wooden door with a core in it; you also gave the name of the manufacturer.

A. The only problems I know of with steel-clad doors are caused by their installation by inexperienced people or the installation of storm doors over them on a side of the house on which the sun shines.

They cannot be trimmed, as wood doors can, so they must be installed correctly the first time and in construction so planned and executed as to minimize the risk of settlement. Storm doors will cause them to overheat, buckle and even cause the seal on any glass insert to break, allowing condensation to form between the panes; this happens because their insulated core is so efficient. Only screen doors should be used, if desired.

The refrigerator-like or compression weatherstripping on steel-clad doors is very effective in controlling infiltration—a large component of energy waste—and they do not warp as wood doors are prone to do with changes in the weather.

I do not recall mentioning wooden doors with insulated cores because I was not convinced of their value; they are no longer available, I am told, as they were not satisfactory. Fiberglass-clad doors do seem to be performing well, and look quite a lot like wood.

Warranties

Comparisons of service from window manufacturers

Regular readers of this column may recall some long discussions of window warranties. New windows are expensive, and things can go wrong, so it is important to look at the warranty—not only the number of years, but what is covered, under what circumstances.

Beyond that, it is important to consider the reputation of the manufacturer for taking action and doing the right thing when problems occur. There are two brands—Andersen and Marvin—that I generally recommend because of their long record of outstanding customer service, often going beyond what is definitely covered in their warranties.

There are other brands whose records in this regard are not so good. However, because a book has a much longer shelf-life than a newspaper column, I'll refrain from making negative mention of a brand name here. If a company does improve the quality of its customer service, it shouldn't be saddled with criticism that might be read ten years after I write it!

That said, before investing hundreds or thousands of dollars in replacement windows, it is well worth asking for references from customers who can testify to the service received, particularly when problems have arisen, and then checking the references.

Finding date for a window warranty

Q. A haze has formed on the inside of double-pane large picture windows facing northeast. The haze formed gradually and is not affected by temperature changes. It is there all the time and is getting worse.

Eventually, it will be difficult to see out the windows. We believe it is on the pane of glass closest to the inside of the house. There is no identifying trademark on the windows. Is there anything we can do to correct the problem?

A. Unfortunately, the only solution is new glass. The seal between the two panes has failed, as it often does in time. There is no way to get rid of the haze and to reseal the dividers between the glass panes.

Look at the dividers between the panes, if you haven't already done so. Often, there is a date of manufacture and some identifying mark stamped on these even though there is no identifying marking on the glass itself. If you do find a date and code, ask a local glass company if it means anything to them. They may be able to tell who the manufacturer is and whether or not the glass is still under warranty. The length of the warranty depends on the manufacturer. In some cases, it may be as long as ten years and even more.

Insist that glass warranty be honored

Q. Both sets of atrium doors in our four-year-old house have insulated glass. There is moisture between the panes in both stationary panels but there's no such problem in the panels that open. The local dealer said he'd talk to the representative of the company but we were told that the damage must have been caused in shipping or installation. How can we resolve this situation?

A. All insulated glass is guaranteed for between five and ten years, depending on the manufacturer. Complain forcefully in writing and keep up the pressure until you get satisfaction.

Product warranties may be longer than contractors'

Q. Ten years ago we had an addition built that included a sliding glass door in the dining room. A few weeks ago I noticed that moisture had appeared between the double glass on one pane of this door. It looks as though the rubber gasket at the corner of the glass has shrunk and left a gap. Is there anything that can be done to seal the glass if the gasket is the problem?

We had a home improvement company do the remodeling and therefore have no guarantees on specific materials used.

Also, the replacement windows put in the old part of the house are Andersen, double-hung, vinyl-covered wood windows. The plastic covering has peeled on several of these leaving patches of raw wood exposed to the elements. Can you offer any advice? In hindsight, I realize we should have been more knowledgeable about the materials used. As seniors on a fixed income, we can't afford to have the windows replaced again.

A. Don't blame yourselves for not being more knowledgeable about the quality of materials used. Andersen windows rate at the top of the stack with three or four other brands. To investigate the reason for the peeling of the PermaShield vinyl covering, call or go to the nearest building supply house handling Andersen products (many do) and ask to have the roving Andersen representative for your area come take a look. He or she may suggest and implement repairs or tell you if you are entitled to new windows, as ten years is a short life span for such windows.

As to the sliding glass door, the separation of the gasket has nothing to do with the moisture between the two panes; it's there only as a shock absorber, water and wind sealant.

The problem is due to a break, however tiny, in the metal divider that separates the two panes and the glass. It cannot be fixed. Although not aesthetically pleasing, it doesn't materially affect the insulation value of the glass.

You may also be entitled to a replacement at no cost except for the installation; look on the divider strip and read the initials and year stamped on it. Call a large glass company and ask them who the manufacturer is and how long it warranties the glass. Although most insulated glass is warranted for five or ten years, some carry a 20-year warranty. Certainly worth a try.

The fact that most contractors don't warranty their work for more than a year doesn't affect the warranties of the products used. Go for it.

Comfort and Energy Efficiency

Insulation needed around window frames

Q. My 15-year-old Andersen windows feel very drafty around the frames. To find out why, I removed the molding from one window and found a space between the 2×4-inch studs surrounding the window and the window frame itself. Should this space be insulated and, if so, how?

A. Yes, these spaces should have been insulated. Low expansion spray-foam insulation is great for the job, but you must use caution in applying it because it expands.

First, wedge tightly, without distorting the window frame, two sticks of wood horizontally and two vertically, spaced evenly, to hold the window jambs and the head and sill in place. This will protect the frame from bowing in as the foam cures. Next, foam according to the directions on the can.

The next day, use a sharp knife to cut off any insulation that is protruding past the edges of the frame, and remove the sticks. You do not need to fill the entire cavities with the foam for it to be effective; irregularities are okay.

Stopping night heat loss

Q. I have very large insulated windows looking into my back yard from both my dining room and living room. The problem is the heat loss through them during the nights. I have thought of storm windows but they are so large—I am not sure I can get storm windows that big.

A. Glass companies can make storm panels in very large sizes. The problem may be the installation. You would have to get one of their people to come and tell you whether or not they can accommodate your window sizes. The only drawback is that dirt will eventually get between the main window and the storm and you will have a difficult time removing the storm to clean the glass.

Foam insulation has been squirted into the space between the new window frame and the house framing. Excess foam has been trimmed away.

There is another solution, if you are mostly concerned about night heat loss. You can install insulated shades over the windows inside. They come in a variety of shapes. One very attractive type can be ordered from Gordon Window Decor in Colchester, Vermont, www.cellularwindowshades.com.

Cold air can shrink cheap vinyl windows

Q. Last fall, I built a 16×20-foot sunroom on the south end of my old house. I wanted to cover 80% of the three exposed sides of the addition with windows to absorb lots of sunshine whenever nature provides it. I chose double-hung vinyl windows to minimize maintenance.

I live in an open area with no shelter from the wind. On cold, windy days, these windows let cold air in through the side channels of the bottom sashes. When the temperature is below freezing and the wind is blowing hard, there is moisture on the glass. In severe cases, ice builds up on the lower part of the upper sashes.

I am very disappointed and called Home Depot, where I purchased the units. They referred me to some place in New Jersey and a representative came to inspect the windows on a cold, blustery day this past March. He said the windows were properly installed but had no answer as to why cold air was coming in. Have you got an answer to this problem?

A. A number of makes of vinyl windows in the lower price range have this problem because the vinyl shrinks in cold weather. You can go into a showroom and be shown that the windows are so tight that a piece of paper inserted around the frames cannot be pulled out without tearing it. But when the frosty temperatures of winter come along, you would have no trouble pulling several thicknesses of the same paper out. The solution that comes to mind is to install storm windows.

Overheating and UV Damage

Controlling heat from windows

Q. How can I control the heat generated by the sun coming in through my west-facing windows? It makes the house intolerably hot in the afternoon.

A. There are several strategies. You could install vinyl or bamboo roll-down shades outside, and lower them as the sun reaches the windows. This is the most effective solution, but you'll have to restrain them with nylon cord fastened at the top through the shades' hardware, and at the bottom through eye screws fastened to the window sills or other parts of the building. Otherwise, the wind will blow them all over the place and damage them.

Or you could purchase roll-down sun-reflecting shades or solarized sheer pleated shades and install them inside. Look in the Yellow Pages under Window Shades. With these, it is best to have the windows open to allow the heat that builds up between the window and the shade to escape to the outside.

Or you could have reflective film applied on the interior of the glass itself. It will slightly darken what you see outdoors but this should not be a significant problem.

Bamboo roll-up shades along a deck. Notice the lines used to raise, lower and protect the shades from blowing in the wind.

UV protection

Q. Our main living area gets quite a bit of afternoon sun and I hate closing the draperies to protect my new navy upholstered chairs. Is there anything I can apply to the French doors and adjacent patio windows to provide UV protection?

The only product I can find is a vinyl film available by mail order that is installed on the exterior of thermal windows. I am not sure this would be the best solution and I am afraid it would be difficult to keep clean. Any suggestion would be greatly appreciated.

A. You can have a window covering specialist install a 3M Scotchtint or equivalent film on the inside of the windows. These films work year around, a desirable feature as UV rays are just as damaging in winter, when there is snow on the ground bouncing the rays inside, as they are in summer. These films come in different tints, help reduce heat in summer, and retain winter heat as well. They are quite scratch-resistant. If you prefer to be able to remove them, they also come as roller shades.

Shading odd-shaped windows

Q. Is there a way to shade odd-shaped south- and west-facing windows to keep the house cooler in the summer? These windows take in so much heat, the house gets very uncomfortable.

A. Shade shops can install a permanent film that will reduce solar gain on the odd windows. There are also roll-down shades made of the same film material if you want to remove it at various times. Other types of shades can be used for odd-shaped windows as well. For example, a Wisconsin reader sent me a postcard depicting an arched window with a fan-shaped shade, available from JCPenney.

Bamboo roll-up shades rolled up when not needed. Note the soffit vents.

Storm door causes damage to insulated main door

Q. We had a "best quality" metal storm door with a foam core installed over our main door. When the glass on the storm door is in, the inside door gets very hot if the sun beats on it and last spring the plastic molding on the inside main door melted. And, in winter the storm door's inside glass panel is always wet. Is there a remedy to these problems other than removing this expensive storm door?

A. Afraid not. Foam-core metal doors are so energy efficient that storm doors are not needed with them. If you install one and the sun hits it, the plastic molding will get deformed and even melt, as yours did, and the metal skin on the door will also get deformed. Dark colors will make matters even worse. We've seen an entire condominium project with this problem. All the primary doors had to be replaced and all storm doors removed.

The condensation problem is probably caused by the tightness of the storm door. Upon opening the primary door, a rush of warm moist air hits the cold storm door panel and condenses. Removal of the storm door will fix both problems.

Cleaning and Polishing Window Components

Best window cleaner

Q. Now that spring is here, do you have a suggestion on the best window cleaner? Commercial products I have used have not been too successful.

A. *Consumer Reports* tested a number of formulae several years ago and found the most effective one to be made of one teaspoon of liquid dishwashing detergent, half a cup of sudsy ammonia, one pint of rubbing alcohol, and enough water to make a quart.

Removal of residue from glass

Q. I have a problem that appears to have no solution. Our window panes seem to be etched by oxidation from our aluminum storm window screens. This has taken place over 20 years and the windows always appear dirty. We have consulted with a number of people, we have tried muriatic acid, nail polish remover, household glass cleaners, etc. but this has not solved the problem.

If we use a razor blade, some residue comes off but not enough to make the windows clean. If you can solve this problem, you will be helping a lot of people.

A. Try white vinegar straight out of the bottle. It does wonders for removing residue from glass.

Water causes film on windows

Q. My large windows have developed a white film caused by a sprinkler system installed above them, which sprays them intermittently throughout the day. What can I use to remove this film?

A. Now you've got our curiosity up! You didn't say why you spray water on your windows. Not fair! Try to remove the chemical deposits with Lime-A-Way. Use the pour bottle and apply the product with clean white clothes. *Do not* let it contact metal. Wear eye and skin protection, and old clothes. You can also try white vinegar.

Cleaning varnish from windows

Q. Some of the stain and varnish I used on my new windows got on the glass. The manufacturer insists that razor blades not be used, but that is the recommendation I get from everyone else. Mineral spirits or other paint thinners have been suggested but if I get some on the wood, I ruin my finish job. Besides, mineral spirits leave an oily film on the glass. Any recommendations?

A. Used with care, a razor blade should do just fine; that's what most painters use to remove paint from glass.

As an alternative, you could apply masking tape to the wood sash members and carefully put paint thinner, mineral spirits, or paint remover on the splatters with a small paint brush and wipe it off as soon as it has softened them. Remove the masking tape and wash the wood adjacent to the treatment with a damp sponge to make sure the thinner or remover has not crept behind the tape and is not affecting the finish. Any oily residue can easily be removed from the glass with water and a little ammonia.

Plastic storm panel is cloudy

Q. We have a clear plastic panel in our storm door. Despite trying several methods to clean it, it is still dull and cloudy. Is there anything that will make it bright and clear again?

A. Have any abrasive cleaners been used on it in the past? This will ruin the finish. I know of no way to rejuvenate it, but why not simply have it replaced with a new hard acrylic panel such as Lexan? It would resist scratches and remain clear.

Removing scratches from Plexiglas windows

Q. My ten-year-old Plexiglas interior storm windows have become hazy and scratched. They are installed with Velcro in the fall and removed in the spring. I am looking for a polish or method to restore them to their original clarity.

A. Plexiglas is quite fragile and requires very gentle handling. Minor surface scratches can be removed by sanding them out with 400–600 grit "wet or dry" sandpaper and buffing with muslin and a fine grit buffing compound. Polish it with an antistatic cleaner-polish such as Brillianize, www.brillianize.com; 800-445-9344.

Dingy film builds on skylights

Q. My skylights have developed a rough, greyish film that looks awfully dingy. I tried to clean them with glass cleaner, using paper towels, but it did no good. I assume this film is caused by pollution. Is there a safe way to remove it?

A. I assume that your skylights are made of plastic material; if they were glass, the cleaning you did should have worked. If this is a correct assumption, using glass cleaner was a mistake. It may have irreparably damaged the plastic.

But you may want to try the industry's recommendations for cleaning acrylic material. Wash with plenty of mild detergent or soap and lukewarm water. Use your bare hands to feel and dislodge any foreign material. To perform the final cleaning, you can use a soft cloth or chamois but make sure it is very wet. Rinse thoroughly. Dry only by blotting with a clean damp cloth or chamois. (Never use anything dry as it may scratch the surface; it will also build an electrostatic charge that attracts particles in the air).

If that does not work and you suspect pollution to be the culprit (the deterioration may be simply age-related), you may try cleaning the skylights with either kerosene or a good grade of VM&P naphtha. Do not use both substances at the same time.

If your skylights have minor scratches, try polishing them with a good grade of polish, using a small pad of soft cotton flannel dampened with water. Rub with a circular motion. After the application of the polish, wipe the surfaces with a damp cloth to remove the static charges.

Do not use spray waxes as they may contain harmful agents that would damage the acrylic material. If you follow these instructions from the industry, you might recondition your skylights to the extent you would like, but they may never look like they did when new. If pollution has actually eaten into the plastic, there really is nothing you can do to make then look good again.

Mortar stains on window sills

Q. The contractor who installed two glass-block windows left a mess of white mortar on my outside red brick window sills. I don't believe he will be any help in resolving this matter. What's worse, he complimented me on these decorative bricks, noting how attractive they are. Is there a product to clean the mess up?

A. The contractor should have cleaned his work up with a solution of muriatic acid, as any competent mason knows.

You should get him to come back to do it, as this is a nasty job that involves handling a very potent acid. If not, then call another mason, making sure he or she is experienced in cleaning masonry with acid.

Water stains on window sills

Q. What can I use to remove or lighten water stains on the top surface of the wooden window sills of my 30-year-old house? The stains appear to have been caused by condensation. Very little of the original varnish is remaining.

A. Remove all the remaining finish. Mix oxalic acid crystals in water until you obtain a saturated solution. Use a plastic or glass container to mix, do not use metal. Apply with a paint brush and give it time to bleach the wood. When satisfied with the results, wipe the residue with a sponge or clean cloth dampened with white vinegar and let dry.

Then, apply a clear wood preservative on the bare wood of the entire sill tops; let dry and apply two to three coats of polyurethane varnish, sanding lightly between coats.

Removing paint from window trim

Q. What is an easier way than sanding to remove paint from window trim?

A. Use a non-flammable, semi-paste paint remover and ventilate thoroughly. If an inside trim, that's a job for warm weather. Follow directions carefully. Wear rubber gloves.

Removing dried putty and reglazing

Q. How can I remove old dried up putty from my windows? Should the frames be primed before applying the new putty?

A. The most widely accepted method of removing old putty is to soften it up with a soldering iron. If you plan on using an oil-based putty, you should prime the sash where the putty will be put to prevent the bare wood from absorbing the putty's oil and causing it to dry prematurely.

Removing tape from painted window frames

Q. How can I get 3M two-sided tape off of painted aluminum windows?

A. Pull as much of the tape off as you can and remove the rest with Avon Skin-So-Soft, hair spray, or laundry spray left on for a few minutes. Other substances worth trying include Clear Guard, Armor-All, Turtle Wax Bug & Tar Remover,

Goo Gone, regular cooking oil, and—hold onto your hat—peanut butter. Whichever you use, leave it on for a few minutes and wash off with detergent and water.

Removing old caulk

Q. What is the best and easiest way to remove old caulking around my windows and doors? The caulking is very old, cracked and moldy and I would like to redo it before painting my house. I've heard that the best way is to use a soldering iron to soften it and a putty knife to remove it. This sounds pretty labor-intensive to me.

A. The method you describe is an old stand-by for removing putty on windows. You may want to try 3M Caulk Remover—a cream that the manufacturer claims will loosen all old caulks, regardless of the type, in several hours.

It comes in an 8-ounce bottle and is available in hardware and home centers. Painted caulk may need two applications and it must not be used near plastic tiles or refinished bathtubs.

Removing mildew and fungus from window frame

Q. We recently bought a house in which the garage had been converted into a room with carpet on the floor and a huge tinted window where the garage door was. The wooden frame of this window and the area around it are covered with mildew and a fungus.

How should we remove these black stains? The room has no ventilation or heat. Should we put a fan and a heater there? My husband is not handy at all, so we need you to be very specific.

A. Remove the mildew with a solution of equal parts of water and fresh Clorox Bleach. If any stains remain, try a household cleanser such as Comet or Bon Ami,

Mildew has grown in a corner and stained this window. Too much condensation and not enough air flow caused this problem.

using a soft scrub brush. Wear eye and skin protection and cover the carpeting with plastic; have old towels handy.

If, by absence of ventilation, you mean the big window does not open, that was a mistake and you may want to have some changes made to it or a new window put elsewhere in the room. Having heat would also help, and certainly make the room more comfortable in winter. Best wishes.

Mold on vinyl seals around window

Q. Our Andersen windows are approximately 15 years old. Black stuff has developed on the vinyl that seals around the window. We don't know what it is or how to clean it. Can you help?

A. The black stuff is probably a mold that developed because there was repeated condensation on the vinyl seals. Use TSP-PF following the directions on the container carefully. It is available at paint or hardware stores.

Rust stains on vinyl molding

Q. The white vinyl molding at the top of my window frames has rust stains from the awning hooks. I have replaced the hooks with non-rusting types. How can these stains be removed?

A. Use auto radiator cleaner or a saturated solution of oxalic acid in hot water. You'll need very little oxalic acid and you can buy a small bottle in a drug store. Apply either of these products with a soft bristle brush. When the rust stains have disappeared, wipe the area with a damp cloth and rinse with plenty of water, using your garden hose. Mix oxalic acid in a glass or plastic container, never metal.

When dealing with strong chemicals, always wear eye and skin protection and dispose of the leftovers with care, following the directives of your sanitation department.

Cleaning aluminum storm doors

Q. Our aluminum storm doors are 50 years old and in need of a good cleaning. What do you suggest?

A. You should use a mild soap or detergent solution. Recommended cleaners are Lux Liquid, Swan Liquid, Dishwasher All, Spray Nine, Cascade, Ivory Liquid, Ivory Snow and Joy, among others.

Removing white corrosion from screens

Q. How can I remove white corrosion from my aluminum screens? I have used Clorox bleach and water with no results.

A. White vinegar should do it. Use it full-strength with a soft brush. Treat both sides. It would be best to remove the screens and put them on a flat surface such as a piece of plywood covered with an old sheet, so as to put as little pressure on the screens as possible. When you are satisfied with the results, rinse them with your garden hose and let them dry before putting them back.

Repairing Damaged Windows and Doors

Minor repairs are often needed, to keep windows and doors operating as intended, and to eliminate squeaks.

Replacing various window parts

I often receive letters asking how to obtain replacement parts for older windows and doors—cranks, latches, clips, control mechanisms, balances, and the like. If the manufacturer is unknown or out of business, or no longer supplies the parts, the best source I have found is Blaine Window Hardware, Inc., 1919 Blaine Drive, Hagerstown, MD 21740, tel. 1-800-678-1919. Their Web site is www.blainewindow. com. If possible, you should send a sample of the part in question to get the exact replacement.

Replacement locks for Andersen windows

Q. Where can I find replacement locks for our 35-year-old Andersen casement windows that are otherwise in good condition?

A. Andersen is one company that can provide spare parts for almost all their products, depending on age; that is becoming rarer and rarer. Call their customer service toll-free number: 888-888-7020, or go to their Web site at www.andersen-windows.com to find their on-line parts catalog.

Window seal is broken

Q. Four years ago, we purchased a small cape that sat vacant for the first two winters. As a result, one of our insulated glass kitchen windows became quite milky looking between the two pieces of glass. Is there anything that can be done to rectify this condition short of replacing the entire window?

A. The seal between the two panes of glass broke allowing moisture to penetrate. There is nothing that can be done to repair the existing glass. But you only need to replace the affected sash, which is cheaper and easier to do, usually, than to replace the glass in the same frame.

What to do with a rotted sill

Q. My living room window has dropped down over an inch because the sill has rotted away beneath it. The sill was covered vinyl, but evidently water seeped behind it causing the wood to rot all the way to the brick foundation below.

Would you suggest removing the window and all the rotten wood and replacing it with new wood, or just scraping out the rotten wood and patching it with cement or wood putty, sanding it down and painting it? I am a 74-year-old widow and would like to find a carpenter to make the repairs before leaving for the winter.

Not only the sill has rotted from rain damage, but you can see the damage on the window as well.

A. If the entire window has dropped as you mention, it's time to remove it and start all over, using pressure-treated wood as a base covered with pine trim primed on all sides before installation. To find a capable carpenter, ask your neighbors or a local building supply store for names of reliable people.

Windows stuck shut by paint

Q. I forgot to open my windows after painting them. Now they are stuck. How can I free them?

A. Buy a tool made for the purpose in a hardware or paint store. It is pear-shaped and has teeth all around. You insert it between the sash and the frame and wiggle it back and forth to cut the paint film.

Repairing window pulley ropes

Q. The ropes holding the pulleys that keep my old windows open are broken. None of the young contractors around here know how to repair these. How can I repair them?

A. On the sides of the window jambs, there is a molding called a window stop. It hides a pocket in which are located the weights. Remove this stop, then unscrew the pocket's closing panel to gain access to the weights. Buy sash cord in a hardware store. There must be old-time carpenters in your area, even retired ones, who are familiar with this type of window; so ask around.

Replacing window balances

Q. The springs on several of our windows have sprung and disappeared into the frames. We can't get them down. Nor can we find any shop that will help us and we don't want to replace the windows. Your suggestions?

A. Find an experienced carpenter or handyman familiar with window balances. He should be able to fix the existing balances or get replacement parts from Blaine Window Hardware (see above).

Lubricating combination windows

Q. Our public library has aluminum combination storm windows. They don't work! Many are stuck and can't be closed, which leaves us with no insulation during the winter. Is there a safe and relatively easy way to get the windows to slide freely up and down? If so, how do we prevent this from happening again?

A. Spray WD-40 between the stuck sashes and the edges of their tracks both inside and outside, and give the spray a few minutes to penetrate between them. They should move freely after this.

If the sashes are not tight to the top of the frames, liberally spray down into the tracks as well. While you are at it, lightly spray WD-40 on the lower tracks also. Work the sashes up and down a number of times to spread the lubricant, and add to it if needed.

Making windows easier to open and close

Q. I enjoy your column and always look to see if something will help me. I am an 81-year-old widow living in a home we bought 47 years ago, and I am happy to say it is in pretty good shape. My problem is that most of the windows are hard to open and close. Is there someone I can hire to make them easier to operate?

A. It's great to hear that you are doing what needs to be done to keep your home in good shape. A skilled handyperson or carpenter should be able to make the windows work more easily. It may be that all they need is lubrication of the tracks. If the working parts are wood on wood, this can be done with beeswax; if they are metal, WD-40 should work well. Good luck.

Windows lubricated too well

Q. Several years ago, I used a silicone spray to lubricate the vinyl tracks of our wooden double hung windows which were difficult to open and close.

It has worked too well. The windows have gotten to the point where they will no longer stay in place when raised. How can I remove the silicone?

A. After several years, the problem is more likely due to weakening or loosening of the spring balances of the window sashes, the silicone having more than likely worn off by now. Find out from the dealer who furnished the windows, or the manufacturer, if you know who they are, how to tighten the springs. Or have an experienced carpenter do it for you.

Repairing aluminum storm windows

Q. My aluminum storm windows are quite old. The molding that holds the glass pane to the frame has severely deteriorated. I cannot locate what I need to replace it in any hardware stores. Can you help me?

A. You should be able to get replacement vinyl glazing stripping from a glass shop.

Stopping hinges from squeaking

Q. Last year, after painting the inside of the house, we replaced all the hinges and doorknobs, as they looked dingy in comparison to the newly painted walls.

Unfortunately, all the doors now squeak very loudly. We used brass hinges. Is there anything I can apply to the hinges to stop the squeaking?

A. Push the hinge pins up about one inch by inserting a heavy nail or nail punch to them from the bottom and tapping gently with a hammer. Cover the adjacent surfaces to protect them. Spray the hinge pins with WD-40. Tap them back in place with a wood block and a hammer so as not to damage the finish. Swing the doors back and forth to work the WD-40 down the pins.

Repairing or replacing roll screens

Q. Our house is over 60 years old. Among the nicest features are copper screens in the windows in the front of the house. They are Chamberlin Roll Screens. They roll up when not needed but are ready anytime. Due to age, some of them are beginning to rip across the bottom.

We tried to take them apart, figuring we could take the end of the screens off, cut the bad parts, and put them back together, but we could not find a way to remove the end of the screens. We have no idea how to even begin to find out if this company is still in business. If they no longer exist, do you have any idea how we can repair these screens or whom we should contact.

A. You haven't said so but I believe you may have Pella windows. Their casement windows have roll screens similar to those you describe. If this is correct, you may be able to get your screens repaired by a local glass company. Unfortunately, Chamberlin is no longer around and Pella cannot repair screens that old. They do not even have replacement screens.

For those of you who have more recent problems with Pella windows, you can call their national service number 800-547-3552 to be directed to the service center closest to you.

Rattling doors

Q. I just bought a house built in the '60s. All the doors rattle. Is there a way to eliminate this problem?

A. You can move the strike plates back until the doors are tight against the door stops. This will require puttying the present screw holes and drilling new holes. Or you can purchase Door-Tite strike plates.

Door-Tite strike plates are used extensively by weatherization contractors and utility companies to make exterior doors seal tighter against the weather. They are also useful to stop interior doors from rattling. These ingenious devices have a stepped feature that allows the door bolt to engage any of its positions.

Doors swing shut

Q. Our interior doors squeaked so we oiled the hinges and now the doors swing shut all the time. How can we make them stay open?

A. You'll have to adjust the hinges in the door jamb. The problem is due to the bottom hinge being farther out than the top one or the door jamb not being plumb in either direction.

If an accurate level shows the jamb to be plumb, move the bottom hinge in or the top hinge out. If the jamb is not plumb from front to back, moving the hinges as indicated should also solve the problem. If the hinge side jamb is tilted either toward the other jamb or away from it, add a piece of cardboard shim under the top hinge or the bottom hinge respectively until the doors stay put in any position.

Repairing interlocking weatherstripping

Q. The weatherstripping on our front door is made of interlocking metal strips that no longer work and make it difficult to open and close the door. Can you suggest a better system to replace what we have now?

A. Have you tried to repair the system you have with pliers? If it is not badly damaged or chewed up, it's worth it as this is a very effective system. An alternative is removal and replacement with one of the many weatherstripping systems available in hardware and building supply stores. You could also hire an experienced carpenter, preferably an older one who has had experience with this weatherstripping system, to repair it for you.

Installing curtains on a steel door

Q. How can I put up curtains and a pull-down shade on a new steel door without drilling holes?

A. You may want to try fastening the hardware with epoxy glue, but it's really no big deal to drill a hole in the skin of the door and install the hardware with short sheet-metal screws.

Patio door no longer slides

Q. My 23-year-old patio sliding door no longer slides. Application of a lubricant helps for just a few pushes. The manufacturer is out of business. How can I restore it to its original ease of sliding?

A. The wheels have probably developed flat spots from skidding on a track with grit on it or maybe just from old age.

Lift the sliding panel out (or have a competent carpenter do it) and check this out. New hardware can probably be obtained from Blaine Window Hardware, Inc., 1919 Blaine Dr., Hagerstown, Md. 21740 (301) 797-6500. You'll have to send them a sample unless you know exactly what part to order.

Patio door slides too easily

Q. I have an unusual problem with the sliding glass door I installed six years ago and wonder what I did wrong—it slides too easily.

Visitors are constantly slamming the door closed, causing the house to rattle and the door panel to bounce back several inches. Other than packing dirt in the track, do you have any idea how to solve this problem? My current "Thank you for not slamming" sign doesn't work.

A. Should you be so lucky as to have such a sliding door! Most people complain of the opposite. Putting dirt in the tracks? You're a funny guy! Here is a suggestion for a sign that gets a lot more attention than your polite urging: DON'T EVEN THINK OF SLAMMING THIS DOOR!

Wooden sliding door warps

Q. We replaced an aluminum sliding patio door with a wooden one with low-E glass. The new door is aluminum clad on the outside but unfinished on the inside. We haven't stained or painted it yet. Recently the middle interlocking strips have not met and the sliding section must be pushed in for them to interlock. Is there a simple remedy for this condition?

A. Probably not at this point. The wood stiles have warped because the unfinished inside faces have absorbed moisture and swollen. You should wait 'til the heating season has been in full swing for a while and try to keep your house as dry as possible. The stiles may straighten out and allow the weather stripping to interlock. If so, paint or stain them quickly.

Pocket-door roller came off track

Q. The closet in the entryway of our home has a pocket door that rolls into the wall. The roller on top of the door came completely off the track and fell to the floor. How does one go about taking the door out to put the roller back up?

A. Check to see if your door unit is of the type that has an opening slightly wider than the door width and retains the door with one little nylon guide on each side at the bottom of the jamb. If it is, all you have to do is to remove one of the guides to be able to swing the door out and remove it. But if it is not, in most cases, the casing—*i.e.* trim—and one side of the split jamb will have to be taken off one side of the doorway.

But if the carpenter who installed it was really sharp, what he or she may have done is to put a full height strip on the leading edge of the door with screws to be used as a door pull, by carving recesses for fingers at the proper height. If that is the case, all you'll need to do is to unscrew the strip to pull the door out.

Repairing hollow-core doors

Q. Several of the hollow-core doors in my house have holes punched through the thin veneer. Is there a way to repair them or must they be replaced?

A. You can apply new plywood sheets over the existing with panel adhesive. If the holes are on the closing side, you'll have to move the hinges and latches to accommodate the extra thickness. Weigh the cost and labor involved against the cost of replacing the doors, as new hollow-core doors are relatively inexpensive.

Wet spot in middle of older glass panel

Q. We moved into a '70s house this past summer and, now that cold weather is with us, we have noticed a strange thing: One of the insulated glass panels in our living room has developed a sizeable wet spot right in the middle of the glass. That spot is about a foot high and 6 to 8 inches wide, and there are beads of condensation on it that begin to drip down as it gets colder outside. What is going on, and what can I do about it?

A. Insulated glass in the '70s and earlier had a divider only ¼-inch wide between the two pieces of glass. Glass is not perfectly flat, and your problem is caused by the two sheets coming in contact with each other in the middle of the field. This is not uncommon on large fixed-glass windows. After the energy crisis of the early and mid '70s, the dividers were made thicker to increase the efficiency of the air space between the panes which is ⅝ to ¾ of an inch. There are two things you can do about it. One is to replace the glass panel with a thicker divider, and the other is to install another pane, either inside or outside, to obtain quadruple glazing.

Paint, Varnish, and Other Finish Work

Painting aluminum storm windows

Q. What is the best way to paint my unpainted combination aluminum storm windows? The frames are pitted and oxidized from 35 years in the weather. I have almost a gallon of latex house paint left that I would like to use if possible.

A. Remove the oxidation by cleaning the aluminum with a moderate abrasive cleaner such as Scotch-Brite brand, made by 3M. Then prime it with zinc chromate or a primer such as Zinsser's Bulls Eye 1-2-3 and, when dry, apply your left-over latex paint.

Refinishing varnished window trim

Q. The finish on the Philippine mahogany woodwork around our windows is beginning to flake and peel off where the sun hits it. I can't tell if it was stained prior to varnishing. I want to refinish it with polyurethane. Any suggestion on where to start? Should I stain it and, if so, how do I get the right color stain?

A. First, you have to remove the damaged varnish, and possibly all the varnish if you want to apply a stain. Use a non-flammable paint and varnish remover, and provide plenty of ventilation. Follow the directions on the container and protect skin and eyes. Dispose of the residue responsibly.

The bare wood is now ready to be stained, and the right color is the one you choose; you'll have to stain all of the woodwork, as it will be nigh impossible to match an old stain that has been exposed to light and sun. Now you're ready to apply the polyurethane varnish; choose one that will withstand the sun so you won't have to do it again so soon.

If you choose not to stain, just sand off the loose varnish, feather the edges between sound varnish and bare wood, lightly sand the sound varnish, and apply new varnish.

Orange juice dulls marble sill

Q. We live in a retirement home. I put a cup of orange drink on the marble sill of the window but a gust of wind knocked it over and I didn't notice it right away. When I cleaned it up, it left a dull spot. How can I restore the shine?

A. The acid of the drink etched the marble's polish. The dull spot is the real marble under the polish. One product that can be used to repolish it is a Goddard Marble Care Kit, available in hardware stores.

Stripping and refinishing a fiberglass door

Q. I have a fiberglass front door that is an absolute mess. I've polyurethaned it about seven times in the last seven years. Much of the original stain has come off from sanding before putting on the polyurethane. I would like to strip the door down to the bare fiberglass and start over with stain and polyurethane. Is this possible? How do I strip it, and what type of stain and polyurethane do you recommend?

A. Strip the remaining coats of polyurethane on the fiberglass door with a gel-type polyurethane remover until you are down to the fiberglass itself. Stain the door with a gel stain and apply a UV-filter polyurethane. Minwax and Zar are two manufacturers of gel stain and UV-filter polyurethane. You should find all you need for this job in paint and hardware stores.

Don't use stain or dark paint on vinyl windows

Q. Please recommend what to use to stain Andersen exterior white vinyl windows and a sliding door to match a musket-brown soffit and fascia. I don't want to use paint.

A. Andersen does not recommend staining their Permashield (vinyl-encased) windows and doors. To change the color, you are limited to paint, and then only with very light colors. And even then, Andersen does not warrant that the paint will adhere or last for any length of time.

The intensity of a color is measured by its Hunter L value. White vinyl units can be painted any color that has a Hunter L value greater than 60. For comparison, White has an L value of 85, sandstone has an L value of 69, and Andersen's dark brown Terratone has an L value of 35.

As you can see from these recommendations, you should not paint your white vinyl windows or door musket brown, as it is too dark; doing so could deform the vinyl, which I have seen happen when people have not followed Andersen's advice. The darkest color you can use would be slightly darker than sandstone.

If you decide to paint, rub the surfaces to be painted with a 3M scouring pad and soapy water, then wipe them with acetone (you can buy these supplies in hardware stores). Then apply an approved paint color.

Refinishing older unpainted window sills

Q. The windows in my home have fairly wide, unpainted oak windowsills. Over the years, they have become damaged because of rain coming in open windows. Since I am not handy, I need someone who can refinish them. I contacted one local wood flooring refinisher who said they didn't do this type of work. Do you have any suggestions on how I can get my windowsills refinished?

A. First, you may want to try several other floor finishers in the hope that you will find one flexible (or hungry) enough in the dead of winter to tackle your small job. But if this does not work, any skilled handyperson or carpenter should have no problem sanding the affected areas and refinishing them.

If the sills are water-stained, brushing them with a bleach solution made up of equal parts water and fresh Clorox bleach may remove the stains. The entire sills will have to be treated in order to avoid having different shades of wood. If the Clorox solution does not do the job, try Oxalic acid (see previous Q&As for drections on how to mix and use). Once they're ready, it's best to use three coats of polyurethane varnish.

Painting vinyl shutters

Q. Is it possible to successfully paint faded vinyl shutters? Mine get the full sun during the day and look pretty grubby. If it is possible, what kind of paint should I use?

A. Yes, you can paint vinyl or fiberglass shutters successfully. Make sure they are absolutely clean and dry. You can clean them with any household detergent but rinse thoroughly. Prime with Zinsser's Bulls Eye 1-2-3 and paint with 100% acrylic latex paint.

Sealing knots on pine door

Q. The pine door jambs in our house have knots that are bleeding through the white paint. We had a similar problem in our last house even though we used shellac on the knots before priming and top-coating with a latex gloss paint.

In our new house, we used UH Stain Stopper to prime the pine with, but this has not worked, and having these brown spots on all our white jambs looks terrible. Can you recommend something that will work?

A. The best product to seal knots is 4-lb orange shellac, but it's hard to find so you may have to settle for 3-lb orange shellac. After it has dried, coat it with Zinsser's Bulls Eye 1-2-3 so the top coat will adhere to it.

Smoothing ripples on plywood door

Q. The front door of our home faces south and the sun shines on it a good part of the day. This has caused the outer layer of plywood to develop raised ripples in the middle of the door.

Should I buy a new door or should I sand the ripples with a power sander, prime and repaint? My concern with the latter is that I might cut through the layer of plywood and ruin the door. Should I sand the ripples and apply an overlay sheet of ¼-inch exterior plywood, then prime and paint it? I'd like to save this door which is, otherwise, in excellent interior condition.

A. The best solution depends on how bad the ripples are. Plywood veneer is very thin. The ripples may be caused by the entire top layer absorbing water through small cracks, expanding, and becoming separated from the underlying layer.

If that is the case, you face a delicate job of repairing it. You would have to cut small slivers of the rippled layer, but only enough so that the opposite sides of the cut-out areas join when reglued and weighted down. To do all of this, you would have to take the door down for quite a while.

However, if the ripples are only the raised grain of a sound plywood sheet, light sanding should be enough. Either do this by hand or use a vibrating sander with medium sandpaper.

Applying a ¼-inch overlay is an option but you will either have to make it smaller than the door itself to clear the frame, or else rehang the door, which will make it stick out inside by the thickness of the overlay. Wouldn't it be simpler, when all is said and done, to replace the door?

Stripping layers of paint from doors

Q. There are 25 doors in our very old farmhouse; they all need repairs and are covered with many layers of paint and other finishes. I can handle the repair part but how should I get the old finishes off so they can be refinished? I have tried a variety of strippers with little success; some finish comes off but it takes a lot of hard work and it's a very slow process.

I recently saw someone on TV use a product that came in a large pail similar to drywall joint compound and looked like it when applied. It was troweled on, then covered with a sheet of paper-like material. When this sheet turned brown, the job was done and the paint was removed in one step. Are you aware of this product?

A. You may be referring to Peel Away, manufactured by Dumond Chemicals in New York City. It has been used commercially for some time, and is now available to do-it-yourselfers. It is available in many paint stores, but if you have difficulty finding it locally check the company's Web site, www.dumondchemicals.com.

An alternative you may wish to try is Savogran's SuperStrip, a non-flammable, heavy-bodied remover made for specially difficult cases, such as multi-layered paint and varnish coats, or else take the doors to a commercial paint and varnish stripper. You can probably get a good recommendation for a local company doing this through a paint store in your area.

Garage door panels have checked

Q. My two garage doors, facing west, have painted plywood panels. The plywood faces have checked and cracked. What can I do to prevent this?

A. Plywood is a tough wood to control and checking is fairly common. Sand the rough surfaces, fill large cracks with an exterior wood filler, prime bare areas with an oil-based primer and paint the doors with a quality exterior latex. Prime and paint the back of the doors to prevent moisture absorption from behind.

Sunlight damages varnished door sills

Q. The oak sills of our atrium door had weathered to the extent that there was no finish left on them—they had turned grey and there were some cracks in them but no rot. This spring, I sanded them and applied three coats of spar varnish but I can already see signs of deterioration of the varnish. Can you recommend a technique for protecting these sills that will last a reasonable period of time?

A. The sills must be exposed to a lot of sun. Ultra-violet rays of the sun will destroy varnish in short order. Varnish, under such conditions, needs to be reapplied every year. You might want to see if a marine store has a boat varnish that has some UV protection.

Painting dark window frames a lighter color

Q. All the window frames of the house I have just bought are stained in a dark color. I want to paint them white. Should anything be done to them first?

A. If no varnish was applied over the stain, simply sand the surfaces lightly and prime with an oil-base primer, followed by the finish coat of your choice. If the woodwork is varnished, you'll have to remove it with a gel chemical paint remover. Use plenty of ventilation and follow instructions, then prime and paint.

Moisture Problems

Many of the questions we've received about windows involve water, which can damage all components of a house. Sometimes leaks are the problem, but more often the condensation and ice on the windows originated elsewhere in the house.

Why storm windows sweat in winter

Q. In my previous house, the insides on my regular windows sweated in winter, but in this house, it's the insides of the storm windows that sweat. Can you explain to me why, and what can I do to prevent it?

A. In your previous house, the storm windows, if you had any, were probably quite loose and allowed a considerable amount of air circulation between the regular windows and the storms thereby cooling the glass of the primary windows. In your new house, the storm windows are tighter than the main windows. Warm, moist air exfiltrates around the primary windows and condensation occurs on the inside of the storms.

Possible solutions are as follows:
- Tighten the window latch that's in the middle of the window.
- Press rope caulking such as Mortite around the perimeter for the winter.
- Install interior plastic storm windows.
- Crack open the storm windows (but that's an energy waster).

Window condensation caused by high humidity

Q. The previous owners of my house had new triple-glazed windows put in. During the winter months, I get condensation and fogging on the sliding windows. What can I do to stop this?

A. With triple-glazed windows, there isn't much more that you can do except reduce humidity in the house and ventilate frequently. Excessive moisture can come from a wet basement or crawl space, bare soil in a crawl space (it should be covered with plastic), firewood stored in the cellar, a dryer vented in the house instead of to the outside, a large amount of water-loving plants, clothes being dried indoors, etc. Correct these and you should see some improvements.

New windows sweating and puddling

Q. Our one-story home was built in 1952 and had good-quality wood windows. Last year we replaced them with vinyl double-glazed windows and, over the winter, had a terrible sweating problem. The bow window in the living room was especially bad, with water puddling on the sills.

The furnace is two years old. The insulation was increased ten years ago. We're now told the house is too well insulated.

A. Your house, with insulation blown into regular stud walls, is nowhere near "too well insulated," but it's obviously tighter that it was. The old wood windows apparently allowed enough infiltration to prevent the condensation problem. Keep in mind that a well-insulated and tight house, coupled with what may be a new efficient furnace with make-up air from the outside, no longer has as many air changes per hour as before the new furnace was installed.

Have you done anything that increases your production of moisture? Added new plants, hung wet clothes indoors to dry, etc? If so, consider changes.

If you have no other practical way to reduce indoor humidity, you may need to find ways to increase ventilation. You could ventilate the house frequently on mild days, or for short periods every day. It will help to use bath and kitchen fans, if you have them, or to install an air-to-air heat exchanger.

Moisture from skylights

Q. My four skylights still have a moisture problem in spite of the fact that I did what the manufacturer suggested to correct this problem—insulate the tunnel leading to them. Could we seal off the area by making a frame around the openings at the bottom and put Plexiglas in to keep warm air from the skylights?

A. Your idea is a good one but, in order to work, the seals around the Plexiglas frame must be tight. Otherwise, you may end up with a worse problem, as moisture will find its way into the confined spaces, which will now be much cooler, so there will be more condensation. You can avoid that to a great extent by using Magnetite storm window panels. They are hermetically sealed to the adjacent surfaces by means of magnetic strips—much like a refrigerator door.

You may also be able to reduce or solve the problem by reducing the relative humidity in the house. To do that effectively, you have to identify the sources of moisture that can be curtailed or eliminated and do something about it.

Bay window leaks

Q. Can you help me correct a very frustrating situation? Last November, I had a bay window installed in the ground-level family room, which has an exterior brick wall. The window has leaked ever since, between the wall and trim on the upper left-hand side. The second story is covered with aluminum siding.

The contractor has come back four times to correct this problem; the last time, they replaced the bay window roof but it is still leaking. I have caulked the second floor window above the new bay window and the siding where it abuts the window, but this has not helped. When I do a water test on the bay window and its roof, there is no leak, but when I do it on the second floor window and the siding, it leaks. The window company rep says he may have to take the siding off and install a liner on the wall under it. I would like your opinion on this.

A. You are fortunate to be dealing with a responsible contractor who is sticking with the problem and is willing to go to great lengths to correct it. The question to ask, in light of what you have told us, is whether the leak may have been there before, but remained undetected until the bay window was installed. If this proves to be the case, you have to ask yourself whether it is pure chance that it was discovered so fortuitously, or whether there may be other areas where leaks occur still undetected. They may eventually lead to serious damage to the house.

Although caulking can be helpful in sealing joints to prevent water leakage (and air infiltration), a much surer way is proper flashing. You should have a very experienced home inspector, general contractor, or siding contractor check your house for what may prove to be an improper siding installation.

Storm windows need ventilation

Q. I just had new combination windows put on the house over the main windows that have leaded glass. All the upstairs windows have lots of moisture on the inside of the combination windows, while none of the downstairs ones have any. The contractor added putty to the new windows but it didn't help. Any ideas?

A. It didn't help because it was the wrong thing to do. The upstairs combination windows are plagued with condensation because they are tighter than the primary leaded glass windows. Warm, moisture-laden air bypasses the primary windows and hits the cold glass of the storms. What the contractor did was to make them even tighter.

The downstairs windows do not have the problem because drier outside air is drawn inside to make up for the air exfiltrating around the upstairs windows.

To eliminate the condensation, you have to provide some outside ventilation of the space between the two sets of windows. This can be done by removing any caulking the contractor put in at the bottom of the storms or by drilling a few holes in their frames just above the window sills. There should be drainage holes at the base of the bottom rail of the storms so that rain water that gets through the screens in the warmer seasons is not trapped.

Sweating of steel-framed basement windows

Q. Our house is relatively new. The basement windows are steel-framed and sweat a lot during the winter, causing water to run down the inside of the finished walls and ruining our painted drywall. Several carpenters have told us that the only solution is to replace the windows with aluminum or wood ones, but that is expensive and messy. Is there another solution?

A. Expensive, yes. Messy, not necessarily if done by skilled people. Aluminum windows should have a thermal break or you would have the same problem.

Yes, there is another solution that has worked well in a number of cases. Have a skilled carpenter build interior storm panels tightly fitted to window stops, fastened to the frames and weatherstripped. Another possibility is to install magnetic storm panels, also on the inside; Magnetite is the original panel developed by MIT in Cambridge, Massachusetts. Look for a dealer in your Yellow Pages.

Low-cost way to stop window sweating

Q. I am a tenant on the seventh floor of an apartment building that has single-glazed windows. They sweat in cold weather and the dampness on the sills is causing mildew. Can you suggest anything to lessen the problem?

A. As a tenant, you certainly don't want to invest a large sum of money in having either interior or exterior storm windows installed. But you could try to have your landlord do it for the protection of his or her investment. If that does not succeed, consider clear plastic storm windows that are heat-shrunk with a hair dryer. They are practically invisible and distortion-free, if installed properly.

Mold growing on new window frames

Q. Please help. About one year ago we replaced all the windows in our home. They are double-hung, oak-framed. We were told to seal the oak with beeswax (which we did), allowing the natural beauty to remain.

Over the course of the last year, we have noticed black mold growing on the frames, mainly on the wood of the top window where the window locks are, and on the bottom window where the handles are located to open the window. Our two bedroom windows are now polluted with this mold. We have tried cleaning with Clorox solution and leaving the bathroom window open when we shower. We also run the fan, which is vented to the outside. The mold continues to grow rapidly. What could be causing this?

A. I am not clear as to whether the mold is growing on all the window frames or only on those in the bedroom. If only on the bedroom windows, it may be that you keep the bedroom cooler than the rest of the house and that the moisture from the bathroom, if it opens into the bedroom, is creating a higher level of relative humidity (RH) in the bedroom. Both of these conditions would encourage mold.

However, if all the window frames have mold, it sounds as if the relative humidity is too high in your house and this may be due to the fact that you replaced old windows with far more efficient ones, allowing fewer air changes.

You mention that the mold has developed over the course of the last year. Did this occur only during cold weather? If not, excessive humidity may not be the only problem. The beeswax may not have been pure and may contain some sugar from the honey-making process; this can encourage the growth of some types of mold.

If it is only a winter problem, you will need to reduce the sources of the excess RH. They can be from water-loving plants, clothes being dried indoors or a dryer not properly vented outdoors, a crawl space with a bare dirt floor, firewood stored inside, the use of a humidifier, a small house with four or more people, long hot showers, etc.

The morning condensation is caused by the cold nights, especially if you lower shades at night. The interior air in contact with the glass is cooled to the dew point. The window seals are unlikely to be broken.

Remember that a house not having central air-conditioning in summer absorbs a lot of moisture during the hot weather and that its release takes time in the fall and the early part of winter. This is why I always advise ventilating houses thoroughly in the late summer and early fall when the temperatures begin to drop.

Preventing water damage under patio doors

Q. I am a carpenter contractor in Oregon who installs a number of sliding and patio doors, either new or as replacements. I have had some call-backs because of water damage under some of these doors although I caulked them as recommended, and I have encountered rot under older units. Do you know of a way to avoid this problem?

A. Yes, and it's manufactured right in your home state. It's called Jamsill Guard, it's a pan made of ABS plastic with the various parts bonded together with ABS cement. Contact Jamsill, Inc., 1-800-526-7455 or www.jamsill.com.

Seasonal reminder: Fall ventilation reduces winter moisture

During the winter months, the greatest volume of mail I receive from cold regions is about excessive moisture problems. These can be mitigated with lots of ventilation in the fall, even if you have to wear sweaters because the house is chilly. Ventilate your house during the beautiful, breezy fall days to let the summer's humidity evaporate, but remember that it takes days to get results. If you haven't done this yet, take advantage of any warm days so as to avoid or lessen condensation problems on your windows as the temperature turns colder in December and January.

Miscellaneous Issues

Coating windows for privacy

Q. I have a large window that opens onto a park but also allows my neighbors to look inside. I have looked into a variety of solutions to this privacy problem and the one that makes the most sense is to have the glass etched with acid or sand blasted on the bottom 8 inches so. I would still have the view above but the privacy below. What do you think of this solution?

A. It is a lot easier to attain the same results with a paint made for the purpose and used in bathrooms. It gives a milky white finish that is translucent. Buy it in paint or hardware stores.

Fiberglass screens may cause odor

Q. This fall, we noticed a smell in the downstairs northwest corner room of our home. At first, we thought it smelled like gas and called the gas company to have that checked. The smell persisted, so we emptied the room and cleaned it thoroughly, and couldn't find any particular source. We noticed that the smell happened during the day when the sun moved around to shine on the west side of the house. In the evening, when the sun went down, the smell dissipated—even when the heat was on. And on cloudy days it did not smell at all.

It is now late March and the smell persists on every sunny day. It has spread to include the other room on the west side of the house. It smells synthetic. It reminds us of diesel exhaust. We have spoken to the gas company, the local extension service, Orkin, our contractor, and our siding installer. None of them has any clues. The person who put the siding on said he's never experienced this before. We have contacted our carpenter, who suggested that we write to you.

So far this spring, it only smells in those two downstairs rooms. We don't know what to do next, and hope that you will have an idea of the cause of this mystery, and give us suggestions on how to proceed.

A. Have you, by any chance, replaced your windows or their screens recently? It sounds to me very much like you have fiberglass screens which, when exposed to the sun, exude the kind of smell you describe. The fact that you only have the problem when the sun hits the windows, and that the smell subsides when the windows are in the shade, is the most compelling clue.

Remove the screens and see if that stops the smell. If it does, you may want to replace the fiberglass screens with aluminum. A glass shop or hardware store should have replacements.

Security locks for open windows

Q. I have been unable to find security locks for my new vinyl double-hung windows that would permit me to leave them partially open for air while making it impossible for someone to crawl through.

A. True Value Hardware Stores' catalog carries a very effective type of window lock for double-hung windows. These are not always in stock, and your store may prefer to order them only in a full box of 20, which will take care of ten windows as it is best to install two on each upper sash. You might be able to convince the store manager that he or she should carry them as, in my opinion, they are the best I have ever seen and the most effective. They cost about one dollar apiece when I got some by special order a year ago to use in a friend's house.

These locks have a plate that is screwed onto the stiles of the upper sashes about 4 to 6 inches up from the meeting rails. They have a small arm that swings out of the way, parallel to the glass, when you want to open the window fully, but blocks the lower sash when the arm is swung at a 90-degree angle across the top rail. Their great advantage over others is that the arm is locked when in use and can be swung open only by squeezing two small pins, which requires two fingers.

Ugly storm door hides beautiful entry door

Q. I recently bought a home that has a beautiful wood door with a leaded glass window at the front entrance. Unfortunately there is also a very unattractive aluminum door covering it and hiding most of it.

I would love to remove the aluminum door to expose the wood door, but many people have advised me not to do it, saying the wood door would soon be ruined by the weather. Yet I have seen homes, churches, etc. with wood doors not protected by another door. If I kept the wood door covered with spar varnish wouldn't that provide the necessary protection?

A. You certainly could, but keep in mind that varnish does not stand up well to the sun or expansion and contraction of the wood, as temperature and humidity change. It cracks and allows water to get into the wood; this causes it to become grained. You may need to bleach the stains out and revarnish frequently.

Subjected to temperature and moisture fluctuations, the door may bind or the weatherstripping may become damaged. Moreover, there will be an increased loss of heat through the door and stresses to the leaded section.

There are storm doors with a large single glass panel in a narrow frame that may be the best compromise; such a door would protect the primary door from temperature changes and the weather and still expose its beauty.

Check stucco for hairline cracks near window

Q. We have an old stucco house. The window sills are almost a foot wide. For the last couple of years, the Sanitas [wall covering] keeps peeling off and the plaster disintegrating under the large windows in our dining room.

I had a roofer look at it. He sealed the windows outside but we still have the problem. Do you have any idea what I could do besides repeatedly patching the plaster and regluing the Sanitas?

A. The combined problem is caused by the intrusion of moisture into the wall. The windows may not be the problem unless there is condensation on them throughout most of the winter.

I suggest you call an experienced mason and have him or her check out the stucco. Over time, stucco develops hairline cracks that can admit water. If this is the case, the cracks should be fixed.

Door panels shrink in winter

Q. We have an old house with flat panel doors. The panels expand and contract relative to the rest of the doors as the seasons change. I assume this is due to changes in temperature and moisture.

I stripped and repainted one of these doors last summer, priming it with a good quality primer/sealer, expecting to eliminate the panel movement. The ends of the door were also primed to keep moisture out. But this winter the panels have shrunk about ⅛ of an inch. Is this normal or am I doing something wrong?

Are the panels in these doors supposed to float or is there any way to eliminate their movement? How can they be painted so there is no gap when they shrink or the panels don't split as a result of the paint holding them fast to the stiles?

A. Your assumption is correct. Shrinkage occurs in the panels, stiles, and rails of the door, but it is visible along the edges of panels because they are not painted.

Old houses can get very dry in winter, as most are quite leaky. You may be able to lessen the shrinkage problem by adopting a lot of water-loving plants and using a good-quality belt humidifier (not the kind that spews water drops into the air).

To retain some dimensional stability in the doors, the most effective method would be to strip them completely in winter when they have shrunk the most, coat them liberally with a wood preservative, and paint them. But that is not very practical during the heating season as you'd need ventilation, something difficult to provide. Instead, thin the finish paint slightly and coat the bare wood showing. It won't solve the problem, but will look better.

Restoring brass door knobs

Q. All the brass door knobs of my 40-year-old ranch house are badly discolored and tarnished and much of the clear lacquer has worn off from them. What can I do to refinish them or have them restored to their original condition?

A. If they are solid brass, a brass cleaner and elbow grease should recondition them. If they are not valuable, replace them.

Brass knocker difficult to polish

Q. My beautiful and ornate brass knocker has gradually turned black. I have tried cleaning it and polishing it without success. It appears that it was originally covered with some kind of clear finish.

When I scratch parts of the back, the brass shows through. Can you suggest what would remove this black tarnish? Because of the elaborate design on the front, I probably would need to soak it and clean it with a toothbrush.

A. The high copper content of brass is oxidizing and the black is copper carbonate. If off-the-shelf copper cleaner paste and it hasn't worked, here are a couple of alternative suggestions, but with no absolute guarantees that they will work.

Wear heavy rubber gloves and rub an inconspicuous area with a soft cloth soaked with white vinegar. Wait 15 to 30 minutes and see if the carbonate is dissolved. If so, dip the entire piece in a bath of white vinegar for whatever length of time worked on the test patch.

If the white vinegar treatment does not do it and you have a deeply ingrained pioneer spirit, try Sani-flush (sodium bisulfate) or Zud, which contains oxalic acid. But these two are more potent, and not as safe to use as vinegar. Again, try test patches in an inconspicuous area.

When clean, coat the piece with canned, clear methacrylate lacquer. If that is not available locally, use a clear automobile lacquer.

Protecting brass screen door from tarnishing

Q. I have a large screen door on the front of my house on the shore that tarnishes a couple of weeks after it has been cleaned, polished, and coated with a polyurethane finish. How can I keep it from turning green and black?

A. A brass screen door? How unusual! What you have done with it is right and it should not tarnish; that's the puzzler to which I have no sure answer. Instead of varnish, try lacquer next go-around.

Cleaning canvas awnings

Q. The canvas awnings on my windows remain there all year as I have no place to store them. They are sooty, dirty, and have moss on them. How can I clean them?

A. Mix a solution made of 3 quarts clean, warm water and 1 cup of TSP-PF, and add a pint of fresh household bleach. Use a scrub brush. Wear eye and skin protection, old clothes, and rinse thoroughly with your garden hose.

4 Plumbing, Electricity, HVAC

This chapter covers the electro-mechanical systems of a house. Inherently, the questions overlap with those of other chapters. Heating and air conditioning are related to insulation, plumbing is related to the material in the chapter on kitchens and baths, etc. But the concentration here is focused on the direct workings of the systems.

Plumbing

Hot Water

Situating the water heater(s)

Q. In planning our new home to be built, hopefully, next spring, we wondered what advice you could give us on where to place the water heater to be most efficient. What size should it be for two adults and two teen-age children and what fuel do you recommend?

A. Much depends on the layout of the house. For instance, if your house is to be two stories with two bathrooms upstairs as well as your laundry facilities, it is more efficient to have the main water heater upstairs close to the bathrooms. Lavatories are generally used in spurts and it is a waste of hot water to run the faucets until you get some. Tubs, showers and clothes washers are less wasteful that way because the hot water is run for longer periods. You may want to set the water heater's thermostats at 120°F. This will be plenty for bathrooms, prevent the risk of scalding, and lengthen the life of the heater.

The ideal is also to have a small water heater under or next to the kitchen sink as hot water is used in spurts there as well, and the dishwasher needs very hot water. This heater should be set at 140°F for that reason. Most modern dishwashers have heating elements built-in for washing but some do not for rinse cycles, so the hotter the water getting in, the better. You will need a check valve on the cold-water feed to the heater or you will get heated water feedback on the cold side.

The initial cost of two water heaters is greater but the economy in fuel should help amortize it over time and the convenience is great. Electric water heaters are the most flexible for both these uses. Assuming you also will have a powder room on the first floor, try to locate it close to the kitchen, and pipe hot water to it from the kitchen heater.

Be sure that you have the heaters and all pipes insulated—both hot and cold. Copper pipes take a lot of heat out of the water before it gets to the faucets. Also, if your water supply is a deep well, insulating the cold water pipes will prevent summertime condensation, but it must be done thoroughly to avoid having condensation form on the uninsulated sections of pipes.

As far as the type of fuel to choose, if your house will be heated with oil, propane, or natural gas-fired warm air, you may want to consider the same fuel for the main water heater. In this case, it may be best to install it in the basement as it will need to be vented to a chimney or directly to the outside. The smaller kitchen heater should be electric to simplify installation and avoid the venting. If your heating system will be hydronic (hot water), a side-arm water storage tank is a good solution. It may be set so hot water circulates constantly through the pipes to give you immediate hot water at all faucets.

Water heats slowly

Q. When I turn on the hot water faucets in the second-floor bathroom of our 60-year-old home, it takes two or three minutes for warm water to arrive. Since we are contemplating gutting this bathroom to remodel it, what can the do-it-yourselfer do to remedy this situation, or does it require professional help?

A. The length of time it takes for hot water to be delivered depends on the length of the pipes that run between the water heater and the fixtures and the diameter of the pipes, the latter being, perhaps, affected by corrosion in the case of galvanized pipes in an old house. You would see rusty water come out first when you turn the faucet on if this condition exists.

If possible, it would help to insulate the pipes from the water heater to the fixtures. It won't do much good just to insulate them in the second floor bath during remodeling. Another possible option, if you have room, would be to add a second water heater to the bathroom during your remodeling.

On-demand water heaters

Q. Last year, we purchased a 3,000-square-foot ranch home that is a little over 70 feet long. The water heater is in the basement on one side of the house and our master bathroom is on the other side. We waste a lot of water getting hot water to the showers and sinks. The kitchen is in the middle of the house and, again, we have to run the water a long time just to get hot water.

I keep hearing about "on-demand water heaters" and was wondering what you could tell me about them. I really would need something just to get hot water to the kitchen sink and then to supply the master bathroom, which has two sinks and a shower. For the kitchen sink we would just need something small, since we usually use a dishwasher for large loads and the sink for washing our hands and small items. The master bathroom is used every day and wastes the most water.

A. On-demand water heaters offer savings in energy, as they use only the fuel that operates them when hot water is needed; they do not store hot water for future use. You didn't mention the type of water heater you now have, so it is difficult for me to be very specific in my recommendations. However, in most cases it would be difficult for the water savings to offset the cost of an on-demand heater, which may cost $400 to $700 depending on model and size.

In your case, accomplishing what you want—instant hot water in the kitchen sink, dishwasher and master bedroom—will be a sizable investment, as you will need two heaters. As retrofits, on-demand electric water heaters require connections to the cold-water pipe under the kitchen sink and bathroom vanity, capping the hot water pipes, and heavy electric connections. One popular model (the type you would need for the master bathroom) requires 240 volts and three 40-amp breakers. The model needed for the kitchen would also require 240 volts, but with two 40-amp breakers. Gas-fired on-demand heaters are more energy-efficient, but require exterior venting through a wall or roof in addition to a gas line.

You might want to weigh other options, comparing costs and convenience. These include the following:

- Insulate the hot-water pipes in your basement if they are accessible; this will speed the arrival of hot water somewhat as it will reduce the heat loss through the copper pipes. It will also keep the water in the pipes hotter longer.
- Ask a licensed plumber if he or she can install a small circulator on your existing water heater pipes to circulate hot water constantly to all fixtures. This can be done only if there is access to the pipes and fixtures from an unfinished basement ceiling. The pipes should also be insulated.
- Install small electric water storage heaters under the kitchen and master bathroom sinks. You'll also need 240 volts for this solution.

Plastic water heaters

Q. Our water system is very hard on hot-water tanks. Somewhere we heard that there is such a thing as fiberglass hot-water tanks. If this is a reality, do you know where we could buy an oil-fired fiberglass hot-water tank?

A. Unfortunately, all oil- and gas-fired water heaters are glass lined. Apparently, the heat from oil or gas is too hot for any plastic. But, if you wish to convert to electricity, the Marathon plastic water heaters, manufactured by Rheem, are guaranteed for as long as you own your home. Ask your power company about these or check www.marathonheaters.com.

Backward plumbing

Q. Several months ago, I had a new 40-gallon gas-fired water heater installed. The temperature setting is at "normal." Immediately after it was installed, when I was showering, the temperature of the water got colder and colder, requiring me to adjust the faucet to add more hot water. By the end of the shower, the water was still cool even though the faucet was all the way to the hot side. At the suggestions of two plumbers, I had a new cartridge installed in the shower faucet; the balancing device was also checked and found to be working satisfactorily. Is this problem caused by a faulty water heater, or improper installation of the water heater?

A. It sounds to me as if the cold water line was installed on the hot-water fitting of the heater, and the hot water line on the cold-water fitting. To check this out, look for the "hot" and "cold" markings on top of your water heater and turn a hot water faucet on anywhere in the house. Then put one hand on each of the pipes at the top of the heater. If you feel cold water coming through the pipe connected to the fitting marked "hot," you have found the problem. What is happening is that cold water is fed at the top of the tank instead of to its bottom through the dip tube, also called the "cold water inlet." The solution is to reverse the connections.

Ideal hot water temperature settings

Q. Here is a question that has puzzled me for a long time. If the water temperature control of a water heater is set too low, more hot water from the tank is required to, say, take a shower or draw a bath at a comfortable temperature. Conversely, if the water temperature control is set too high, the water can scald but less hot water is needed for any given purpose. What is the proper and the most effective setting for a gas water heater? How about electric water heaters?

A. The proper setting is what suits any family the best. The most efficient setting for energy conservation is generally considered to be 120°F. This is because more energy is lost through the jacket as the differential between the heater's water temperature and the ambient temperature increases.

"Milky" hot water

Q. I had my gas water heater replaced because the water coming out of the old one was milky. Now the same is happening with the new one and the plumber who installed it doesn't know why. I can't afford another one. What is the problem?

A. Fill a glass with water and watch it for about five minutes. If the water begins to clear up from the bottom, it will tell you that the milky condition is due to gases in the water being released into the atmosphere. This happens when water is heated and cannot hold as much gas as when cooler.

In your case, it may be due to too high a temperature setting. Try lowering it to 120°F. if it is at 140°F.—a setting often used for dishwashers. It may also be caused by the free hydrogen film on the sacrificial anode in a new heater, which protects the tank against cathodic corrosion, but this will disappear within a year.

Too-high pressure from the main water pipe may also contribute to this condition, as can solder fingers that solidified during the connection of the heater, but this is far-fetched and uncommon. The fact that you had this experience with the previous heater tells you that it has nothing to do with the old or new heater, and replacing it again will not solve the existing condition.

Insulating gas water heaters

Q. I recently had a new gas water heater installed. It appears to be insulated with ordinary fiberglass. When I told the gas company serviceman I intended to put on it the insulating jacket just removed from the former electric heater, he said I should not do it because the additional insulation would cause the tank to sweat and rust through from the outside. How could this occur?

A. I have a hard time visualizing that happening, since the two insulating jackets would keep the outer metal jacket warm. What he may have meant is that an insulating jacket for an electric heater should not be installed "as is" around a gas heater. The top of gas-fired heaters should not be insulated so as not to interfere with the draft hood—and neither should the very bottom where the control and air ports are located.

Solar hot water problems

Q. The joint of the pipe feeding solar heated water to the heat exchanger that heats domestic water in my house keeps coming apart at the exit tee from the gang of solar panels. I have to re-solder it every couple of months. The temperature of the return line reaches 220°F., but is it enough to melt solder?

And what about anti-freeze? I have used propylene glycol made for solar systems at $18 per gallon; I have also used the type used in RVs which costs about $3 per gallon and have noticed no difference.

A. The solder you have used should hold; perhaps the joint was not clean enough. At this point, it seems that you should call in a professional solar installer to investigate as there are a number of possibilities such as: 220°F. is too hot (glycol degrades and becomes acidic over 180°F.); inadequate circulation; sensor location; wrong location for the feeder pipe; etc.

As for the anti-freeze, the type used in solar systems contains inhibitors and can withstand higher temperatures.

Hot water runs slowly

Q. The hot water faucets in my 33-year-old house give off about one-third of the water they should, compared to the cold. Any idea what causes this?

A. First, check to see if the cold water feed to your water heater is fully open. Another possibility: If your water is heated in a coil in your boiler, the pipes may be encrusted with calcium that restricts the flow, like arteriosclerosis does in people. If that is the case, you'll have to have a plumber run acid through the pipes to dissolve the deposits.

Shower turns too hot and cold

Q. Several months ago we had our powder room and upstairs bathroom remodeled. Ever since we have had a problem that the plumber cannot resolve.

When someone is showering and cold water is turned on elsewhere, the shower water becomes scalding and, if hot water is turned on, the shower water becomes very cold. Watering the lawn also changes the temperature of any water used in the house. The plumber told me there is nothing he can do about it.

A. Your plumber is not up to date with modern technology. First, he should have used a ¾-inch water line until he got to the point of teeing-off to each faucet with ½-inch lines.

It's too late to do that now, but you can have the shower valve changed to a balanced-flow valve. All faucet manufacturers make them; they keep the water temperature even regardless of what other fixture is turned on. It will only help at the shower, but that's where it's most crucial.

Emergency shut-off for water heater

Q. Some time ago, I recall reading about a product that will shut off the water supply to a water heater if and when it leaks. I could kick myself for not paying more attention at the time. I hope you can give me the name of the product and the address of the manufacturer so I may contact them directly.

After suffering the damages caused by a heater run amok, your help would be greatly appreciated.

A. The product is called WAGS and is manufactured by Taco. WAGS stands for Water and Gas Safety Valve. It must be installed by a certified technician and you can find the nearest one by looking Taco up on their Web site: www.wagsvalve.com. Follow the prompts to find the nearest certified installer.

WAGS can be used for electric and oil-fired water heaters as well as gas. It is totally mechanical, with no electric connection. Your heater must be set in a drip pan at least ¾-inch deep, and wide enough to allow the device to sit next to the heater. When the heater starts leaking and the water level in the pan reaches the opening on the WAGS, it causes a fibrous element to dissolve to activate a spring-loaded piston that shuts off the water supply. For gas heaters, it also shuts off the gas valve. Therefore, the leakage is restricted to the contents of the water heater.

Water Color and Quality

Hard water stains

Q. We just put in a water softener because we have very hard water. How can the mineral stains in the bathtub be cleaned?

A. Try a product like Lime-Away or Zud. You should be able to find these in hardware stores and in the cleaning-supply aisle of supermarkets. Read and follow the directions on the container, as both of these products have caustic effects on some surfaces, and care is required in handling them. Wear rubber gloves.

Calcium deposits slow refill of toilet

Q. We have lived in our 35-year-old split-level home for 10 years. Our water is very hard. We've noticed a considerable change in how long the toilets take to refill after flushing, especially in the last six months—as long as three to four minutes. I thought it might be caused by mineral build-up in the pipes. Do you concur, and what do you recommend to correct the problem?

A. Your diagnosis is correct. Calcium deposits are restricting the diameter of the pipes, similar to plaque in arteries. A water softener should correct this condition but you will probably have to replace the inner workings of the toilets; it's not worth the cost to try to clean them. As to the rest of the piping in the house, if you have no serious problem with flow restriction in them, just live with it. The only other choice would be replacement.

Milky-colored cold water

Q. I have had some minor plumbing work done in the bathroom. Now the cold-water tap emits milky-colored water for the first minute or so. If the water is left to sit in the bowl, it will clear up in a minute. The water has excessive air in it. How does it get in the water and what can be done about it?

A. Did you have a new faucet installed? If so, the aerator may be the cause. Unscrew it and see if it solves the problem. If it does, you may want to try a different aerator, available at a hardware store.

Treating rusty water

Q. Whenever we shower, our bathtub gets brown. We have the same problem with our sinks. What is the problem and what can we do to get these stains off? I have tried all kinds of cleaners without success.

A. Either you have old galvanized pipes that are mixing rust with the water passing through them, or else you have water with a high content of iron or sediment. You can have the water tested by the health department.

If the problem is caused by the pipes, the solution is to replace them before they start leaking. However, if the problem is with the water itself, you should have an iron (rust and sediment) filter installed near the entrance service or just past the pressure tank.

There are two kinds of iron in water. Most iron comes out in oxidized form and is controlled by a water softening system. But ferrous iron or iron in unoxidized form cannot be treated by a water softener. You would need to add an aeration system followed by a dedicated backwashing iron filter. If you also need a water softener, the aeration system and the backwashing filter would have to be installed before the water gets to the water softener. Have a water treatment specialist analyze your water and propose a solution.

If you haven't already, try using Lime-Away or Zud to remove the stains; one of them should work. Heed the cautionary statements on the containers; they are potent chemicals.

Blue shower floors caused by acidic water

Q. About ten years ago, I replaced the galvanized pipes in my house with copper. We are on city water, which is very soft and slightly acidic. The floors of the showers are blue from leaching copper. Is this a problem with the pipes themselves or with the water?

A. The bluish-green color you describe is generally an indication that the copper pipes are being eaten by acidic water. It can shorten the life of copper pipes considerably depending on the degree of acidity. You may want to have a water specialist test your water and make recommendations.

Sand in the water

Q. Our 20-year-old artesian well is 300 feet deep. Recently we have had sand coming out of our faucets. Someone offered to install a sand divider down the well for $500. Is it a good idea? Our pump was replaced a year ago, 10 feet from the bottom of the well. The sand is plugging our faucets and ruining our clothes.

A. Well walls do collapse at times. Perhaps the pump should have been put farther from the bottom. What the person is proposing is to install a substrainer. It's a plastic sleeve with slots that prevent sand from being sucked into the pump. Sand can ruin a pump, as well as other parts of your plumbing. The price quoted seems high as substrainers cost around $100, and the labor to pull the pump out and install it shouldn't be that much; perhaps another $100. Get another price.

You may also want to have a rust and sediment filter installed just past the pressure tank to remove any sediment that might get through the substrainer. Use heavy-duty cartridges so they last longer.

Bad Smells

Note: This section covers miscellaneous odor problems, but be sure to also check the section later in this chapter on plumbing vents, as inadequate venting is a major cause of bad smells.

Sewer smell may mean toilet needs tightening

Q. We noticed a pronounced sewer smell in our bathroom. Our landlord had changed the wax seal on the toilet about a year ago, but for the past month there has been a terrible smell, which seems to be coming from the toilet.

Also, the tile around the base of the toilet has suddenly been discolored. We also noticed that the overflow drain on the sink is clogged, but even if we block off that smell, there's still a strong smell like sewage in the bathroom. Any suggestions would be greatly appreciated.

A. The fact that the tiles around the toilet have become discolored would indicate that there is leakage at the joint between the toilet and the closet bend on which it rests. It may be that the toilet needs to be tightened to the floor.

You'll notice that there are two bolts on its base. If the china caps have been put over the bolts and nuts, remove them and hand-tighten the nuts. Do not use a wrench to force them, as it could crack the base of the toilet.

But if the bolts and nuts are tight, you may need a new wax seal.

Slow leak may cause musty smell

Q. There is a musty smell in my stall shower. I poured Clorox bleach down the drain but the smell persists. There is a shower door and I noticed that the tiled step into the shower has a crack where there is an odor. However, there is no visible evidence of any leaking in the bathroom or ceiling below. Help!

A. There could be not enough wetness to show a leak but enough to cause the wood underneath the tiled step to be wet. You should not use the shower for a few days, and let the wood forming the curb dry by providing high heat in the bathroom during that time (with the door closed), and caulk the crack.

Urine smell in bathroom

Q. There a smell of urine in the bathroom of my ranch house. I was advised to have the vent pipe above the roof snaked out but that did not help, so the wax seal of the toilet was replaced and I caulked around the base of the toilet. The smell persists. Any suggestions?

A. A smell of urine is not generally indicative of a blocked vent pipe or deteriorating wax seal; you would experience a sewer smell instead. The problem may be due to urine that splashed onto a nearby wall or other surface, or under the rim of the toilet, or even under the toilet seat itself.

Odor comes from kitchen sink drain

Q. We hope you can help us with an odor problem that seems to come from our garbage disposal or drain in our double kitchen sink. The developer of this relatively new townhouse tried three different disposal units and also replaced a piece of the drain pipe under the sink but we still have the odor. We have tried baking soda with vinegar and Disposer Care, recommended by the disposer's manufacturer. Nothing has helped.

A. It does not sound as if the disposer is the cause of the odor. You might try pouring a mixture of equal parts bleach and water in both drains. You may also want to undertake a regular cleaning schedule by pouring a solution of Super Washing Soda down both drains. You can buy it in the laundry cleaning supplies of your supermarket. The instructions for this procedure are on the side panel of the box.

Showering causes strong plastic smell

Q. Within the past two weeks, the fiberglass tub unit in our five-year-old house has been giving off a strong plastic odor when we use the shower. The odor is strongest when hot water is run. Is the plastic material decomposing so soon after its installation?

A. It sounds as though the resin did not fully cure and there must be cracks in the finish around the unit for the odor to come back into the bathroom. Blisters might develop in time if they haven't already begun. Flash a strong light on the surfaces and check them out. Call a fiberglass repair specialist for an evaluation and possible remedy. Find him or her in your Yellow Pages under Bathtubs & Sinks—Repairing & Refinishing.

Sewer odor comes from sink

Q. Help! I have never come across this problem in your column before. About three weeks ago, I noticed a foul, sewer-like odor coming from the little overflow hole in my bathroom sink. It has gotten worse and become unbearable. I tried putting baking soda down the hole and the drain, but that only helped for one day. The sink is not clogged—the water goes down smoothly. Can you tell me what is causing this odor and how to get rid of it?

A. Is the sink vitreous china, or is it made of a plastic material like cultured marble? If it is new and made of the plastic material, the odor may come from the outgassing (the release of gases or vapors by a material over time) of the plasticizer—a rare occurrence. In an older sink, the odor may be due to the accumulation of bacteria at the end of the overflow.

Try this first: Put some fresh Clorox bleach in a spray bottle and spray it copiously into the overflow hole. If that does not do the trick, remove the pop-up stopper, seal the end of the overflow by stuffing a rag tightly down the drain a few inches (be careful to have enough of the rag sticking out to be able to remove it), and pour bleach down the overflow.

If the pop-up stopper is captive (tied to the control rod that operates the stopper), you can free it by unscrewing the knurled nut that ties the control rod to the waste pipe under the sink and pulling it out enough to free the stopper. You will see that the stopper has an offset ring on the bottom. Put the control rod back and hand-tighten the knurled nut. When you are done, put the stopper back, turning it until the offset ring is clear of the control rod.

Hot water smells rotten

Q. I have an unusual problem that is causing me grief. Ever since I moved into my house, my hot water smells like rotten eggs. A friend who also has a well said that she has the same problem, and advised me to open the well and pour 10 gallons of bleach into it, run water from the hose into it and let it sit for 12 hours, then run the water for 30 to 45 minutes. I have done this and it seemed to work for a week or so. But then the smell came back. Is it coming from the water heater or the well? What can I do to get rid of the smell once and for all? Please help!

A. Your friend's suggestion is used to disinfect a water supply that has bacterial contamination. Your problem, however, is in the hot-water tank, so there are two possibilities:

- The magnesium sacrificial anode may have corroded (it is designed for the purpose of protecting any exposed metal parts inside the tank). You can replace the anode, or have a plumber do it.
- A sulfur bacterial growth may have developed in the hot-water tank. It is harmless to humans, but does cause an odor of rotten eggs. Chlorination is the solution for that, but instead of having to go through the effort of pouring chlorine in your well every week, you may want to have a water specialist test for this possibility and recommend a solution.

Dry traps

Q. I recently moved into a seven-year-old house that has a roughed-in three-piece bathroom in the basement. Quite often, when I open the bathroom door, I notice a foul sewer odor. I intend on having a plumber connect the toilet and basin and plug up the shower drain. Will this take care of the problem?

A. The odor is coming from the dry traps of any or all of the three fixtures. All you need to do to stop it is to keep water in the traps. Pour some in regularly. Having the plumber do what you suggest should take care of it, but don't plug the shower permanently; you or the next occupants may want to have it installed later. The plumber can plug it with an inflatable bulb, or with a rag and a thin concrete cap.

Noisy Plumbing

Water heater gurgles

Q. Our gas-fired water heater gurgles loudly when it is heating water. Why is this and how can we correct it?

A. Rumbling noises are usually caused by scale that has built up inside the tank or sediment that has accumulated in its bottom. Attach a garden hose to the drain spigot at the base of the tank and drain it while it is refilling, until the water runs clear. If this does not solve the problem, call a licensed plumber.

Clattering noise in exhaust outlet

Q. Our bathroom ceiling fan probably exhausts through the roof. It produces a constant clattering noise as the wind hits a metal shield that we can't locate. A roofer told us that he can't do anything about it because we have a sloping roof. I can't believe this and the clattering is driving us nuts.

A. The clattering you hear is indeed made by the wind flap that is found either at the aluminum roof or wall jack or on the outlet sleeve of the fan housing. It is caused by a combination of positive pressure exercised by the warm air inside the house and negative pressure from wind coming from certain directions.

I don't understand why you're not sure whether or not the fan exhausts through the roof; it's easy to find out. If there is a roof jack and air comes out of it when you turn the fan on, that's it. If there is an attic, it's also easy to locate the duct, if there is one. The answer to your problem may be to replace the jack with a spring-loaded one or, if that's not possible, to screw the exterior flap shut and discontinue using the fan, if your sanity is at stake.

Bathroom fan sounds like air hammer

Q. My bathroom fan sounds as if someone is working with an air hammer. I've taken it apart, cleaned it, and re-installed it with no success. The fit between the fan housing and the duct is so tight that there is no room for padding. What can I do to make it more quiet?

A. Replace it with a quiet fan; they are not that expensive. The blades on your fan may be out of balance or the axle or bearings wearing out.

Pipes make snapping sound

Q. In order to remodel my bathroom, the outside wall of the house was opened up to allow removal of the old tub and insertion of a new, all-in-one glass fiber tub/shower unit. Since then a loud snap occurs approximately ten minutes after taking a shower, then five to ten minutes later, and again twenty to thirty minutes later.

The contractor re-opened the outside wall but he and the plumber found nothing unusual. Can you suggest a cause for this bizarre noise?

A. The waste piping was probably replaced with plastic pipe, which is rubbing against framing or restrained by it. The water pipes may also have been changed to plastic and suffer from the same problems. You don't hear them snap when you use the shower because of its noise, but they probably snap as they expand. When the pipes cool off, they snap again as they contract.

If my diagnosis is correct, there really is nothing to be concerned about and you should try to learn to live with this sound, which is common to plastic pipes.

Too much pressure causes noises

Q. I recently replaced my corroded, restricted supply water line to the house. Since then, when my tenant upstairs takes her 5 A.M. shower, the initial water flow noise is very loud. Also, my downstairs faucets pound when I first open them. Is there any way to cut down on the noise?

A. It sounds as if the new water line provides much more water to the house than the old corroded one, and the added volume—along with the city pressure—is causing the noise. Try reducing the pressure or the flow of the water entering the house by turning down the entrance valve. You may also need to have a plumber install a small pressure tank to absorb the shock when first opening a faucet.

Pipes thump when taps turned off

Q. Recently, the water pipes in my house have developed a very annoying "thump" when the taps are turned off. The main water line is in the crawl space under the house. What is causing this and what can be done about it?

A. If you are on a municipal water system, your plumbing fixtures should have water-hammer arresters. These are small tanks with a bladder filled with air, which provides a cushion against the vibrations caused by the sudden shutting off of a solenoid valve or cartridge faucet. If you don't have any, they should be installed.

If you do have water-hammer arresters of the diaphragm type, they may need replacement. Or, you may have water-hammer arresters that have filled with water. If this is the case, turn the main water supply off at the entrance to the house, open all the faucets, and let the plumbing system drain out. Shut them off and turn the water back on.

If you are on a private well, the pressure switch may be set too high. Normal settings are 20/40 or 30/50 for turning the pump on and off.

Insulating plumbing sounds

Q. The plastic waste pipes in our new home, built last year, are very noisy when a toilet is flushed or someone takes a shower. This is particularly annoying in our master bedroom which is directly below our daughter's bathroom.

Is there a cure for this other than open the walls and replace the pipes? A contractor suggested blowing in foam insulation in the walls.

A. Replacing the pipes with cast iron seems pretty drastic. Blowing in foam or other insulation may be effective, but that will depend on the space available between the pipes and the wall finish. Toilet waste lines are 3 or 4 inches in diameter in walls that are either 3½ or 5½ inches thick and, if the pipes are close to the finish of the wall, it may not do a bit of good.

This may be the case in the ceiling of your master bedroom, since a closet bend drops down about 8 inches and the ceiling joists may not be very much deeper. You could try it and, if it does not work, you could add sound deadening board to the ceiling and apply new ⅝-inch drywall over it.

Banging water heater

Q. What could be causing our 10- to 12-year-old gas water heater to make banging noises when heating water? It's got progressively worse in the last six months in spite of the fact that I drain several gallons out every month or so.

A. A build-up of lime on the bottom of the tank. Lime precipitates and calcification occurs when water is heated at or above 140°F. The deposits expand and pop when the heat comes on. When you replace your tank with a new one, think of lowering the temperature to 120 or 130°F. This will reduce calcification and prolong the life of your heater (authorities have said it can double it) as well as save energy.

Too-hot water causes pipes to bang

Q. Ever since I replaced my gas-fired water heater both hot and cold pipes bang when I turn off a faucet. I've tried draining the system to force all air out of the pipes but the problem still exists. The banging even occurs when the toilet stops filling up after flushing.

A. Today's gas- and oil-fired water heaters have very fast recovery and may, in many instances, heat the water so fast and high that it causes the temperature and pressure relief valve to open up.

Your new heater may also have its thermostatic control set too high. Lower it and see if it solves the problem. Your old heater was not as efficient and was probably coated with mineral deposits that tended to insulate it to some extent and reduce its efficient recovery. If lowering the thermostat does not solve your problem, or the thermostat is set at the minimum acceptable range to you, the solution is to have a plumber install a small expansion tank.

Toilets

Learning to live with water-saving toilets

Q. We are having a problem with our Kohler water-saving toilet. It does not flush waste down completely; consequently, we have to flush several times, which ends up by wasting water. Sometimes, it helps to hold the handle down until the flushing is complete. What can we do, short of replacing the toilet?

A. The tank on this particular toilet holds 3½ gallons of water but is designed to use only 1½ gallons per flush. The other 2 are there to provide weight to push the first 1½ gallons down. Holding the handle down helps, as you have noticed, as it allows the remainder of the water to follow. You need to use this procedure only when flushing solids.

Flushing stopped

Q. One of my toilets has suddenly stopped flushing properly. The water just swirls in the bowl and often solids do not get flushed even after two or three flushes. What is causing this sudden problem, and what can I do about it short of having the toilet replaced? My other two toilets do not have this problem.

A. There could be several things going on. Is the drain plugged in any way? Kids have a way of dropping things in that don't belong in a toilet. To test the draining power, take a 5-gallon bucket and fill it ¾ of the way with water. Then see if the toilet will flush with a quick dump of water. If the water doesn't go right down, try a plumbing snake to see if there is an impediment in the toilet's "S" trap that can be dislodged. Or the toilet may have to be pulled up and the drain checked.

Improper flushing also can be caused by an obstruction in the jet hole at the bottom of the bowl that starts the flushing. Less frequently, it is caused by encrustations in the rim holes of the bowl that start the swirling of the water. Or it can be caused by too low a water level in the tank.

To clear the jet hole of any obstruction, shut off the water supply to the tank or hold up the float in the tank with a piece of wire. Flush the toilet and very gently pour about a cup of muriatic acid into the bowl. Be very careful handling muriatic acid, as it is extremely toxic; wear rubber gloves and pour from the container the acid is sold in. Never pour muriatic acid into a metal container and never use metal tools with it. You will find muriatic acid in hardware stores. Close the lid and wait a few hours; doing this overnight is best. Then, let the tank fill up again and flush the toilet after shutting off the water supply or using the wire trick again. Take a short-handled screwdriver or similar tool and ream out the jet hole.

If this does not solve the problem, pour about a quart of fresh Clorox bleach into the tank and flush the toilet. Then use an Allen wrench of the appropriate size to ream out every one of the rim holes (you'll need a mirror to find them).

If these steps do not fix the problem, raise the water level in the tank to the top of the overflow tube, even if the water is at the waterline mark inside the tank.

Leaking toilet flap

Q. The other day, we were sitting in the living room when, suddenly, we were startled by the toilet, which started filling as if it had been flushed. Later, it did the same thing, and it has ever since. This is quite disconcerting, specially in the night, and an awful waste of water. What is causing this and how can we cure it?

A. The most likely cause of these inadvertent flushes is a tank ball or flap not sealing properly on the flush valve seat. As a result, the water in the tank leaks slowly until the level reaches the point where the filling mechanism is triggered.

This may be due to a small piece of foreign material that has become lodged preventing a tight fit. Lift the tank ball or flap and run your hand around it to check it out and clean it. If this does not correct the problem, you may find that the rubber has become soft or pitted; the mechanism may then need to be replaced.

Low water refill

Q. After our toilet is flushed, it takes a very long time for the water to refill the tank again, and there is never more than a couple of inches of water in the bowl. Can you help?

A. The slow refill problem may be due to the supply valve being partially shut, an obstruction in the water supply to the tank, or the ball-cock assembly needing replacement. The very low water level in the bowl may indicate that the plastic refill tube has been dislodged and no longer provides water to the bowl through the down tube (sometimes called the overflow pipe).

Urinals

Q. As a matter of curiosity, please comment on why home builders do not install urinals in bathrooms. Seems to me they would be more sanitary and less frustrating for the clean-up crew. An ancillary benefit would be the death knell of the ongoing debate: seat up or seat down!

A. Your very original letter was my comic relief for the day; thank you.

Unfortunately, urinals are very expensive; the cost of the unit, including the flushing mechanism, is around $500, to which must be added the cost of the water and waste pipes. There is also the question of room in most bathrooms.

I don't see how a urinal would simplify the job of the clean-up crew; it's another fixture to deal with. Better to train the male users to wipe the bowl rim after use. And, as to the age-old debate about toilet seats, it's a hard one to win. Try bargaining.

Faucets, Sinks, Tubs

Faucet is difficult to operate

Q. The faucet of my bathroom sink is pulled forward to turn water on. It has become very difficult to operate. I have squirted oil into the part to no avail. What else can I do?

A. The problem is in the inner workings of the faucet, be they cartridge, ball, ceramic disc or tipping valve. There may be a need for lubrication with a special grease rather than just oil, or some part is worn and needs replacement.

Unless you are handy, it is a job best left to a plumber but, if you want to attempt the repair yourself, get Reader's Digest *New Complete Do-It-Yourself Manual*.

Faucets spraying hard jets

Q. My bathroom sink faucets are spraying water in hard jets instead of the normal flow they used to have.

A. Remove the aerators and soak them in white vinegar or replace them.

Faucet reassembled backward

Q. One of my faucets was taken apart to put in new washers. When it was reassembled, the faucet operated in reverse; instead of pushing the handle back to turn the water on, it now has to be pulled forward. How can the problem be corrected?

A. The spindles were reversed when the faucet was reassembled—the left spindle was put on the right side and the right on the left. Or if there is a plastic cuff over the spindle, it may be in upside down. Either way, it should be easy to reassemble correctly to get back to normal.

Water flows slowly after replacement of washer

Q. After I replaced the washer on my hot-water faucet, it no longer functions as before. When turned on, the water will flow for a few seconds then practically shut off. This occurs several times before I can get a normal flow. What's causing this and how can I correct it?

A. The new washer is thicker and more resilient than the old one which, in time, became compressed and developed a recessed ring where the faucet seat embedded itself when tightly shut. The new faucet has not had time to adjust to these conditions and hot water causes all parts to expand, reducing the passage of water.

It is also possible that you did not tighten the screw that holds the washer in place securely enough and that it has loosened up from the temperature changes. This causes the water to get behind the washer and shut off the water flow. Check that first, but if it's tight, be patient, it will work itself out in time.

Replacing a sink stopper

Q. My bathroom wash bowl is in good condition except for the metal stopper and the ring around it, which are pitted. How can this be repaired?

A. The simplest thing to do is to replace the pop-up piece and the flange that screws into the tail pipe. A plumber can do that in a few minutes. If you have other

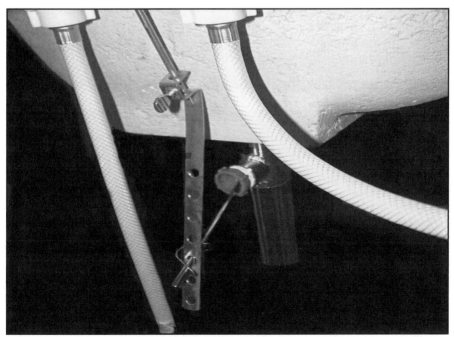

This is the backside of a bathroom sink with the stopper connection

plumbing problems, make a list and have them all taken care of at the same time to amortize the cost of the call.

If you prefer to tackle the job yourself, buy the parts from a hardware store or a willing plumber and ask for instructions; it's not difficult to do.

Water restricted in kitchen faucet

Q. I am having a problem with my kitchen faucet. I can't get the water to run fast in either the hot or cold sides of my single-lever faucet. I just get a little coming out. The water runs fast in all other fixtures. I have a well. I live alone and don't have much of an income but I am a handy person. What can I do about it?

A. Is this a recent phenomenon or has it always been like that? If it has been a problem since the house was built, there may be an obstruction from a piece of solder stuck in the kitchen faucet cartridge. That would require taking the faucet apart. But first check under the kitchen sink to make sure the shut-off valves to the hot and cold water are fully open. If they haven't been operated in a long time, they may be frozen and you may risk breaking them if they are the usual flimsy oval metal valve handles, so be careful in working them. The best way to avoid breaking them is to buy a Gordon Wrench (see Resources).

If it is relatively recent, and the valves are fully open, I would check the aerator on the spout of the faucet. Since you have a well, it is possible and likely that there is sediment blocking the aerator; it's a fairly common occurrence. If this is the case, one permanent solution is to have a rust and sediment filter installed on the water line just past the pressure tank. It should have a by-pass so that you can still have water in case the cartridge gets clogged and you can't get it replaced immediately. Use heavy-duty cartridges so you won't have to replace them as often; they cost the same as standard cartridges but last much longer.

Flow restrictors for shower heads

Q. Where can I buy flow restrictors for shower heads?

A. If your local hardware store doesn't carry them, a plumbing supply house does. Or ask a plumber to sell them to you.

New parts for old plumbing fixtures

Q. I have an old cast-iron free-standing tub and a sink that is bolted to the wall. I want to keep them in my remodeled bathroom. Are there replacement plumbing parts such as drains and faucets for these old tubs and sinks? Also, the outside of the tub has been painted. Is there anything I can do with that?

A. You should be able to get replacement parts from Dinapoli Plumbing Parts, 137 Herricks Rd., Garden City Park, NJ 11040. Their telephone number is 516-746-1570, or go to the Web at http://www.dinapoli.com.

You haven't said whether or not you want to remove the paint from the tub or paint it a different color. To remove the paint successfully, you would have to know what kind of paint was used. If it is epoxy, it will be difficult to remove. You can-paint it with epoxy if all you want is a different color.

Water Supply, Pipes, Connections

Sweaty tank and pipes

Q. My water storage tank and controls are in a closet on the first floor as there is only a crawl space under it. The tank and water lines sweat. This keeps the floor of the closet wet all the time. What can I do to prevent it?

A. If you insulate the tank and water lines, you'll only move the problem farther down the lines into the walls or floor system. In my experience, the best way to handle this common problem, particularly with deep wells that have cold water, is to place the storage tank on two 4-inch-thick concrete blocks set in a 24×24-inch metal pan, 2 inches deep with all seams soldered. This collects moisture safely and lets it evaporate into the surrounding air.

Waterlogged expansion tank

Q. Water is coming out of the pressure relief valve of my boiler at the rate of a full bucket a day whenever the boiler is fired. It does not leak when the burner is not on. What can be the problem?

A. It sounds as though the expansion tank is waterlogged. Try this: With a nail, push on the pin in the center of the valve used to pump air in the tank; it looks just like the valve on a car or bicycle tire.

If a little air, and only air, comes out, the bladder can be pumped up again. Try using a bicycle tire pump or call your service technician. However, if water comes out, it means that the bladder has a pinhole and became filled with water. The ex-pansion tank will have to be replaced. It's not too expensive.

Air in the well water

Q. I have a problem with my well-water supply. I get sporadic bursts of air when I turn on any faucet in the house. I have a captive air tank for storing the water sup-ply. The vinyl bladder bag was replaced as a precaution. The well was checked out. The pump was removed and checked for leaks. A faulty check valve was replaced. But I still have air coming out of the faucets.

A. I assume the entire pressure tank was replaced as I am not aware that it is pos-sible to just replace the bladder. The old tank probably had a snifter valve, which worked in concert with a back bleed valve in a "T" in the water line about 10 feet or so down from the pitless adapter in the well casing. New tanks do not have snifter valves and do not need back bleed valves. If the back bleed valve was not removed as part of the recent repairs, the pump should be pulled out until the valve is acces-sible and it should be replaced with a coupling. This should solve your problem.

Durability of different copper pipes

Q. I understand that type M copper water pipes have thinner walls and don't last as long as type L. Someone told me if I have type M I can anticipate having the pipes in the house replaced in a few years. Obviously that's of great concern. What's the scoop on it and how can I tell what I have?

A. You can tell as follows: the writing on K type copper is black; on L type it's blue and on M type it's red. However, although its true that M type copper pipes have thinner walls, don't panic. The worst enemy of metal water pipes is acidity of the water—a low pH (neutral is 7). Have the pH of your water supply tested and if it's in the mid to low 6 range or lower, talk to a water specialist about installing a system to raise the pH to neutral. Your pipes should then last a long time.

Sticking water valves

Q. I went to turn off the main valve to my water supply the other day and found that I could not turn it off. The valve is stuck in the open position and I realize that, sooner or later, I may have an emergency when I need to turn it off. I sprayed it with WD-40 and let it soak for a while, but it still won't budge.

Short of calling in a plumber, is there any way that you can think of that will help me? I thought of replacing the circular handle with a ratchet to get more leverage, but I don't want to damage or strip the spindle.

A. Try gently loosening the valve with a pair of channel locks (a type of pliers with many adjustable positions; all homes should have this tool). This should free the valve. Then, work it back and forth several times. When the valve moves freely, open it fully and back it up slightly. Try to remember to turn it a little every month. If you cannot move with the channel locks, you probably should call a plumber.

Gordon Wrench for sticky valves

Q. A few weeks ago, you mentioned a tool called a Gordon Wrench. I have been looking for one ever since but no one seems to have heard of it. Where can I find one?

A. For those who may have missed the description of the Gordon Wrench, it is an ingenious plastic tool used to operate the often frozen oval, chrome-plated pot metal valves found under toilets and bathroom lavatories. These valves are only used when the water supply needs to be shut off for repairs or in an emergency. As a result, they become stuck and any attempt to operate them can lead to breakage and injury, as these valves are very fragile and often in hard to reach places.

Robert Gordon, a retired engineer, invented it and sells it direct. You can order it through the Web at www.gordonwrench.com. The site shows what it looks like, how it works, the price list, and other information. You can also order it through the mail by writing The Gordon Tool Co., Inc., 14851 Jeffrey Rd., #22, Irvine, CA 92618-8022 or by calling 949-552-7613. Please call only between the hours of 9 and 5 Pacific time, as Mr. Gordon works from his home. The price for one wrench is $9.75 including shipping and handling in the U.S.

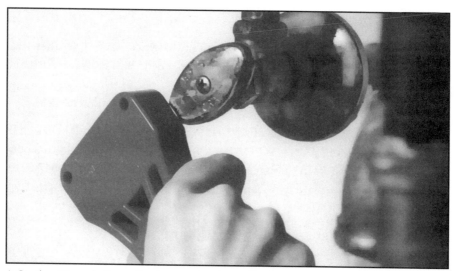

A Gordon Wrench fits perfectly over the shut-off valve

Laundry flooding: a word of caution

Having witnessed the unfortunate experiences of three people I know whose homes were badly damaged by flooding caused by the break of a clothes-washer hose, I urge all of you to shut off the two valves to the water supply of your clothes washer when it is not in use.

Consider having a plumber install a single-lever valve in lieu of the too-often-found regular valves. The advantage of a single-lever valve is that it is easy to operate and visually tells you if it is closed or open. It is well worth it. You may also want to change the hoses to the kind with mesh reinforcement.

Single lever shut-off valve connected to a washing machine: left is closed, right is open

Cast iron replacement parts

Q. I cannot find replacement drain covers for my basement sewer line. These two covers are made of cast iron, to which is attached a bell. They have corroded and no plumber, plumbing supply house or hardware store can tell me where to get replacements. Can you tell me where I can obtain these hard-to-find items?

A. I hope you have saved the corroded parts as you will need to send them to JHL Foundry. Their mailing address is P.O. Box 1084, Mt Pleasant, PA 15666-1084 but their UPS address is RR4 in the same town. Their phone number is 724-547-8210. They make cast iron replacement parts but they need a sample to make sure they can duplicate yours.

Clogged softener causes low water pressure

Q. The water pressure at the tub and sinks of our 30-year-old house is getting very low. We have a well and a water softener. What are the cause and solution?

A. Check the salts in your water softener. They may have gotten clogged and need replacement as they do periodically. If, in addition to the water softener, you have a dirt and sediment filter, the cartridge may need replacement.

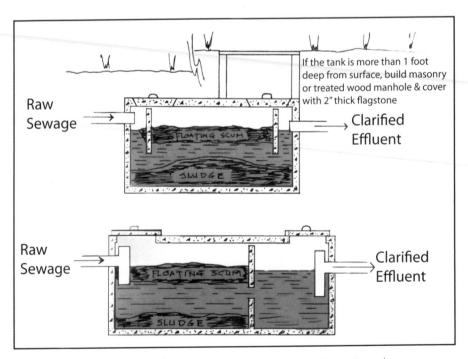

Two types of commonly used and approved precast concrete septic tanks

Septic Systems

Septic maintenance

Q. I have just had a new septic system installed and would appreciate your suggesting some reading material pertaining to operation and maintenance of septic tanks, drain fields and sewer lines.

A. The rules are very simple: do not flush anything you haven't eaten first, use only white toilet paper, and have the tank pumped every three to five years to prevent too great a build-up of scum and sludge that could be flushed into the field and eventually clog it. The operator of the pumper (also referred to as the "honey wagon"), if experienced, can tell you at the time of the first pumping whether three, four or five or more years between pumping is adequate. If you want a good understanding of rural plumbing systems and at the same time to be entertained, the best book is *Country Plumbing; Living with a Septic System* by Gerry Hartigan— published in 1984 but still widely available on-line or at used bookstores.

Avoid septic additives

Q. I have a question about the use of products like Ridex, etc., in septic systems. I see it advertised on television by a presumed septic system contractor who states you should use it regularly. An employee of a local septic company told me not to use it, because it breaks down the solids into very fine particles that then flow with the water into the leach field, increasing the potential for failure. Based on your experience, what is the correct scoop?

A. The employee from your local septic company is absolutely correct. He or she obviously knows a lot more about septic system health than the purported septic system contractor I also see pitching an enzyme product on television.

From all the research I have done over the decades, there is no need for any additive to a septic system; all the bacteria needed for proper functioning of the system are already in the human intestinal tract. However, to ensure continued good health, septic systems should be pumped every three to five years. The person who gave you the good advice can also tell you how frequently you should have your system pumped by looking at the condition of the contents when he or she comes to pump it next time.

Pumping a part-time septic tank

Q. Our septic tank, installed in 1969, is used only 3 months a year. So far it has never needed pumping out.

A. A system used only three months of the year has a great recovery time during which the leach field has a chance to dry up and oxygen and bugs a chance to clean it up. It's like having a dual system you can alternate every year.

But you make a mistake in not pumping the tank out on a reasonably regular basis. Solids, in the form of sludge at the bottom and scum at the top, build up over time, reducing the amount of liquid being stored and treated. When the solids represent a large part of the mass, there's a risk of particles being washed into the leach field thus contributing to its early clogging.

The general recommendation is to have the tank pumped out every three to five years—depending on its size and the number of occupants in the house. But since yours is used only for 25% of the time, you can safely wait 10 to 15 years to have it pumped out if the use is fairly light during the three months of occupancy.

Antifreeze in the septic system?

Q. We have used automotive antifreeze in the drain pipes of our summer cottage. Does it harm the septic system? If it does, what will it do?

A. Harsh chemicals do septic tanks no good. They kill the bacteria needed to digest and treat human wastes dumped into the system. Buy non-toxic antifreeze from an RV or camping goods store.

Where is the septic tank?

Q. When I bought my house a few years ago, the previous owner wasn't able to tell me the precise location of the septic tank and leach field. The old idea of watching where the grass first greens up in the spring or where the snow melts most quickly didn't work for me. Is there an easy, foolproof way to pinpoint them short of digging up the yard? I don't have an immediate problem, and only two of us live in the house, but I am contemplating having the tank pumped out. The previous owner claimed that it had been done within the seven years prior to my purchase.

A. Hire a septic pumping contractor who has a detector that can locate the tank when you are ready to have it pumped, which should be done every three to five years on average.

A septic tank in place in the ground, with the lines hooked up

Overflowing toilet

Q. I have had a problem with a toilet overflowing. A plumber worked on it and it seemed to work for a while but it began to overflow again. Each time the plumber was called but the problem recurred. Finally we decided to replace the toilet, unfortunately with one of the new 1.6 gallons type. To this day, I never know when it is going to overflow and must keep a plunger handy. I have had several different plumbers try to correct this problem but it is only temporary. I would appreciate your input before I go bankrupt.

A. It sounds as if the problem is more in the sewer line. Could there be something partially blocking it? Another possibility, if you have a septic system, is that it may be overdue for pumping. If you haven't had the tank pumped in many years, it may be full of solids which cause a back-up if too much water is discharged into it at one time—say, if you flush the toilet during or shortly after someone took a bath or a shower or the clothes or dishwasher washer were used.

And if the leach field is failing, it may take a while for the effluent to be absorbed, causing a back-up in the system. It may be a good idea to have a septic specialist investigate.

Drains

Drain too small

Q. Since we put an apartment in the basement of our double-wide mobile home, the waste water from our washer backs up in the bathtub before draining away. What did we do wrong?

A. I assume your washer backs up into the basement bathtub. Your washer may drain into a 1½-inch line. It is too small for the powerful drainage of the washer. It should drain into a 2-inch line.

Shower drain freezes

Q. The drain in our upstairs bathroom shower freezes in the winter. The pipes are located inside my son's closet and the former owners had installed an access panel. Upon further investigation, a cold breeze can be felt along the wall in my son's room to the left of a heating vent and to the drain area at floor level.

We have tried putting a heater in the closet on very cold nights. We had some-one put extra insulation in the attic. The last two winters, we've had plumbers come out and defrost or replace the drain. It even froze and broke on us. No one seems to know how to stop the breeze or find out where it's coming from. Should we call a roofer? I hope you can help because this is getting costly.

A. From the sketch in your letter, and from your description of cold air along the wall near the heating vent, it is clear that there is no insulation in the stud space in which the heat vent is located. In homes built before the mid 1970s, it was fairly common to install heat ducts in outside walls in lieu of insulation.

Open the access panel and see if there is room behind the drainpipe to inject foam insulation between the drain and the wall sheathing; do not put foam in front of the pipe, as you want some heat to get to it. Foam can also be blown into the rest of the cavity to seal the area next to the heat duct and behind the duct, even if there is only a very narrow space in which to do it. Foam as deep down as you can reach.

You can buy cans of foam in hardware and building supply stores. Since you are probably not practiced in the art of foaming, buy the type that does not expand too much to avoid having a mess on your hands. When done, this should improve the situation immeasurably.

Water drains slowly in sink with disposal

Q. I have a new double-bowl sink and disposal. Water drains fine from the bowl that doesn't have the disposal but drains very slowly from the bowl to which the disposal is connected and the bowl fills.

When I turn the disposal on, the sink drains fine. We have snaked the pipes and used every drain cleaner imaginable to no avail. What could be the problem?

A. The new disposals have very small openings to allow more grinding time within the unit so that garbage will be ground much finer. As a result, water will fill them and the sink when the disposal is not running. This is a normal condition.

Gentle way to clear drains

Q. Our bathroom sinks have become quite sluggish and I can't remove the gizmo that keeps water in, in order to clean the drain. I don't want to use any of the harsh chemicals available because I am sure it would not be good for our septic system. Is there a gentler alternative?

A. There is. Buy washing soda in the laundry section of your local supermarket and follow directions on the box. It works very well. The most common is Arm & Hammer's Super Washing Soda. Do not confuse it with baking soda.

Cement-clogged drain

Q. When the plumbing fixtures were installed in our new basement bathroom, we tried the shower and found that the floor drain was plugged. I removed the drain cover plate and found that the obstruction is 10 inches down from the floor. It appears that cement used to install the floor tiles fell into the drain and hardened. What can I use to soften up or dissolve this cement? Or is there another way to get rid of it without having to chip it out?

A. Who did the tile job? The tile contractor should be made to correct the problem he or she caused. However, if you did it yourself, here is a way to attempt to remove the plug, which is probably in the trap.

If the drain pipes are plastic, carefully pour muriatic acid in a plastic funnel placed in the drain, avoiding all contacts with any metal parts. Pour enough acid so that you can see it in the tail pipe. Watch if it drains and at what level it stabilizes; you want the cement obstruction to be bathed in the acid. Give it time to work; keep an eye on it with a flashlight. When the acid has drained, turn the shower on and see if it works fine. If it drains slowly, use a plunger, but only if you have water and not acid in the trap. If this does not do it, repeat the operation.

You may want to get a pressurized can made for flushing sinks from a hardware store, or buy an attachment to your garden hose made for this purpose to power-flush the drain. If everything else fails or the drain pipes are metal, the pipes may have to be replaced.

Basement plumbing

Q. We are moving to a country home and would like to have a toilet and a shower in the basement. However, the sewer line to the septic system is 3 feet above the basement floor. Can this be done?

A. Yes, but it will be expensive. A sewer ejector pump can be installed in a sump. The waste water will be pumped up when the level in the sump activates the float.

How long does a sump pump last?

Q. I am concerned about the longevity of my sump pump which has worked hard during our very wet spring. Should I install a second pump as a back-up in the same crock with a higher float level in the event the original pump fails, or should I install another crock and pump to share the load?

A. A good-quality sump pump should last for years even with frequent usage. You should not be overly concerned about its giving up the ghost unless you know it's a cheap model. In that case, you can buy insurance in the form of a good-quality submersible sump pump (cost about $100), install it in the present sump, and save the older and cheap model for an emergency. My bet is you'll never need it.

Plumbing Vents

Leak may be at vent stack

Q. Our bathroom has what appears to be a leak in the ceiling from the attic. Exploration reveals no leak in the roof but the ceiling itself is spongy in places, and damp. Could condensation be the cause? There is no exhaust fan.

A. It could be, but another possibility is a leak around the collar of the plumbing vent stack that goes through the roof in that area. Tie a towel around it in the attic to check it. If it gets wet after a series of rains, you have found the culprit. The neoprene gasket may have cracked and may need to be repaired in the form of polyurethane caulking.

Plumbing vents are usually on the roof, as shown here. In any event, they should extend at least 1 ½ feet above the eaves.

Vent clogs during cold weather

Q. I have a problem with my atmospheric vent stack on my roof. When it is cold, the top of the vent gets clogged with snow, causing a back-up sewer odor inside the house. Any suggestions?

A. The vent gets clogged from ice. Snow would melt from the heat the vent generates, but ice forms because of the high moisture content in the stack. Your vent stack is probably too small in diameter. If there is access to the attic, it should be changed to a 4-inch size where it comes out of the insulated space.

Another way to keep vents from freezing

A Wisconsin reader solved the common occurrence of plumbing vent stacks that exit through roofs sometimes freezing shut in winter causing plumbing problems (including sewer smell in the house). She painted them black under the assumption that they would absorb solar heat since the sun is generally shining when the temperature is very cold. She has not had the problem since, so we can assume that her theory was correct. But, that would only work if the plumbing stacks are exposed to considerable solar time during the day, i.e., they are not on the north side of a steep roof.

Roof vent odor

Q. In spite of the fact that we have our septic tank pumped out every three years, there is a sewage odor coming out of the roof vent. Is there something wrong with the septic system or is this a venting problem?

A. The odor is caused by the wind creating a negative pressure over the vent and sucking the gases out. Install a 90-degree elbow over the vent facing the prevailing winds, and adjust it as needed until you find the right angle. Do not cement the elbow. It needs to remain adjustable.

Vents too short

Q. We would like to ask you about a problem that we are having at our log cabin. When the plumber hooked up our toilet, sink, bathtub and kitchen sink on the main floor, he used two "cheater vents" instead of running a vent up through the roof. Everything seemed to work fine, except that we would get a gurgling sound in the bathtub when you let the water out of the kitchen sink and vice versa—but everything seemed to drain all right and nothing was backed up.

We've heard from different people about the pros and cons of using "cheater vents." Meanwhile, we've had a different plumber install another bathroom in the basement and he ran a 2-inch vent pipe out through the wall and up 3 feet from the kitchen drainpipe. This seems to eliminate the gurgling sound from the tub or sink, and the toilets seem to flush better.

The problem we're having now is the odor coming from the new outside vent pipe—it smells like sewage. It's not constant, but comes and goes and is very unpleasant. The vent pipe is located on a back wall of the cabin and is near a window that's level with the first floor, but the cabin is one and a half stories and no matter how high we go up with the pipe, it will still be near the upstairs windows. Is there a filter system that we can put on the vent pipe, or should we cap it off and live with the gurgling and use the cheater vents? Can you help with this situation?

A. The second plumber didn't do you any favors. A vent pipe must go through the roof or, in the case of an installation like the one he did, should be higher than the eaves of the roof and should not be installed near a window.

Now, you'll need to have the pipe relocated away from both the upstairs and downstairs windows and extended to 1½ feet above the roof eaves. This may still cause you to get a sewer smell when the atmospheric conditions are propitious, so you may need to install a 90-degree ell on top of the pipe (do not glue it on. Just push it in place). Turn the ell facing the roof ridge to start with and, if you still smell sewage, turn it toward the prevailing winds until you have it just right.

Blocked vent

Q. I live in a 40-year-old ranch house. In the last two years, I have had a strange problem with the plumbing. The drains in the bathtub and kitchen gurgle when I flush the toilet. I have not had this problem before. Have you any explanation as to why this is happening, and if so, how can I rectify this problem?

A. It sounds as if you have a venting problem. When a toilet is flushed it displaces air into the vent system, which is there to equalize the pressure created by the flushing and prevent the very problem you're having. The fact that this problem developed only in the last two years indicates that your vent stack is partially or fully blocked by some foreign matter, perhaps a bird or squirrel nest. You should have a plumber or Roto-Rooter snake out the vent system.

Gurgling sink

Q. For a long time there has been a prolonged glug, glug sound emanating from the kitchen sink when the water drains out. What causes it, and how can this noise be stopped?

A. The kitchen sink waste does not appear to be connected to the house vent stack or to be vented on its own through the roof of the house. Thus, as water is drained out of the sink, it causes air ingestion through the waste pipe to even out the negative pressure created by the water flowing down the drain.

The glug, glug sound is air passing through the sink trap creating fluctuation of the water in it that acts as a seal to keep sewer gases out of the house. There is a risk that enough water may be sucked out of the trap to allow gases to enter the house. Since the gurgling sound is harmless in itself, you have the choice of ignoring it and just letting water flow in the kitchen drain for a few seconds after the sink is drained to refill the trap, or to have the kitchen sink properly vented.

Toilet drains when another is flushed

Q. We have lived in our house for 50 years and have recently developed a new problem. Our second-floor bathroom is directly over the one on the first floor and, when the upstairs toilet is flushed, the water in the other toilet is drained. This necessitates flushing it to put water back in the bowl. Any suggestions?

A. It probably means that something has recently happened to plug the atmospheric vent stack that should protrude from your roof. When this vent is plugged, draining or flushing one fixture may cause another fixture's trap to empty as make-up air—to replace the air displaced by the rushing water—is drawn in through another fixture. You may need to have a licensed plumber check this out.

Exhaust Vents

Proper venting of exhaust fan

Q. A year ago we installed an exhaust fan/light combination in our bathroom. The fan is vented through the attic by an elbow attached to the sewer vent. Now it's leaking around the unit, the result, we presume, of condensation. What do we do?

A. First, you must disconnect the fan duct from the sewer vent. You have created what can be a serious problem. Sewer gases can, under certain conditions, be sucked back into the house, *i.e.* when your furnace is working or you use your fireplace or wood stove, or when you turn on the kitchen fan, for example.

Instead, run the duct across the attic's floor joists with a slight pitch to the outside, making sure insulation fills the joists' spaces so the duct is lying on top of them. Vent the duct to a gable wall by means of an aluminum jack equipped with a spring-activated flap, if you can find one.

Cut 3½-inch-thick glass fiber batts in half lengthwise and place one set snugly on each side of the duct. Then lay a full-width set of batts directly on top of the duct and the side insulation. The duct must be snugly surrounded by insulation for it to work. This should eliminate condensation.

Q. Your recommendation is to vent the fans through a gable wall. My house is a ranch house with a 5-foot-high attic and, if I understand what a gable is, we don't have any. What do I do?

A. A "gable" wall is any end wall with a peak in it, even if it is a shallow peak as on a ranch house. The reason a gable wall is best for venting is because the outlet to the vent can be high enough to avoid any bathroom odors blowing back into nearby windows. If your roof is sloping on all sides or you are constrained in other ways from using your gable end, the vent can exit on any outside wall, preferably away from any opening windows.

Best pipe for venting bathroom fan

Q. You have mentioned using a plastic pipe schedule 20 to vent a bathroom fan. I have never seen or heard of this type of pipe. Where can I buy this funnel and what size pipe do I use?

A. The pipe in question is a "schedule 20" (indicating the thickness of the plastic) PVC drain pipe with a "bell" end. It is 4 inches in diameter, and you should use the solid type (as opposed to the perforated type used to collect or discharge water). Make sure the bell end is facing toward the fan. This kind of pipe is not as heavy as drain pipe but is perfectly adequate for venting, and will cost less.

Ice forms on ceiling-fan exhaust

Q. Our bathroom ceiling fan has created quite a problem. In winter, ice forms in the vent pipe, which goes straight up through the roof. When it melts, water drips or runs down on top of the toilet. Now the paint on the ceiling around the fan is peeling off. Any suggestions?

A. Yes. Keep the toilet lid open so water drips into the bowl, and keep an umbrella handy. All kidding aside, this is a common problem because those who install these fans do not pay attention to the laws of physics. The only way a bathroom fan should be vented in temperate and cold regions is through a gable wall; never through the roof or into an attic or a soffit.

The duct should be laid on top of the joists with a slight pitch to the outside and surrounded by insulation on all sides. This is easily done by snugging fiberglass batts on each side of it and placing others on top, making sure cold air cannot sneak in. This keeps the warm, moist air from cooling off too fast and condensing too soon and certainly from running back into the bathroom.

Bath and dryer vents must be separated

Q. When we modernized an old two-story duplex earlier this year, I asked the contractor to follow your instructions in one of your columns recommending installing bathroom fans on interior walls and venting them down through the basement and outside. It wasn't practical in our case, so he vented two showers and two clothes dryers, that are back-to-back on the second floor, up through the attic and horizontally along the attic floor to a vent hole in the eaves. There are 20 vent holes in the eaves and a cupola on the rooftop.

We now have one apartment rented, and are finding lots of lint coming out of the dryer vent in the unoccupied apartment as well as condensation in the shower compartment. It appears that the exhaust from the occupied apartment is emptying into the other instead of going out of the eaves vent. What do you advise?

A. Too bad you didn't show the contractor another one of my columns mentioning the fact that a bath or kitchen fan, or dryer, should never be vented into the eaves of a building. If you have two separate ducts discharging out of the same vent hole in the eaves, the discharge from either apartment is going to turn right around and go through the other duct, as all air movement through your attic is from the eaves up through the cupola.

And, if you separate the ducts so that they vent through different holes some distance apart but still through the eaves, the lint and moisture will then be directed up into the attic where you certainly want neither. But, if you have combined the two showers and two dryers into common vents, the air movement from outside will cause the discharge from either apartment to short-circuit back into the other where they are tied together.

The solution is separate ducts for each of the showers and each of the dryers (four in all) going out through a gable wall and terminating in a good-quality jack equipped with a spring-loaded flap. Be sure all ducts are surrounded with insulation to retard the formation of condensation.

Dryer should vent outdoors

Q. We recently put an attached garage on our house, and the dryer vent, which used to be on an outside wall, is now venting into the garage. I plan to insulate the garage, but only heat it occasionally with a wood stove if I have car work to do.

I have heard that venting your dryer into the house during the winter is okay, as it adds moisture to the dry winter air. Do you think I should add pipe and vent the dryer outside? If I do, does this pipe have to run uphill all the way? Are there any guidelines as to how flat or steep the pipe has to be?

A. The main problem with venting a dryer inside is lint accumulation. It should not be vented in the garage for the same reason. You can run the pipe flat or at a downward slope; it does not have to slope upwards. If you can, extend it from its present outlet to the nearest outside wall even if it requires a bend. But keep the duct with as few bends as possible and with no "droops," as these can collect condensation that may eventually block the exhaust.

Never vent fans into soffits

Q. The bathroom fans in my two-story home are vented into the two-foot-wide aluminum soffit. Can you describe the most practical way to remedy this situation? I want to avoid creating new problems such as a leak in the roof by venting them through it.

A. You're right! Bath and kitchen fans should never be vented into soffits, attics, gable or ridge vents, basements, or crawl spaces. In cold climates, they should not be vented through the roof either, as condensation runs down the vent, stains ceilings, drips on the floor, and rusts the fan and its housing.

The proper way to vent bath and kitchen fans is through a gable wall. In cold climates, the vents should also be insulated. This is easily done by placing fiberglass batts on each side and on top.

Venting exhaust from middle of house

Q. How can I install a fan in a first-floor half bath that is in the middle of the house? I am stumped, as there is a second floor and I'd rather not cut too many walls and ceilings to do it.

A. If the basement ceiling is open, install the fan in a wall and duct it down to the basement and outside through a band joist.

Be aware of the fact that the chosen wall may have blocking at midpoint or plumbing within the stud spaces. Place the fan below any blocking and check for pipes from the basement.

Condensation impedes exhaust

Q. Several years ago, I replaced my windowless bathroom's fan with a larger one to handle the humidity. However, mold grows on the ceiling and in the glass dome of the light fixture, and the ceiling paint is cracked.

The vent holes in the ceiling fan seem very narrow and, when I hold a flame to the fan, it hardly flickers. My husband thinks condensation in the hose in the attic may be responsible. Your suggestions would be helpful.

A. Your husband may have put his finger on the problem if, when the fan was installed, the vent pipe used is of the flexible plastic type and there is a dip in it. I have seen this problem a number of times: the dip fills with condensation, and no exhaust takes place. Eventually, the plastic rots, and the water is dumped onto the insulation and the ceiling below.

In my experience, in most climates with cold days in winter, condensation will occur and run back down into the fan housing, causing rusting, water stains, paint peeling, and worse. This is why I recommend running the vent in rigid plastic pipe to a gable wall—and not to a soffit, ridge vent or through the roof, and certainly never discharging into the attic—pitching slightly toward the outside and surrounding it with fiberglass insulation.

Moisture and smells from neighbors' fan duct

Q. We live in a small apartment building. It used to be a large private house that was remodeled into a four-unit apartment house on two floors. Our problem is that our bathroom is constantly plagued with mold or mildew and, yet, we are only two of us living in the apartment and we use the fan whenever we shower in the morning before going to work.

Our neighbors do not have this problem but, when they use their bathroom, we seem to get some odors and can hear their fan running. What do you think is the problem?

A. I bet that when the remodeling was done, both your bathroom's fan duct and your neighbors' were tied into one outlet. It may be that all four apartments have their fans' ducts tied together. If your apartment is the last one in the ducting, you get everybody's moisture and other unpleasant aspects of this error.

This can be verified by asking the landlord to check the attic, if accessible, or with the contractor who did the job or by using a smoke candle in each of the apartments. Put the candle close to the fan and let it be drawn up into the duct one at a time to see which is the culprit or if all are. If, during this test, the smoke comes out of your fan, it tells you that the ducts are tied together.

Correcting this problem may entail some tearing up if the attic is not accessible. Or you can seal the fan with plastic and use a window for ventilation, if you have one.

Bathroom fan sometimes optional

Q. The seven-year-old house I just bought has a window but no fan in the bathroom. I am concerned about the steam generated when I take a shower; high levels of humidity and mildew that could, in the long run, cause damage to the walls.

I don't want to open the window in the winter since it would make the room cold, nor in the summer as I have central air conditioning. Am I concerned for no reason? Should I install a ceiling fan and should I let it vent the humidity into the attic? Wouldn't that create another problem?

A. Whether the humidity generated by your showering will eventually cause a problem or not depends on the size of the house, the number of occupants and their own bathing habits, other sources of moisture created by your lifestyle, etc.

Go ahead and see what happens without installing a fan. Opening the window for a few minutes after you have finished in the bathroom, and with the bathroom door closed, is not going to cause a great deal loss for heating or AC, and may save you the headache of having to deal with mildew later.

On the other hand, leaving the window closed and the bathroom door open will allow the moisture to dissipate throughout the house, which may not be bad at all, depending on how much additional moisture is generated in the house.

If you decide that you need a fan, it certainly must not be vented into the attic. As you sense, that would create other problems. It should be vented outside through a gable wall.

Electrical Systems

Wiring Issues

Finding the right electrician to rewire a house

Q. My house is over 100 years old. It has no insulation. Before I insulate it, I need to have it rewired. I still have the old porcelain knob-and-tube wiring. How do you find a good electrician, and what would be considered an average estimate? Is there anything I should look for? I have a four-bedroom house. The basement is unfinished, and there is an unfinished area over all but two rooms.

A. You should definitely have the knob-and-tube wiring replaced before insulating the house walls. The danger is that once these old wires are buried in the insulation, their own insulation—which is often brittle from age—may overheat and cause a fire.

You didn't say where you live, but you should be able to find a licensed master electrician qualified to replace your wiring; just be sure that he or she is licensed by the state authority in charge of licensing electricians, plumbers, gas technicians, etc. There is no way I can tell you what this conversion will cost. Since so much of your house is accessible from below, it makes the job that much easier and less costly. To ensure a fair comparison, ask two or three licensed electricians to give you a price, but remember that the lowest price is not always the best. The way you relate to the electricians is more important. And don't forget to ask for references.

Replacing aluminum wiring

Q. The 22-year-old house we are considering buying has aluminum wiring. Should we be wary of it? We understand that some, not all, junction boxes were rewired using copper connectors. If all were similarly rewired, would that eliminate the problem? What about the service box? And, how well does aluminum wiring age? Will we have to rewire the house? One electrician said rewiring the remaining junction boxes will do the trick; another says steer clear of the whole thing. The eager sellers have reduced the price considerably. We love the house but we are concerned.

A. It is common to find multi-conductor—or stranded—aluminum wiring for entrance cables and appliances such as ranges, but that type of wiring is not usually a problem. Single-conductor aluminum wiring can be a problem as it expands and contracts at a different rate from the brass binding screws and plates of the switches, receptacles and breakers to which it is connected.

A competent licensed electrician can easily detect a problem. You should be concerned if you notice certain bad signs such as warm cover plates, a strange odor, any indications of arcing, static sounds on an AM radio, or flickering lights. However, it is possible there may be no problem, in which case you should leave everything alone.

Problems can be minimized or prevented by the proper amount of torque on the terminal screws and the application of anti-corrosion paste, as should be done on multi-conductor main and branch terminals.

There are a number of relatively simple strategies to correct problems. For example, the breakers, switches, and receptacles can be changed to the "CO/ALR" type that is compatible with aluminum branch wiring. Or copper pigtails can be connected to the aluminum wiring and then to the existing terminals—if the boxes are large enough to accommodate the additional connections.

Lights flicker

Q. A few weeks ago the lights throughout our house began flickering. We have aluminum wiring. This occurred only on occasion. The power company came out twice, checked the line coming into the house, replaced the meter, and assured us the problem was internal.

The electrician is continuing to look for loose connections but believes that a loose wire would not cause flickering throughout the house. Any suggestions?

A. I hope that by now your electrician has located the appropriate loose wires as that has to be the problem. Lights could be flickering throughout the house if they are randomly placed on the same circuit. Tell the electrician which lights flicker at the same time; he or she should be able to trace it back to the proper breaker.

Other possibilities that would cause widespread flickering are a loose connection at the neutral entrance wire or at either of the hot legs. The power company would probably not check that as it is inside the panel. They're concerned with the outside stuff only.

Backward wiring can damage appliances

Q. Somebody told me that one should be careful in plugging in any appliance that has a wide-prong plug because it could be damaged if the wiring is not correct. He could not explain more. What is he talking about?

A. What your friend is referring to is the proper polarization of the receptacle. If the receptacle has reverse polarity, that is to say that the hot wire (the black one) is attached to the neutral terminal (the silver colored one) instead of the hot terminal (the gold colored one), the integrity of the appliance plugged in is in jeopardy.

The correct connections of any three-prong plugs can be easily checked with a small tool available in electrical supply houses, hardware and building supply stores. It is a simple matter to reverse the wires so the black one is connected to the gold colored terminal and the other to the silver colored one, but make sure the current to that receptacle is off before working on it.

"Exercising" circuit breakers and GFCIs

Q. I read in a government publication titled "Home Electrical Safety Audit" that circuit breakers should be exercised once a year by flipping them on and off at least a dozen times. Is this a good practice?

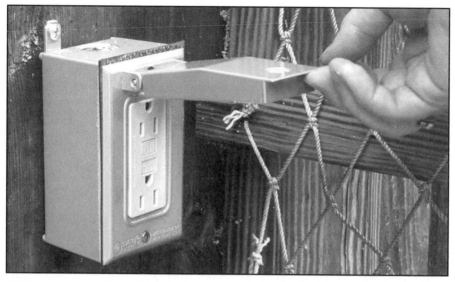

GFCIs must be used in kitchens, bathrooms, and any other part of the house with exposure to water.

A. Who would argue with a government publication! However, some other publications mention that it should be done every six months; take your pick. (Relatively few people actually do this, but that doesn't mean it's not a good idea.) Needless to say, make sure that any computers or major appliances that may be on the circuit are turned off and/or unplugged.

Ground fault circuit interrupters (GFCIs) should definitely be tested frequently—like once a month; there is a test button on them for the purpose. Reset them after testing, or the plug(s) will not work. You will find GFCIs in bathrooms, laundry rooms, near the kitchen sink, outdoors, and everywhere there is water nearby, or inside the electrical panel as special breakers. The exercising keeps the connections solid and firm.

Grounding prong can be at top or bottom

Q. I am about to do some serious electrical work on my house—a handyman's special now turned into a handyman's nightmare. I had given up hope of getting an answer to a perplexing question, but then I thought of you.

The electrician who put in my service told me that my state requires wiring for multiple family units be done according to the National Electrical Code which, in turn, requires that the grounding prong be up on all outlets. This seems backward to me. Can you provide some insight on if and why this is so?

A. There is no such requirement in the NEC, or any code that I know of. Your electrician is mistaken on this score. There may an argument for what he told you, though. If a plug is not fully inserted into the receptacle and some metal object falls on it, the ground leg would prevent the object from making contact across the hot and neutral, thereby causing a short-circuit. But receptacles are installed both ways; it's up to you or your electrician.

Lights dim when neighbor's AC starts

Q. Our next-door neighbors recently completed a renovation and installed a larger compressor for their air conditioner. Every time their air conditioner compressor starts, our lights dim briefly. Should I be concerned about this?

A. It sounds as if your house and your neighbors' house share the same transformer. That transformer may not have the capacity to handle the additional load of your neighbors' new compressor, which could cause a surge that makes your lights dim. Call your power company and tell them about the problem. They may need to replace the transformer with one of greater capacity.

Lighting

Recessed bathroom lights turn off and on

Q. The recessed lights which the electrician installed in our new bathroom turn themselves off when they get too hot and then back on when they've cooled. This is very annoying but the electrician tells us that this type of light is now required. We need all the light we can get in this bathroom. What can we do?

A. Recessed lights, for a number of years, have been equipped with a thermal cut-off to prevent them from overheating—which can be a serious problem now that we use higher levels of insulation in ceilings. This is to avoid the danger of fire. They are known as IC fixtures.

But your problem is probably caused by a bulb with too high a wattage; recessed fixtures have the maximum wattage that should be used embossed inside the housing, and it is usually 60 watts. Check this out and change the bulbs if necessary; that should take care of it. If this doesn't give you enough light, you may have to add additional fixtures. Another solution is to get rid of the recessed fixtures and replace them with surface-mounted ones.

Are heat lamps a health danger?

Q. I recently read an article in a health magazine about the potential long-term harmful effects of sun lamps in tanning salons. How does this relate to combination fan-light-heater ceiling fixtures in bathrooms?

A. First, it's worth noting that heat lamps are different from sun lamps. A red or white heat lamp would have no tanning or burning effect, while a sun lamp could burn a bald head under it. None of these bulbs provide room heat; only radiant heat to someone in direct line with the bulb.

That said, you would get more ultraviolet rays walking or gardening in the sun than from standing under a sun lamp while drying after a bath.

Clean fluorescent lights work better

Suggestion from a reader: "In your column you talked about a person having problems with the fluorescent lights in their kitchen. I had a similar problem. I tried replacing the switch, ballast and bulb, but the problem persisted. Like you, I discovered that if you flip the switch several times, it would finally go on. This usually worked, but I thought that there might be a better solution. While doing a search on the problem on the Web, I came across a technical bulletin that indicated that this problem would occur during humid weather if the bulb is dirty or dusty. I tried cleaning the bulb, and it finally worked properly. You might want to pass this suggestion on to your readers. I hope that this is helpful."

Thank you; it's a great suggestion that I will promptly try it on my recalcitrant fluorescent lights!

Miscellaneous Electrical Questions

Run generator from outside only

Q. We moved into an 18-year-old house last year. During the inspection, the inspector showed me a generator sitting in the basement. He said that it was a very nice unit that probably cost a few thousand dollars. But he said that we needed to hire an electrician to make it run again. Later, I found out from the previous owner that the generator hadn't been used since her ex-husband moved out 17 years ago.

Recently, a handyman who did some jobs for us saw the generator. He said it runs on natural gas so, once it is plugged in, it will run again. Sounds simple, but not to someone (me) who is scared of everything running with gas and electricity. Is it safe to have a generator in the basement? I did some research on the Internet and found out the unit is supposed to be installed outside. What can I expect from a machine not running for 17 years? All I want is an emergency power supply for the sump pump. Is it easier to just buy the battery-operated set?

A. It is never safe to run any unvented fuel-burning appliances inside. Combustion results in a number of gases, one of which is carbon monoxide, "the silent killer." Your generator should be moved outside before being serviced and used again. Even after 17 years, it may still work fine.

Generators are used to provide electrical power when power is not available on-site or when there is a power interruption, so it does not run on electricity—it makes it. If your generator is powered by natural gas, contact the supplier of the natural gas and ask them if they service the type of unit you have and to connect it to the gas supply. You will still need an electrician to make sure the generator is operational and to connect it to the house's electrical system. If the generator is powered by gasoline or diesel, an electrician can handle the entire job.

Electrical outlet makes clock run fast

Q. One of our electrical outlets makes our clocks run fast. At first, I thought the clock I plugged into it was malfunctioning so I bought a new clock. The same thing happened. Then, I plugged them both into a different outlet in the same room, and they were fine. What's going on?

A. According to a master electrician friend who also has taught vocational school for many years, the only possibility that comes to mind is that high frequency is being induced into the circuit into which you first plugged the clocks; this would cause them to accelerate.

This may be caused by ham radio or other electronic equipment using high frequency. But this should apply to all outlets on the same circuit. So, to verify this hypothesis, you should determine if the other receptacle into which you plugged the clocks in the same room is on a different circuit. You can do that by having someone turn off the breaker that controls the speedy receptacle while you watch a lamp plugged into it. When that lamp goes off, plug it into the other receptacle and see if it lights up. If it does not, both receptacles are on the same circuit and we continue to have a mystery.

Replacements for old-fashioned light switches

Q. Several of the light switches in my 1920s house are of the two-button type, and two are broken. Where can I find replacements?

A. These will not be easy to find in most hardware stores, but push-button switches are obtainable from several sources on the Internet. One such source is the House of Antique Hardware at www.houseofantiquehardware.com.

Heating and Cooling

Health and Safety

Carbon monoxide detectors

Over the years, you have read my recommendation to buy and install carbon monoxide (CO) detectors on each level of your house. A recent event that could have had tragic consequences prompts me not just to remind you, but to exhort you to do it now if you haven't done so already.

Good friends of mine live in an old house in the country. They have been heating with coal for years because they prefer its even heat to the auxiliary oil-fired capability of their furnace. They haven't had a CO detector in the house all these years, but finally bought and installed a plug-in type detector just before the heating season started. During the holidays, at about 2 A.M. one morning, they were awakened by the screeching of the detector. Its digital readout registered 200—a lethal dose over time. Not being able to put the coal fire out, they opened all the windows in the house in spite of the cold night and went back to bed to stay warm.

After a while, the house was so cold that they closed the windows; shortly after that, the detector screeched again so they re-opened the windows. This went on for the rest of the night. They had a technician come to examine the furnace, and he found a crack in the heat exchanger. Had they not installed the CO detector, they would no longer be with us and would have left two young adult daughters without their parents.

Unfortunately, putting off installing CO and smoke detectors can have catastrophic results. In fact, such procrastination or negligence was responsible for the deaths of two young men after a day of skiing several years ago in my home state of Vermont. The investigators found a CO detector in its package on a shelf next to their boiler room, and a smoke detector that had been disabled. Had the CO detector been installed, these young men would still be alive today.

Please, if you haven't already done so, go out and buy a good-quality plug-in (with battery backup) CO detector for each floor of your house, and install it according to the instructions in the package.

Schedule testing of smoke detectors

All smoke detectors need to be tested regularly, including the fall, as we approach the heating season. Test them by pushing on the test button. If they are solely battery-operated (as opposed to hardwired to the electric system), you should change the batteries as you turn your clocks back. It is not worth the risk to rely on a battery that is one year old. If they have any life left, use the old batteries on something less important or recycle them properly.

Appliances should be vented

Q. You have recently written that all fossil fuel appliances should be vented outside. In the '40s, we replaced our vented gas range with a new range that is not vented to the outside and I haven't seen a single vented gas range for sale anywhere.

We just installed a brand new ventless fireplace in our living room. It is true that, when first installed, it set off both smoke detectors and the carbon monoxide detector half a house away. The gas company sent someone to adjust it and we have had no problem since. We do keep a window cracked as recommended in the fireplace literature when it is in use.

But when we cook with the oven and four burners all at once, they use more gas than the fireplace. For well over 40 years I have vented my gas dryer into the basement in the winter and have had no problems. I believe you may have needlessly scared some readers with your comments in this case.

The metal cap on this chimney can cause the gases from its flue to be sucked back into the house as the other flues provide make-up air.

A. You may have a very leaky house and if you wish to have a window open during the winter to provide fresh air for the fireplace, you are also wasting energy. People living in the tighter houses of today should use vented appliances or provide fresh air to the boiler by other means. Having investigated fatal accidents caused by carbon monoxide, I am very conscious of the problems this gas can cause when it becomes concentrated for whatever reason. It's a warning all should heed.

Using the wrong chimney caps is dangerous

In the course of my consulting work, I often see dangerous situations on chimney tops. Many chimneys have multiple flues—sometimes as many as three. For a number of good reasons, the flue liners that protrude from the brickwork are topped with either masonry or metal weather caps. These come in different shapes.

Most of the ones I see are flat metal caps with slightly downturned edges to shed water. There is no problem with these caps when there is only one flue in the chimney, but there is a potentially deadly situation when there are two or more flues capped with these types of caps. The flues are usually only a few inches apart and the caps are wider than the flues. In many cases, these caps almost touch each other and, in most cases, their legs are only a few inches high—another problem (there should be a clear space of a minimum of 10 inches between the top of the flue liners and the weather cap).

As one appliance is fired—be it a boiler, furnace or fireplace—the gases from the combustion hit the weather cap and are forced sideways. Unfortunately, the fired appliance creates a negative air pressure in the house that must be made up by outside air drawn into the house to equalize the pressure. In houses built in the pre-energy crisis of the early '70s, there are a lot of air entry points in the house and this is helpful. But in the tight houses built since then, the easiest and often only point of entry for this make-up air is another flue. So the combustion gases, con-

This chimney with the wythes separates the two flues safely.

strained by the caps, are drawn back down into the house, creating an extremely dangerous buildup of carbon monoxide gases in the house.

Another type of weather cap is shaped like a tunnel. The same dangerous situation can occur if one of these caps is installed so it faces an adjacent uncovered flue or if two or more of these caps are facing each other. I recently saw a chimney that had three of these caps lined up to form a long tunnel with very little space between each of the caps. These caps are fine and safe, but only if they are installed so that their sides are parallel to each other.

In chimneys built by experienced masons and capped by a slate or concrete cap, the flues are separated by what is called wythes—walls of bricks or stones built between each flue preventing the gases from one flue from being sucked down into another. The same should be done—in this case with metal dividers—if flat weather caps are used.

I urge you to check your chimney tops and take appropriate corrective measures if you find the conditions described above. They may save your lives or prevent the ill effects caused by the inhalation of carbon monoxide (CO). And be sure that you have functioning CO monitors in all areas of your house as recommended by health officials.

Duct coated with asbestos

Q. I am preparing to sell my house, which was built in 1952. A heating duct for the bedrooms passes through my unheated attached garage. This duct has an asbestos covering. The duct is fastened to the gypsum board or plastered ceiling, leaving three asbestos-covered sides exposed.

I am told that because of the asbestos the house will not pass inspection, but that if I cover the asbestos it will pass inspection. I thought I would cover it with fiberglass insulation batts. None of the insulation comes in a width that would wrap around the heating duct. I believe it would need to be a minimum of 35 (preferably 40) inches wide and anything up to 70 feet in length. I don't suppose that it would have to be insulation material. Can you suggest a material that I can use to cover the heating duct, and, if so where I can purchase it?

A. If you are referring to a pre-purchase building inspection for a prospective buyer, be aware that the Standards of Practice of the American Society of Home Inspectors (ASHI) do not direct inspectors to pass or fail a house inspection. If the passing or failing grade is meted out by your local authorities, that's something else entirely. But the Consumer Products Safety Commission (CPSC) and the EPA do not mandate the removal of asbestos that is in good condition. They recommend encapsulating it if it is in need of repairs, and otherwise just leaving it alone.

The simplest thing to do in your case, to ensure that there won't be any hitch with a concerned buyer, is to have a carpenter build a box around the duct. Although not needed, fiberglass insulation can be stapled in sections in the framework of the box to increase the existing insulation provided by the asbestos that was put there for that purpose.

Product improves wood-stove safety

A very effective way to reduce creosote formation—and staining—is to use ACS (Anti-Creo-Soot) daily following directions on the spray bottle. Used daily, ACS converts creosote to an inert powder instead of the corrosive and smelly liquid it is. I recommend it highly, having used it every wood-heating day in my wood stove for close to 30 years.

For the readers who are not acquainted with ACS, it is a catalytic water-borne formula that changes the chemistry of the gases generated by wood-burning and prevents the formation of the very dangerous type III, glaze creosote on the walls of chimneys that can lead to chimney fires and is very hard to get rid of.

The deposits from these gases, with regular use of ACS, will be in the form of a very light brown ash similar to that found in oil burning. It is very easy to sweep it off the chimney walls at the end of the season. And ACS, if used daily, will also change existing type III creosote into the same harmless brown ash. Chimney sweeps love it because it makes their work a lot easier.

ACS can be purchased from many chimney sweeps or stove shops, or ordered from any number of Internet stores, including www.northlineexpress.com .

Smelly oil spill

Q. The oil company providing us with fuel overfilled the underground tank. The oil went over my river rocks and got on the side of my foundation. The pipe is close to a cellar window, so every time I open it I can smell the oil. What can I do to eliminate the smell? I have already used cat litter.

A. It sounds as if your underground oil tank is not equipped with a whistle fill-vent alarm. Some oil companies will not supply fuel oil to such tanks, as it's a guessing game with potential results like those you have experienced. You should ask your fuel supplier to install such a device so you won't have a spill happen again.

As to cleaning the river rocks; how big are they? Can you move them to some safe area where they can be cleaned without penetrating into the soil? You can try to clean them and the affected area of the foundation by rubbing Speedy Dry (buy in automotive stores) on them or using Spray 9 (buy in hardware or janitorial supply stores). Then, lay them on a plastic sheet after cleaning them and place them in a sunny spot and let the sun do the job over time. To eliminate the odor, use Odor Kill spray (buy in plumbing supply houses).

Have you dealt with the contaminated soil around the spill? If not, and there isn't too much of a spill, you should dig up the contaminated soil and place it on a plastic sheet in an area out of the way as the treatment will take a long time (a year or more). Mix cow manure with the soil and cover it with another plastic sheet to keep water out of it; turn the mixture over every once in a while. Once all smell is gone out of the pile, you can use it as compost in your garden.

Removing oil from tank

Q. The heating system of the house I recently bought was changed from oil to natural gas prior to my purchasing it. After moving in, I discovered that the oil tank, left in the basement, is full of oil to the top (270 gallons). I would like to have the tank removed from the basement and, therefore, need to have the oil pumped out or drained out. How should I go about it?

A. Call heating oil dealers and ask if they will pump the oil out and remove the tank for you at no charge, the oil being their compensation.

Underground oil tank endangers water supply

Q. Our 40-year-old underground fuel tank is near our well. I worry about it leaking. Is it true that water would seep in before oil would leak out? It has been nicked twice by backhoes.

A. Water may seep in if the holes are above the oil level but, if the holes are below, oil will seep out. You can have a pressure test run by a fuel oil dealer equipped to do it, but it's expensive. It may make more sense to just have the 40-year-old tank replaced; it's probably time. Oil leaks can contaminate the aquifer for miles around, not just your well.

Safely retiring an underground oil tank

In an earlier column, I advised a reader, if he decided not to remove a no-longer-used underground oil tank, to fill it with sand—a very tedious project and one difficult to accomplish thoroughly.

Upon researching the subject further, I have become aware of a faster and more thorough system, but one which is not a do-it-yourself project. Your fuel oil dealer can direct you to a contractor who can pour a cement-sand slurry through the filler pipe. The advantage of this system is that the slurry completely fills the tank and will harden in time, whereas sand alone cannot. Therefore, when the tank eventually rusts away, settlement will be kept to a minimum.

But removal is still the best method, and may be the only one permitted in your area. Your fuel oil dealer can advise you of your options.

Oil smell can signal danger

Q. There is an oil smell coming from my 20-year-old furnace after the burner has shut off but while the fan is still running. The smell seems to be coming from the registers. The serviceman installed an outside air intake near the furnace because he said that this was caused by the flue gases being drawn down the chimney because air escaping at the top of the house was being replaced that way.

This has not cured the problem. Do you have another thought?

A. There may be cracks in the heat exchanger and this should be checked immediately, as it is dangerous. When the burner comes on, the metal heat exchanger expands and any small cracks close up. But after the burner shuts off and the fan begins to cool the exchanger down, the cracks open up again and that is when you begin to smell the fumes. Heating contractors have devices to check this out.

Bringing in fresh air for heating system

Q. I am thinking of installing a duct from the return plenum on my forced air furnace to the outside, to bring in fresh air which will be warmed and distributed through the house. It will have a damper, which can be closed on rainy or humid days—or should it have an automatic damper, if that is not too expensive?

A. It is a good idea to install a duct from the outside to the return air duct of warm air furnace in houses that have excessive humidity because they are too tight, or the occupants generate a lot of moisture, or a new high-efficiency furnace has reduced the number of air changes in the house. But it should only be a small duct—no larger than 4 inches—to avoid condensation on the inside of the furnace that would lead to rust and premature destruction.

Use a round duct; install a manual damper which should seldom, if ever, need to be closed but which will allow you to regulate the amount of fresh air and install a dryer-type wall jack outside with the flap removed or blocked open.

Install a piece of ¼-inch mesh hardware cloth over the opening outside to keep out rodents, birds, and large insects such as bumble-bees. Smaller insects will be captured by the furnace filter. Insulate the portion of this duct that is inside the building to prevent condensation and dripping on the floor.

Avoiding allergens from old ducts

Q. We are planning to have central air conditioning installed in our 40-year-old house. Our three-year-old oil-fired furnace has a humidifier system. The ducts are metal except for one plastic section. Should we be concerned about health problems, *i.e.*: bacteria, fungi, etc., since the cold air will flow through those old ducts?

A. There is no reason that I am aware of why you should have any trouble as long as you make sure that the humidifier is emptied, disinfected with household bleach, and thoroughly dried before the cooling season starts. That should be done at the end of the heating season in any case, whether there is air conditioning or not.

You may also want to have the ducts cleaned professionally to remove accumulated dirt and dust in them that could be a breeding ground for bacteria and a source of allergens.

Clearing mildew from ducts

Q. Is there a natural product that can be sprayed into the ducts of our forced-air heating system to clear any mold or mildew that might have accumulated in them? We had the system professionally cleaned about five years ago.

A. Do you have any evidence that there is mold or mildew in the ducts? If you are not using an in-furnace humidifier, there is probably little chance there is a problem. You probably have air-conditioning as well; this dehumidifies the summer's warm, moist air and should help keep the ducts dry.

I am assuming that your ducts are made of metal. The lining of fiberglass ducts is more prone to the growth of molds.

There is a product used by certified EPA applicators called Oxine that is used to disinfect ducts but its use is recommended only when there is definite evidence of a problem. It is not a do-it-yourself job. In any event, the industry recommends vacuum cleaning warm air systems' ducts every three to five years, so you may want to have that done again soon and, if you have a mold problem, that would be the time to treat the ducts.

Noisy Heating Systems

Reducing noise from return vent

Q. My townhouse has a large return duct for the air conditioning and heat in the living room. It is so noisy that it's hard to converse, and I must turn the television up to hear it. Can something be done to reduce the noise?

A. The noise can be due to equipment noise or to air noise. A qualified heating and air conditioning contractor can determine which it is and make the repairs. To correct either will probably require opening the wall that conceals the duct.

If it is equipment noise, there may not be a flex joint isolating the duct from the furnace; if it is an air noise, the duct will probably have to be changed to a larger one lined with fiberglass, and it may even need to contain some insulated baffles and elbows to bounce the sound around.

Noises from new furnace boiler

Q. We replaced our boiler three years ago. In the first year, we put up with assorted thumps, bangs and gurgles because the installer said it would take time to settle in. The same thing happened during the next heating season and a repairman performed various maintenance checks to no avail. And we've had the noises again this past heating season. The baseboards were bled, so that is not the problem. What do you suggest?

A. New boilers have very little water in them and they heat very fast, which can account for the noises that have plagued you. My expert has solved similar problems by adding a T in the feed and another one in the return, and installing another circulator between the two and wired to the burner to give more flow through the boiler. He told me that this problem is more prevalent with boilers that have an output of over 100,000 BTUs. Discuss this with your heating contractor; it may be what you need.

Steam boiler makes banging noise

Q. My house is heated with a Peerless steam boiler two-pipe system. When the boiler is cold and pushing steam, there is a bang-bang-bang noise in the pipes. What is causing this? The boiler is 12 years old.

A. There are several possibilities that come to mind if the banging occurs when the boiler starts generating steam. Here are a couple:

- The pipes may not have the right pitch. This can cause water to pool in a section of pipe. Then, when steam is generated, it pushes this water to the nearest fitting, causing the banging. Water puddles in any section of pipe will also cause steam to condense over them, which will result in a vacuum and cause the water to bang.
- The steam supply pipes may not be insulated. This will cause steam to condense and result in water hammer—the banging you hear.

There are other possibilities, so your best bet is to have an experienced steam technician inspect your system and correct the problem. Don't put it off, as water hammer can cause damage to some parts of the system.

Booming sound when gas furnace turns on

Q. I purchased a used mobile home a few years ago. During the heating season, whenever the propane gas furnace comes on, there is a loud boom. The former owner told me it was caused by a cold chimney. Is this a dangerous condition? It causes vibrations in that part of the trailer every time the gas ignites.

A. It is not a normal condition and it can be caused by the wrong orifice in the furnace, wrong gas pressure, maladjustment of the air supply to the burner, or wrong-size chimney. The latter is not likely in a manufactured home, so your heating contractor should look into the other possibilities.

Furnace fan hisses

Q. When the fan on our furnace goes on, both for heat or air conditioning, there is a slight hissing sound coming from the vents. Is this normal?

A. There are several possibilities. Was the air conditioning installed at the same time as the furnace, or is it an add-on? If an add-on, is the hissing sound dating back from that time only? It is possible that the hissing sound is caused by the slight restriction of the air flow as it goes through the air conditioning A-coil that is in the plenum above the furnace. It may be perfectly normal but, if you want to be sure, have an air-conditioning contractor check it out.

Hot air ducts expand and pop

Q. When the forced-air furnace comes on, it is accompanied by a sound from the ducts similar to the sounds heard when a house settles. It is causing me to lose sleep. The house is 40 years old and this is the original furnace. Do you have any idea why the system makes such a racket and how it can be fixed?

A. The ducts may be popping while expanding. If much of the ductwork is accessible from the basement or crawl space, your heating contractor may be able to identify the culprits and take measures to control the movement.

Air in hot-water heating system

Q. We live in a condo and have a boiler with baseboard heating units. This has been going on for a couple months. A gurgling sound occurs every time the heat comes on, then continues for several minutes. Is it something that will take care of itself or does it require having a heating person check it out?

A. You should have a heating contractor come and bleed the system.

Heating pipe turbulence

Q. I need information about heating pipe turbulence problem, night and day, in our 19-unit condo. Two new boilers were installed last fall and the expansion tank adjusted. I also understand that most of the units' owners had their zone valves replaced. The blasting continued until the end of the heating season in May.

Should the pipes be drained again? It helped one year but not the previous year. Can you further guide us?

A. If the sound of the water is a loud bang, the problem is with the zone valves. If the sound is of water swishing through the pipes, either the circulator is oversized or you need an air separator. If the sound of water through the pipes is similar to a waterfall, there is air in the system.

If your heating contractor is not able to solve this problem for you, you may want to call in a mechanical engineer. You should be able to find one in the Yellow Pages under "Engineers-Mechanical."

Finding a quiet boiler

Q. I plan to replace my 28-year-old oil-fired boiler with a new 80%-plus efficiency model. I want a quiet model because the room adjacent to the boiler could be used as a bedroom. Do you know of any boiler designed to be quiet running?

A. The Energy Kinetics System 2000 boiler is state-of-the-art and very efficient, but quietness is, after all, very personal. You could also, when finishing the bedroom, take some measures to reduce the sound transmission.

Soundproofing a furnace room

Q. Your recent discussion of soundproofing a furnace room was of special interest to me. I am remodeling my basement and would like to soundproof the injection pump, which is located in the closet of an adjoining room.

I would like more information on several terms you used. What is dense insulation made to deaden sound? What is sound-deadening board? And what are resilient channels? I would also like to put sound-deadening material in the ceiling of the basement before I enclose it with wallboard. Your suggestions, please.

A. Fiberglass manufacturers make a special type of insulation used as acoustical material that is denser than the type used for heat retention. Sound-deadening board is a fiberboard also made to absorb some sound. Resilient channels are metal channels that are fastened directly to the wall framing or through resilient board or wall finish and onto which drywall is attached.

When airborne sounds hit the wall finish, the resilient channels cause it to vibrate and thus reduce the transfer of sound to the framing and the other side of the wall. In other words, resilient channels act as shock absorbers. They should be installed in the room in which the noise is generated.

Use the same system for the ceiling as you would for the walls. You should be able to buy all these items in well-stocked building supply stores. If they are not carried in stock, they should be able to order them for you. Smaller retail building supply stores have more flexibility in special ordering than the larger stores.

Problems Caused by Modern Upgrades

Modern houses are made comfortable with far less fuel than older houses need. But ironically, modernizing sometimes brings problems. For example, old chimneys may drip condensation because modern appliances don't keep them warm, and tight houses may not provide the combustion air needed for burning fossil fuels or wood. Over the years, many readers have expressed surprise at the new problems they face, and have asked how to deal with them.

Dangers in venting new furnace through a chimney

Q. I had a new high-efficiency gas furnace installed and it is causing a problem. A great amount of moisture accumulates in the chimney flue, flows down to the bottom of the chimney and spills over onto the basement floor.

The only way I have found to eliminate this problem is to open the clean-out door at the bottom of the chimney and leave it open during the heating season. How can these two things be connected?

A. Although you were very clever in opening the clean-out door, thus introducing a lot of additional air into the chimney that helps absorb the high level of moisture contained in the fumes generated by the high-efficiency furnace, this is neither safe nor the solution to the problem.

Condensation occurs on the walls of the chimney when the highly humid and cool gases from the combustion process of high-efficiency furnaces come in contact with the cold walls of the flue liner. Less efficient furnaces had much hotter flue gases, which prevented condensation from occurring.

The best way to solve your problem is to have the furnace vented through the wall, as most of them are designed to be, instead of through a regular chimney. The instructions that came with the new furnace undoubtedly state so, and it is surprising that the installer did not know that.

The present installation is dangerous. The condensation contains corrosive chemicals that can cause deterioration of the liner and its mortar, leading to openings in the walls of the chimney through which the gases can leak into the house, spalling of bricks and mortar that can clog the very small opening of the new furnace's flue. This causes gases to flow back into the house or back flow, for whatever reason, through the open clean-out door, with the same results.

The only safe way to use an existing chimney to vent today's high-efficiency furnaces is to run the same diameter flue all the way to the top of the chimney. So why do that when it is simpler to run the vent through a wall as intended in the first place? The installer created a potentially dangerous and life-threatening condition and he should be responsible for correcting it. Once the correction is made, you may want to consider having the now unused chimney sealed with a slate or equivalent at its top to keep the elements and cold out.

Humidity increases with high-efficiency furnace

Q. Our 20-year-old house is heated with a high-efficiency gas furnace and we are beset with a high humidity problem, in the 70% range, in spite of our running a dehumidifier constantly. What can we do about it?

A. You may have noticed a considerable increase in relative humidity in the house when you switched from a standard gas furnace to the new high-efficiency type. That's because the old one created artificial infiltration by sucking in cold outside air through whatever cracks the air could find in order to replace the air the furnace sent up the chimney. This dried up your house by changing the air often.

Conversely, the new high-efficiency furnaces draw air from outside through a pipe going through the wall of the house and exhaust the same air through another pipe generally inside the first one. As a result, they do not create artificial infiltration and the air in the house is not changed every time the furnace comes on.

You should examine your home and your habits, and make changes as needed. Vent the dryer outside, don't dry clothes on indoor lines, use bathroom and kitchen fans, cover the crawl-space dirt with 6-mil plastic, grade the land away from the house, reduce the number of water-loving indoor plants, open windows on milder days to air the house, etc.

A dehumidifier is not very efficient at winter indoor temperatures, and over time uses a lot of electricity.

Dirty condensation from chimney

Q. We recently changed from oil heat to gas heat and have noticed a brownish liquid coming out of the connection of the chimney and the flue pipe and through the chimney blocks. It is now running on the concrete floor. What is happening?

A. While you were burning oil as your heating fuel, soot deposits formed on the inner walls of the chimney. Since you changed to gas and installed what is probably a high-efficiency furnace, cooler gases are sent up the chimney and are condensing on its walls. This causes the oil soot to become soggy and run down the chimney.

The contractor installing the gas furnace should have recommended that you get the chimney cleaned before using the new furnace. Have it done promptly.

You will still see condensation, although it will be cleaner. One way to eliminate the condensation problem is to have a stainless-steel liner of the proper size for the furnace installed in the chimney and special insulation poured between the original flue and the liner. This will keep the gases warmer.

Heat costs rise after AC is installed

Q. I had an air conditioning unit installed two years ago and I am very satisfied with its performance but the cost of heating in winter has risen considerably.

The compressor is in the attic where the floor is insulated with 8-inch batts. I asked the installer about closing all eight room supply vents and the large central return in winter. He said to leave them open. If I close those nine openings to prevent warm air from going into the ductwork in the attic, will this damage the compressor because the attic becomes so cold in winter?

A. Since you have noticed a considerable increase in heat costs now that the air-conditioning has been installed, it's a fair bet your diagnosis is correct; warm air rises through all the registers, gets into the air-conditioning ducts in the attic, and causes a considerable amount of heat loss, even though the ducts may be insulated, as they aren't insulated for winter conditions.

Go ahead and seal the ducts by sticking tight-fitting pieces of 2-inch rigid foam insulation into the ducts, after removing the registers. Poke some cotton or other loose material around to seal any cracks between the foam and the sheet metal.

But before you insert the insulation into the ducts, make a handle so you can remove it in the spring. Cut long strips of duct tape and stick it over the top of the insulation and down the sides, with several inches to spare, then fold the excess over itself, leaving a tab about 2-to-3 inches long for that purpose.

Don't worry about the compressor getting cold; many of them spend the winter outside. You should be a lot more comfortable and reduce your heating bills.

Keeping Temperatures Even Throughout the House

Keeping a house comfortable throughout is partly a function of the mechanical systems, so it is worth discussing here, but be sure to also check the chapter on insulation.

Ventilating attic to reduce summer heat

Q. The upstairs level of our two-story home gets very hot during the summer. I'm thinking about putting a power roof vent to remove the hot air. Would it help if I also put in a vent in the ceiling of the upper level to draw air from the living area into the attic and out the vent? I would plan to cover the hole in the ceiling with insulation during the heating season. The house has a 4-in-12-inch pitch roof and the attic has 12 inches of insulation. There are six 12×4-inch vents in the eaves.

A. Instead of installing a roof ventilator, why don't you increase the attic ventilation by means of a baffled ridge vent? You should also increase the eaves' vents and make sure that air can circulate freely between the insulation and the roof sheathing. This should cool the attic enough that you should not need the attic fan nor the hole in the ceiling. Twelve inches of insulation should be enough to keep you cool if you lower the attic's temperature. You can also use a window fan.

Heating and cooling upstairs of cape-style house

Q. I'd like to improve the cooling and heating in the upstairs bedroom of our Cape Cod house. Would a duct fan be a good solution? I'd like to wire the duct fan off the furnace/AC fan. Can the connecting wire be run inside the duct?

A. Running the wire, or anything else, through the duct represents a code violation. Cape-type houses often have the problem yours has because the heating and air conditioning system is not generally designed to handle the half story under the roof, which would have been considered to be an attic at the time of original construction. Ducts of the right size to handle delivery and return of air are not always easy to install later, when the upstairs is being finished.

Before going to the trouble of installing a new duct fan, why don't you try "constant air circulation"; turn on the furnace fan and let it run constantly during the heating and cooling seasons. These fans are designed to run all the time.

If this does not do it, consult a heating and air conditioning contractor; it may be possible to run another supply or a return duct through a closet. This is a better solution than installing a duct fan and trying to wire it to the main fan.

Better heat circulation needed upstairs

Q. The upstairs rooms of our cottage are too warm in the summer and too cold in the winter, in spite of the fact that there are ducts carrying heat and air conditioning to these rooms. Would putting small fans over the registers in these rooms move more air and make a difference? Would that affect the other rooms? Are there fans for that purpose? Where can they be purchased?

A. There are fans made to be installed inside ducts, under the registers, to increase the amount of heat delivered in rooms suffering from poor distribution of air. But it would be better to have the present system balanced, presuming, of course, that the ducts to the upstairs rooms are sized properly.

You should have a heating contractor survey the system and advise you.

Bedroom too cold in winter

Q. We are unable to use one bedroom in winter because it is too cold. Not much heat is coming out of the duct and the room feels damp. The house was built in 1962; it is built of solid masonry and it is semi-detached.

There is a chimney against the wall of this bedroom, but the fireplace in the living room below is not used. We have had the roof inspected, the furnace replaced, thermal windows installed, and attic insulation added. I don't know what to do next. Someone has suggested that it may be a ventilation problem, caused by a damp roof. Who should I call to help me with this problem?

A. I assume the bedroom is on the second floor. If the duct to this bedroom is set in the solid masonry wall, it is separated from the cold outdoors by only 4 inches of masonry. And if it is coming from the basement, by the time the air gets to the bedroom, it has cooled so much it isn't doing you much good.

Attic dampness may also be a contributing factor. Your utility company may have a service under which an expert could check the attic. If not, call in a home inspector. Then have a heating contractor check the system to see if it can be improved by adjusting dampers to direct more heat to the bedroom or, more likely, by running a new duct to it through interior spaces.

No heat from second-story baseboard

Q. My hot water heating system is 35 years old. It heats my basement and one-and-a-half story house. But there is no heat coming out of the second-floor bathroom baseboard. When I bleed it, water comes out but it won't heat.

My concern is that the feed pipes looping around the house are 1¼-inch black pipes feeding ¾-inch copper pipes to the baseboards. Is there any way I can clean and flush the system without tearing out any piping?

A. Since water comes out when you bleed the bathroom radiator, there may be blockage in the return pipe in the form of rust, perhaps, from the iron pipes. You could try to reverse-flush the system if it is so set up. Otherwise, have a plumbing and heating contractor look into the problem.

Spreading heat to a cold room

Q. We cannot get comfortable in our large living-family room. We have to have the thermostat at 74°F. to be able to sit and watch TV or read without wearing a blanket, while the rest of the house is too hot. This room has a cathedral ceiling and the house is heated with warm air. How can we correct this situation?

A. You may be able to adjust the line dampers in the ducts serving the various rooms. If you have dampers, they are controlled with a lever or wing nut either under or on the side of each duct and the direction of the levers or wing nuts should indicate the direction of the damper inside. Adjust the dampers to the ducts serving the rooms that are too hot so they are at an angle to the direction of flow of the air and open fully the damper controlling the air flow to the living room.

Another thing that would probably help a lot is the installation of a ceiling fan in the cold room. Be sure you get one that is reversible so that in winter you make the blades blow air upward, while in summer you blow air downward.

By blowing air upward, the hot air that has stratified at the ceiling level is forced downward along the walls and toward the center of the room where it is sucked back up. In short order, the room air is mixed more evenly and you will feel more comfortable. In summer, whether you have air conditioning or not, the fan should blow the air downward so that you feel the coolness of the air moving over you.

Buy a good-quality fan and install it at least 12 inches down from the ceiling but no less than 7 feet from the floor. Fans that are too close to the ceiling do not move air efficiently. You can get ceiling fans with timers to turn lights on and adjust the fan speed as room temperatures change.

Heating room over garage

Q. We have been living in a duplex townhouse (with one common wall with the neighbors and three open sides) for 13 years. In the wintertime, the room above the garage becomes so cold that we cannot use it for about six to seven months.

Recently, I changed the garage door to one with thick insulation, put a new ceiling (which is the floor of the cold room) with thick insulation in the garage, and put new windows in the cold room. This has had little effect. The garage and the room are facing the backyard. The wall facing the backyard is insulated.

A. I hope you filled the entire depth of the garage ceiling joists with insulation. If you didn't, cold may be getting between the insulation and the floor of the room above from the sides exposed to the outside. I assume that all other exterior walls are insulated, as you say the one facing the backyard is. If your repair work is well done, you may need more heat in this room. Remember, this room has more exposure to cold than the others since it has an exposed floor.

How is your house heated now? Assuming that this room has heat from the main house system, it may need to be balanced or more heat may need to be drawn from the main source. If you have warm-air heat, you should make sure that the damper to this room is fully open and that there is a cold-air return in the room. If there is not, make sure the door stays open or that there is at least 1½ inches clearance under the door for air to be drawn back to the nearest return air duct.

You may also need to have a fan installed in the ductwork to draw more heat from the main. If your heat is forced-water (a hydronic system), you may need to add more radiation. As a last resort, and if the house uses gas, you could consider a separate heater such as a Rinnai, vented outside.

Constant air circulation aids cooling

Q. When using central air conditioning, is it more economical and/or beneficial to run the fan continuously while waiting for the compressor to kick in? As cold air descends, I think it would be better to circulate the cold air, thereby not causing so much demand on the compressor. Am I thinking right?

A. It is best to run the fan constantly to keep the air in the rooms more even. As you stated, cold air drops to the floor and warm air rises to the ceiling. Constant Air Circulation (CAC), as it is known, is best for comfort.

Furnace ducts in cold crawl space

Q. My father just bought a brand-new ranch house built over a crawl space. The furnace is in the kitchen and that side of the house is perfectly toasty. But, by the time the hot air goes through the ducts in the cold crawl space, the air is cooled considerably and the bedrooms are always chilly, no matter how high he turns the thermostat up. What's the best solution to this problem?

A. Have a heating contractor insulate the ducts in the crawl space with insulation designed for the purpose.

Since the house is new, the builder and his or her heating sub-contractor should get this deficiency corrected at no cost to your father. This problem should not exist in a new house; they should have used insulated ducts, in the first place. Fortunately, insulation can be retrofitted to the exterior of the ducts. But if they used insulated ducts, then the system needs balancing.

Options for Upgrading Heating Systems

Comparing oil- and gas-fired systems

Over the years, many readers have asked for advice on upgrading to various boilers and furnaces. They have usually narrowed their searches to three or four brands or models. For the purpose of this book, it seems more appropriate to generalize a bit, listing some of the considerations in making the choice.

- At the risk of stating the obvious, the more efficient the system, the less you'll spend on fuel and the less negative impact you'll have on the planet. Most new furnaces and boilers have efficiency ratings of between 80 and 95%, while many older systems are in the 50% range. Therefore, upgrading to a new system will almost inherently lead to significant fuel savings.
- The efficiency ratings (officially called Annual Fuel Utilization Efficiency, or AFUE) should be in the product literature or the manufacturer's Web site. You may also find the information on the Web site of the Gas Appliance Manufacturers Association (GAMA) Web site at www.gamanet.org. (The specific Web pages change, but you should find the ratings by first clicking on Consumer Information.) Other useful information is provided by the American Council for an Energy Efficient Economy (ACEEE), at www.aceee.org.
- As a practical matter, most people must balance energy efficiency with cost. If a more efficient model is significantly more expensive, will the fuel savings be enough to pay back the difference over time? If so, how many years will it take to recover the extra investment? Be sure to take all costs into consideration, including purchase price, cost of installation, additional equipment that may be needed (Will the new system require a new expansion tank?), projected maintenance costs, and any tax benefits for energy efficiency. If you are discussing this with a qualified and honest heating contractor, he or she will help in making these comparisons.
- In computing savings, keep in mind that as efficiency increases, the amount of savings between the higher and lower efficiency models diminishes. An easy comparison would be with miles per gallon of various automobiles. You would use 5 gallons of gas to travel 100 miles in a car that gets 20 MPG, but only 3⅓ gallons in a car that gets 30 MPG—a saving of 1⅔ gallons. But you would only save an additional 83% of one gallon if you drove a car that gets 40 miles per gallon, which would only burn 2½ gallons per 100 miles, and only half a gallon more if your car got 50 miles per gallon. It's the law of diminishing returns, which applies equally to furnaces and boilers. The difference between 50% and 80% efficiency is very significant, but boosting efficiency to 90% may yield smaller savings than you would expect.

- Also keep in mind that improving the energy efficiency of the house may have a greater effect on fuel savings than replacement of the furnace or boiler. If you have an inefficient old house, then improving insulation and reducing drafts may be the most important steps to take. This will also allow you to get by with a smaller (and less expensive) heating plant.

Fuel choices when updating a heating system

Q. Our house is two stories and 60-something years old. It is not well insulated. Our only source of heat comes from two wood stoves—one is airtight and the other not—and a couple of oil-filled space heaters. We are tired of being pioneers and want to get a good furnace.

Since there is no natural gas line on our road, we are limited to oil, propane gas, or electricity. We are going to keep our two wood stoves but do not want to rely on them for our main source of heat. What is the best and most efficient type of heat, and can we add air conditioning to it later?

A. Join the crowd of the tired pioneers! There nothing like heat coming on at the turn of a thermostat. Although electricity is very flexible and convenient, it should be dismissed as too expensive. Besides, we should all try to reduce our demand on this source of energy to put off as long as possible the need for new plants.

The choice between oil or propane depends largely on what is the most available in your area. Oil furnaces require yearly maintenance for efficiency, while gas furnaces should receive yearly safety checks. Air conditioning can be added to a furnace anytime.

However, the single best thing you could do is to increase the level of insulation. This would allow you to get by with a smaller and less expensive heating plant, and also insulate you to some extent from the fluctuation in oil or gas prices.

Moving up to radiant and baseboard heat

Q. I have been looking for information on getting off of wood heat. I have an old farmhouse built between 1840 and 1900. I have done a lot of insulating and window replacement, removing the old plaster and replacing it with fiberglass, plastic sheet and wallboard. Many of the windows are double-glazed and have inside storms of Plexiglas sealed to the frames, as well as outside aluminum storms.

The basement has walking room and a crawl space, and separate areas that need special attention. I have a Sears forced-air gas furnace that hasn't been used in almost 15 years. I use about five cords of wood a year. I have been considering a combination of underfloor radiant heat in the kitchen, where most activity takes place, and baseboard for the rest of the downstairs, letting the upstairs get warm as it does now, from downstairs heat rising.

A California company offers a radiant heat package for $4,600 with complete instructions for the capable do-it-yourselfer. Are there options in the Eastern part of the country, where I live?

The next question is fuel. I hear that oil and propane are from the same source and that their prices fluctuate in unison, and that oil is less desirable due to noise and smell. I need to vent from the side since there is no good place for a chimney. Is it good to stick to propane?

A. There are a number of heating contractors who install radiant floor heating systems. Check your Yellow Pages under Heating Contractors; you should find block ads within that category. Call around to get two or three estimates. You may be all right getting a complete package from some faraway company and installing it yourself, but what happens if you need service and adjustments?

Keep in mind that radiant floors must have a much lower temperature than baseboards, so proper zoning of various heating areas of the house is critical. You may also want to consider having baseboard heat installed upstairs. It might be okay for you not to have upstairs heat and rely on warm air rising, but this may be a serious drawback if and when you sell the house. Propane gas (or LP, for "liquid propane") is made from petroleum, so oil and propane prices have a tendency to follow each other. Oil is more efficient, giving off more BTUHs than LP gas, but it does require more frequent servicing and is somewhat dirtier.

Wood and pellet stoves

Q. With home heating oil prices going through the roof, we're considering a wood stove or a pellet stove, which we would run in addition to our forced-air system. Is this a reasonable idea? How much work and maintenance do these stoves require? Will they make a dent in our fuel bills?

A. Air-tight wood stoves and pellet stoves are very efficient ways of heating large open spaces. Many people enjoy the comfort of radiant heat from a burning fire, as well as the aesthetics.

There are drawbacks to heating with firewood, depending on your situation. Handling firewood can be tedious and messy, and dry wood can be quite expensive unless you cut your own. A wood stove requires timely feeding several times a day to maintain an even temperature, although that may not be a problem if it is used to supplement another heating system. Unless the wood is dry and the fire is handled by an experienced person, it can generate a lot of corrosive and foul-smelling creosote. The chimney should be swept professionally at least once a season. You should use the catalytic spray ACS on a daily basis to prevent creosote build-up in the chimney, which could lead to a dangerous chimney fire.

Pellet stoves are much easier to use; you just buy the pellets, assuming they are readily available in your area, and feed them into the mechanism that feeds the stove. Pellet stoves do not need a chimney (as wood stoves do) although they can use an existing one. They can be vented through a wall, like modern boilers and furnaces. They do not create creosote or generate water vapor. They do need to be plugged into an electric outlet but can also be equipped with a back-up marine battery in case of power failure. They have thermostatic controls and operate much like a regular heating system, with no need to fill them several times a day. They are clean and easy to feed.

But anyone considering wood or pellet stoves should work out the cost. A good quality stove costs $1,000 and up (some sell for less). Installation adds to this; wood stoves need a properly-sized lined chimney. Dry wood sells for $200 a cord and up, depending on your location. Pellets, bought in summer when they are cheapest, sell for $200 to $275 a ton (50 bags, 40 lbs each) plus delivery. Consumption will depend on the energy efficiency of the house and the climate. On average, one ton of pellets will last 50 days (one bag per day).

Compare this with the cost of oil for the season and figure out how many years it will take to come out even and begin to save on fuel. And there is also the convenience factor to consider.

Don't convert wood stove to gas

Q. I'd like to install a liquid propane gas log system in a Vermont Castings wood stove I own. Upon inquiring in a fireplace shop, I was told that I shouldn't, because cast-iron stoves have inadequate flue capabilities for gas logs, creating a carbon monoxide hazard.

However, my house is heated with a large LPG heater that has a smaller vent than the stove, so I can't help but wonder whether I have been properly informed.

A. Vermont Castings says no gas equipment is approved for its older wood stoves. The burning and venting systems are radically different. Guaranteed adequate air intake and a non-convoluted flue gas path are essential.

Gas fireplaces as heat source

Q. We have received advertisements for gas fireplaces/stoves with our gas bill. What can you tell us about them? Are they a reasonable replacement for wood stoves cost-wise? Can we install one ourselves?

A. Gas-fired fireplaces with ceramic logs do have high BTU outputs that rival some wood stoves, and they are much cleaner. Their cost is high but so is the cost of good-quality wood stoves. (Choose one that is designed for efficient heating, rather than one that is designed mainly for aesthetics.)

There are models for either propane or natural gas. You can install one yourself but the gas line must be checked by the gas company prior to operation.

Adding humidifier to furnace

Q. I recently bought a condominium with central heat and air-conditioning. Our winters are very dry and I would like to connect a humidifier to my furnace, which is hanging under the ceiling of the storage room. Can this be done?

A. If there is access to the plenum, it should be possible to install a humidifier, but be sure that it is of the evaporative type and not one spraying mist.

Heating and AC-Related Repairs

Welding a crack in a cast-iron stove

Q. My beautiful old cast iron parlor stove has a crack in it and I have been told that I should not use it as carbon monoxide could exude from the crack. Is there any way this can be fixed at a reasonable cost?

A. Cast iron can be welded but a new crack can develop next to the weld. The cost depends on the accessibility of the area to be repaired and its size and shape. The cost would range from $50 to over $100.

   You may be able to fix it temporarily with Rutland Stove Cement or a black silicate stove and fireplace repair caulking. Either one should be available at your hardware store.

Hot baseboards crack plaster

Q. Our house is heated with hot water baseboards that are built into the plaster walls. After patching and painting a room, the heat from the baseboards causes severe cracking around them, where they meet the plaster. I have tried a variety of fillers but nothing has worked. Can you suggest a solution?

A. The best solution would be to cut the plaster back and to install a metal bead that would stand about ⅛ to ¼ inch away from the plaster, leaving a shadow line around the baseboards. This would entail repairs to the plaster, but you would be done once and for all.

Radiant heat causes slab to crack and shift

Q. Our 30-year-old house has copper heat pipes in the concrete slab of the first floor. About 15 years ago, a crack appeared in the floor, and several years ago, branch cracks started to appear. A white, gritty material comes up through the tile floor. I removed the tiles, chiseled out the cracks, and used various hardware-store materials to repair the cracks, but the tiles still heave and white stuff still comes to the surface. How can I fill these cracks to prevent recurrence?

A. Your problem may be caused by water that is too hot. The boiler should be set at a maximum of 140°F. Otherwise the concrete expands too much and cracks. Another possibility is a chemical reaction between the copper pipes and the concrete; this is more serious. The gritty stuff is probably powdering cement.

   Once the cause has been determined and addressed, you might be able to patch the cracks with Thorocrete or a similar product.

Constant buildup of air in baseboards

Q. I am having trouble with my gas-fired boiler but as a widow on Social Security I can't afford to hire an expert. When I turn the thermostat up in the morning, two of the convectors don't heat until I bleed them of air. Some days I have to do this two or three times. What would cause this problem?

A. Your system suffers from one or more problems that are not for the do-it-yourselfer to fix. Air is getting in somewhere, and the place must be found and corrective action taken. Your boiler may not have enough pressure to run properly. It should be 12 to 15 pounds when cold and 20 to 24 pounds when running. The fast-fill valve may be clogged. There may be a problem with the expansion tank.

You should have a competent heating contractor check the system out unless you want to continue bleeding the baseboards every day. Check with your utility providers (gas and electric) for any assistance that may be available to you either through them or your county or state.

Gas furnace smells awful when first turned on for season

Q. Our warm-air furnace was converted from oil to gas. When we first turn it on in the fall, after being off all summer, there is a really bad smell. We put in a new filter and clean the registers and cold-air returns, but it still smells awful. The smell disappears or is very minimal after a couple of days. What can we do about it?

A. All heating appliances exude an unpleasant smell after being idle for an extended time; the dust that has accumulated in or on them is being burned off.

However, you should have the gas company check the heat exchanger; it may be cracked and be responsible for the remaining minimal smell you mention. A cracked heat exchanger can allow exhaust gases to be sucked out of the combustion chamber into the furnace casing, to be mixed with the circulating air from the house. This can be a dangerous situation.

The gas company's serviceman should also check the entire system for safety, including checking to see that there is no return in the furnace area without a supply duct. If there is, the possibility exists for back drafting—in other words, the combustion gases are sucked out of the furnace and mixed with the house air instead of going up the flue.

I presume that at the time of the conversion, you were advised to have the chimney cleaned professionally. Oil deposits on the chimney walls can be desiccated or become soggy, depending on the moisture contents of the gases of the new system. Either way, these deposits may block the thimble into which the furnace flue is connected to the chimney and cause a back-up of combustion gases into the house through the atmospheric damper. This can be deadly. If it hasn't been done, have it done right away.

In any case, it is always advisable to have a heating appliance checked yearly, before the new heating season, by qualified service personnel.

Pipes leak when boiler is turned off

Q. My house is heated by an oil-fired boiler. Although it can also supply domestic hot water, I am not using this feature and have an electric water heater.

During warm weather, I would like to shut off the boiler to save fuel. However, shutting it off causes contraction of pipes and joints and eventually the latter start leaking. Repairs are costly. What is the solution?

A. The pipe joints should not leak regardless of the temperature of the water in the boiler; if they do, this is a fault that needs to be repaired once and for all.

However, the gasket around the tankless coil can, and frequently does, leak because the bolts are not often tightened by service personnel at the time of yearly tune-ups, as they should be. After a while, they are so corroded that they can break if attempts are made to tighten them, so the owner faces an expensive job.

Rust precipitates from water in furnace coil

Q. Our home is heated by an oil-fired hot water system and our domestic water is generated through a coil in the furnace. Frequently, after the hot water hasn't been used for several hours, we get some discoloration in the hot water only.

It seems to come from water that has been sitting in the coil. When hot water is first turned on, it is fine, but when the water gets hot, it is a rusty color for a short period of time. As soon as it is flushed from the system, it's fine again. This happens at all the sinks in the house.

I have been assured by the company that maintains our furnace that there is no black iron anywhere in the furnace and that all water lines in the house are copper. We are on a municipal water system. Do you know of any place where I might get the water tested to find out what this discoloration is?

A. Any iron in solution in the water that sits in the boiler's coil for several hours at the very high temperature the boiler requires to heat the house will precipitate. That is what you see as soon as the water in the coil reaches the various sinks.

Water in a separate water heater is only heated to 120°F to 140°F. The water standing in the coil for an extended period of time is heated to 180°F.

There isn't much you can do except install a filter to remove the iron from the water supply. Is it worth it? This small amount of precipitated iron is not considered a health hazard. You actually ingest it every time you drink the water.

If you want to get the water analyzed, call your state health department or look in your Yellow Pages under "Water Analysis," "Laboratories-Testing" or "Water Softening & Conditioning Equip., Svce. & Supls.."

Furnace pilot keeps going out

Q. The furnace in my townhouse is seven years old. Two years ago, I had the thermocouple replaced because the pilot kept going out. Everything was fine until this past October, when the pilot went out again but, this time, I could not relight it. I had to replace the gas valve, after which I was able to relight the pilot, but I still have a problem with it going out. Every couple of weeks, I either wake up or come home to a cold house and I have to relight the pilot. This is a nuisance.

There does not appear to be a down-draft in my furnace, so what could be the cause? Is it possible that the thermocouple is defective?

A. It is always possible that a brand new part proves to be defective, but it is more likely, from your lengthy experience, that the problem is with the pilot orifice. A pilot light needs to be strong and actually give out a "shhhhh" sound. Perhaps your pilot light is too weak and the orifice needs to be cleaned or reamed out.

However, when the service person comes to clean out the orifice, you should ask him or her to test the thermocouple as well. A specific reading should be between 8 and 25 millivolts. If the reading is lower than 8 and the orifice clean, the thermocouple should be replaced. If the reading starts out okay but fades, there could be too much heat on the cold juncture, drawing down the millivoltage.

Other things to check out include restrictions in the venting, not enough make-up air for proper combustion, and a cold external chimney without a metal liner, causing the flue blockage switch to activate.

Repairing or replacing oil tank

Q. I have been told that oil tanks should be replaced after 15 years due to possible leakage. Mine is 22 years old and in my basement. Please advise.

A. Who told you? There are many oil tanks that are twice as old as yours and doing fine. Moreover, a leak would develop slowly and you would notice oil dripping on the floor. Oil tanks that develop leaks can also be repaired; pin-hole leaks can be fixed with a magnetic device that holds a rubber-like gasket under compression over the hole. Multiple leaks or larger ones can be fixed by putting a stainless steel bottom on the exterior of the tank.

Your oil dealer should be able to perform these repairs if and when they become necessary—unless he or she is the one trying to sell you a new tank.

System Maintenance

Frequency of furnace cleaning

Q. Please settle a dispute between us. One of us thinks the furnace should be cleaned every year at the end of the season, while the other thinks that every other year is frequent enough for cleaning.

A. The important question is what is the source of heat? If you have a furnace or boiler that is oil-fired, it should be cleaned and serviced every year as the build-up of soot in the system can reduce its efficiency considerably.

If the furnace or boiler is gas-fired (whether natural gas or propane), there should be no loss of efficiency from year to year and no need for servicing except that the American Gas Association (AGA) recommends a yearly safety check.

Maintenance of steam boiler

Q. We recently installed a new cast-iron steam boiler. What is the proper maintenance during the summer shut-down for prevention of rust and scale buildup?

A. In a properly designed and installed system, the only maintenance that needs to be performed by the homeowner is to flush the water feeder valve once a month or so, to keep the float from getting stuck by the deposits of the minerals in the water inside the boiler. Do so by opening the valve so a little water is flushed through the blow-off.

If your boiler is oil-fired, it should be serviced yearly by competent personnel to assure efficient combustion and remove any soot build-up on the heat exchanger. Gas-fired systems do not need servicing, but yearly safety checks are recommended.

Removal of filter from air conditioner

Q. My husband removed our air conditioner's filter. Is this a health hazard?

A. Not really. The same air still flows through the filter. It just means your house will get dirty faster. Filters must be kept clean, if of the reusable type, or they should be replaced when dirty, if of the disposable type. Failure to do so makes the fan work harder with poorer results.

Wasps nest in gas fireplace

Q. We have a gas fireplace in our family room, and wasps have taken up residence in it. When the weather warms up, they start coming into the house via the fireplace. Do you have any advice on how to get rid of them?

A. You have a potentially dangerous situation. Have a service technician clear the vent of any nests. Even though the wasps are gone by winter, their nest may cause an obstruction that could create a backup of gases and even cause an explosion.

As long as you use the fireplace in the spring when wasps become active again, they won't try to build a nest in the vent. But as soon as you stop using the fireplace you should cover the vent outside with whatever will work: a plastic bag, a metal or wood box, etc. Just don't forget to remove it in the fall before using the fireplace.

Stacking firewood

Q. Several months ago we read an article warning against piling cut logs on one's property. A neighbor just did this very thing and I am concerned about what it will do as it is close to my lot. Is it because rats or other animals congregate in them?

A. I can't imagine why it would be considered unsafe to stack firewood on one's property. I do not recommend stacking wood against the house unless you stack the logs on wood runners that rest on concrete blocks directly under an eave wide enough to protect them from water, and you plan to use them that winter.

For longer-term storage, they should be set away from buildings, off the ground, as described above, and a piece of plastic or other covering placed over the top of the pile only—not over the sides, as it is important to let air circulate through the wood to dry it. Termites, carpenter ants, and other bugs are a potential problem, but not if the wood doesn't stay there too long.

Changing the type of coal used

Q. Will I create a problem by substituting stove-size coal for the recommended chestnut coal in a Gold Magic Monticello coal-burner? The stove has a deep, cylindrical, fire-brick-lined chamber that holds about 60 pounds of coal. It has a round shaker grate. A large bottom draft controls air for primary combustion, and a secondary air control on the loading door introduces air above the burning coal.

A. Since you have a shaker grate, there is no harm in switching to stove coal; if you had a rocker grate, it would definitely not be recommended, as pieces of unburned coal can get trapped in the rocker grate and damage or even break it.

That said, why would you want to use stove coal instead of the recommended nut coal? They cost the same and, given the proper combustion conditions, give out the same amount of heat—except that stove coal has more impurities (such as pieces of rock) since it hasn't been fractured as much. Because of stove coal's much larger size, it requires a very hot fire to ignite it and a lot of air to maintain its combustion. Lacking this, it does not provide the same amount of heat output per weight. Is someone offering to give you some stove coal for free?

Closing Down a House for the Winter

Precautions for being away in the winter

Q. I plan to be away this winter and need to know the best way to winterize the house. I do have someone who will check the house frequently, and I can shut off the water at the main valve. I can also leave some heat on but what if it fails? What temperature would be best? How do I drain water from the pipes without calling a plumber, which is costly?

A. The cost of having a plumber winterize your house is only a fraction of the cost of repairs if you forget anything. Shutting off the main valve does not protect the pipe on the street side of the valve. Water must be shut off at the street.

There are a number of places where water may not drain out of concealed pipes that do not slant toward the lowest point. The washer and dishwasher also need to be cleared of water that remains in certain sections of their inner workings. A qualified plumber will drain water out of the pipes and blow them out. If you have a boiler, it also needs to be winterized. The plumber will put anti-freeze in it.

Your safest bet is to keep a minimum of heat—the lowest setting on your thermostat. That would probably be 55°F. on an older thermostats or 45°F. on a newer one. Your house checker should make a point of going to the house immediately after any power interruption to make sure the furnace or boiler does come on without the need to push a reset button. Have all of this figured out and written down as instructions before leaving.

Safety tips while away from home

Q. We'll be away traveling in January and February and would like to close the house down. Can you advise us on thermostat setting, light timers and whether we should leave the draperies open or close them up. Any other suggestions?

A. Leave the thermostat at 45–55°F, and open doors to vanities and the kitchen sink so heat can get to the pipes. Install timers on a couple of lights and a radio and set them on the random setting so they come on at different times every day. Notify your local police department; leave a key with a trusted neighbor or friend and ask them to check on the house every other day or so. Stop newspaper deliveries. Don't keep garbage cans out where someone can see that they are not being used. If your mail is delivered, have someone pick it up daily, or rent a box at the post office and file a temporary change of address. Ask your local police for additional suggestions and whether it's a good practice in your neighborhood to leave the shades open or closed, or, better yet, have someone change them frequently.

Alarm systems for a cold house

Q. You mentioned a warning light that flashes when the temperature goes below a certain level and also a phone-activated one. Where can I purchase such devices?

A. The Freez-Warn is a light that flashes red if the temperature drops below 45°F (7° Celsius). A similar device, priced at only $13 to $20, is the Honeywell Winter Watchman. Another type of alarm, called Freeze Alarm, rings a selected telephone number when the temperature drops below 45°F. This is more costly—with models ranging from $110 to $375—but helpful if you don't have anyone you can rely on to watch for a light as they drive by.

Cold-Weather Problems

Outside faucet freezes

Q. The outside faucet in my old farm house freezes when the temperature gets below 20°F. Not only can't I get water from time to time as I need it to clean a compost pail but I am concerned that, when the temperature gets much lower, the pipe will burst. Do you have any suggestion on how to solve this problem?

A. You can buy a foam faucet cover from some hardware stores or big box stores. Manco, Inc.'s Duck brand Foam Faucet Covers are available at Wal-Mart for about $6.00. They look like a bell with a long metal stem going through the top of the bell and terminating with a hook inside the bell. The hook is put around the spout of the faucet and the bell is brought tight to the siding by screwing the wing nut on the outside of the bell. Don't tighten too much or you'll damage the bell.

You may also want to insulate parts of any exposed pipes if they are accessible in your cellar. You will find Duck Brand self-adhesive aluminum foil-covered pipe wrap that is easy to install in the same stores. It's easier to use than foam sleeves if there are short sections of pipe with several bends as often found in old houses.

Or consider replacing the faucet with a deep-wall spout. This shuts off the water inside the wall before it can reach the outside wall. You may have to make some minor plumbing adjustments to mount the faucet or call a plumber to do it.

Frozen AC causes furnace room to flood

Q. We have been living in a townhouse for the last 20 years. Recently, once a week, we have had a flood in the laundry room. Our furnace and air conditioning unit are in this room. The flood is not caused by the washer or the water tank.

A. Based on the sketch you sent me, and considering that the dampening sleeve between the plenum and the duct work is always wet, and that the leak occurs at the base of the furnace, I suggest you call your air conditioning service people. It sounds as if the A-coil of the air conditioner is frozen with ice.

Protecting central AC units in winter

Q. Should the outside unit of a central air-conditioner be covered or not in winter?

A. These units are designed to take the weather and should not be covered. They need to be properly ventilated in order to prevent corrosion. In snow country, if they are exposed to snow fall, you may want to put a piece of plywood over the top, but the sides need to be left open.

Saving Energy

Note: Energy issues are also covered earlier in this chapter, in the section on upgrading of heating systems, and in the separate chapter on insulation.

Turning air conditioner on and off

Q. My question is in regard to establishing a setting for the air conditioner. I don't prefer to use AC unless it is very uncomfortable. I always just shut it off, but was recently informed that it is not a good idea and it should be set higher. It makes sense to me because during the winter, one doesn't shut the heat off and on, but just utilizes the thermostat. I understand it has something to do with the compressor.

A. The simplest thing to do is set the AC thermostat high enough that it only comes on when the outside temperature is so uncomfortable that you would turn it on anyway. However, I see no problem at having it off until you need it. It remains idle during most of the year anyway.

Turning water heater on and off to save money

Q. My oil-fired boiler is very old and it provides me with domestic hot water by means of coils inside it. As I now live alone on a very limited income, I would like to know if it harms the boiler to turn it off and just turn it on once a day to heat water to shower and do the dishes.

A. Technically it should not harm the boiler. (I presume you plan to shut it off by means of the red emergency switch and only during the non-heating season.)

However, practically, you may not save much, if anything. Old boilers contain a lot of water. Heating water once a day to warm the domestic water coil and then letting the boiler cool down may use as much energy, in the long run, as letting the boiler maintain the desired water temperature around the clock.

You may also find it very inconvenient to wait the length of time necessary to have the water hot enough to use for showering and washing dishes. One way to save energy, though, is to reduce the setting on the aquastat that controls the temperature of the domestic hot water.

Timed thermostats

Q. I have electric baseboard heat in my well-insulated house. I find it inconvenient to have to reset the thermostats in every room at night and to have to get up to a cool house in the morning. Is there a solution?

A. Have an electrician install the Sunne Electronic Time/Temperature Programmer. It will allow you to set your thermostats at one temperature and select the times you want the heat on or off. And if you are on a peak/off peak rate have the programmer turn on the heat one hour before morning peak period and off just before peak comes on. You can program it to do that several times a day.

Dark radiators give more heat

Q. Will painting metal radiators black increase their heat output? Will there be such benefits if the radiators are already covered with white or pink latex wall paint and subsequently painted over with black paint?

A. The darker the color, the more heat radiators will give out, but the difference is slight between black and other dark colors. You can paint radiators already painted a light color with a dark paint and get the benefits of the greater heat output.

The only type of paint that has a negative effect on the heat output of radiators is a metallic paint. So stay away from aluminum or any other paint with metallic properties. These actually reduce the efficiency of radiators radically; they should be avoided. But you may paint the radiators with a dark green, brown, blue, red or whatever color strikes your fancy or fit the room decor with very good results; the radiators do not have to be painted black to be efficient.

Reflecting heat from back of radiators

Q. Would it make sense and be safe to put aluminum foil against the walls in back of my radiators to reflect the heat into the rooms instead of heating the walls?

A. Yes to both questions but consider using rigid aluminum sheets instead. Not only would they be a lot easier to insert but you could also easily remove them periodically to clean them—a necessity for them to remain efficient.

Turning heat down and running ceiling fans

Q. We keep the thermostat at 68°F. in the daytime and 62°F. at night in our well-insulated home. There is a 20-foot high peaked ceiling in the great room with a ceiling fan. Our house is heated with forced air.

I read somewhere recently that too great a differential in temperature settings is self-defeating because of the energy required to achieve the daytime temperature. Is this correct and, also, should the fan be running day and night?

A. All the information I have is that lowering the thermostat for a consecutive period of eight hours will reduce your heating costs by 2% per degree F. The fan should be run all the time in a room with such a high ceiling to prevent stratification of the heated air where it does no good. The fan blades should move the air upward in winter to circulate the air against the walls and downward in summer to make you feel cooler.

Saving on utilities in unoccupied apartment

Q. We own a two-family house, and because we are seniors and want peace and quiet, we are thinking of no longer renting the upper floor. Should we leave the electricity and the gas furnace on? We don't want to spend too much money on the utilities since we won't be collecting rent, but don't want to ruin the flat either.

A. The electric meter doesn't run unless you use electricity, but may have a monthly meter charge if there is a separate meter for the apartment.

If there is a separate gas furnace for the upstairs apartment, you should leave it running and set the thermostat to 40° or so. If the thermostat doesn't go that low, (many old ones don't), ask your gas company to tell you whether it's worth changing it. (Would you recoup its costs in gas saved over a short period of time?)

Since there is probably no insulation in the ceiling between the first and second floor, heat from below will keep the apartment warm enough on most days so that the upstairs furnace won't need to come on except on very cold nights to keep pipes from freezing.

Have you thought of renting the apartment for a reasonable price to a working couple or a nurse who is out all day? You may be able to receive income and not have the burden of utility costs with a very quiet tenant who is seldom there.

Insulating heating ducts

Q. With the increase in the price of heating oil, I am looking for ways to reduce costs. I have turned the thermostat down and installed a programmable thermostat. Next, I would like to insulate the metal heating ducts in my basement and attic to reduce the loss of heat from the hot air that travels through them. Some of the ducts are round and others are rectangular and all are easily accessed. What is the best way to insulate them?

A. The best way to insulate the ducts in the basement is to buy duct insulation from a heating contractor or supplier or to have a contractor do the job. Keep in mind that in doing so, you will reduce the temperature in the basement, and the first floor may feel a little cooler. Also, consider what activities are frequently carried out in the basement; will you need additional heat at these times?

To insulate the ducts in the attic (a bad place for them), regular duct insulation is not going to be enough. If they are lying directly on the floor joists, and if there are many, it may be best to have cellulose insulation blown over the existing insulation (to improve the R-factor of the ceiling), making sure that at least a foot of insulation covers the ducts. But if there are few, you may want to snuggle fiberglass batts of the same thickness as the thickness or diameter of the ducts on each side of them and cover them with R-38 (12 inches thick) batts. Just be sure that there are no empty spaces around the ducts for air movement.

Aesthetic Issues

Refinishing radiant-heat slab with wood flooring

Q. Our Levittown ranch is heated by means of a radiant floor. The concrete slab is covered with ugly brown asphalt tiles, over which there is carpeting.

The carpeting has discolored from the radiant heat and we would like to replace it with wooden tiles as a sister-in-law has successfully done. We have been warned that the tiles may crack. Can you recommend it and can you give us the name of a manufacturer that would guarantee the tiles would hold up?

A. A technician for Bruce Hardwood Floors, the country's largest hardwood floor manufacturer, tells me that it can be done successfully, and faxed me their installation instructions. They only recommend the use of laminated parquet or plank products, and never solid hardwood flooring. The instructions are not difficult to follow but there is a kicker: the asphalt tiles must be removed and so must a good part of the adhesive used to install them.

Considering that you must assume that the existing tiles and the adhesive contain asbestos, their removal and disposal must be done by trained professionals.

Bonding tiles to hot chimney

Q. I have made a 4×8-foot mural-relief out of stoneware clay to cover an indoor cement-block chimney. Is there a product that would successfully bond the tiles to the chimney which may get up to 150°F?

A. The best adhesive I could think of is Sikaflex-1a. Their technical services assured me it is good up to 167°F. Apply a bead from all sides and in an X in the center. Press heavily in place. Leave ¼-inch space around each tile to allow for expansion. Get it from masonry and waterproofing supply houses.

Radiator covers

Q. Do you know where I can get radiator covers?

A. One source is ARSCO Manufacturing Co. 3330 East Kemper Road, Cincinnati, Ohio 45241, telephone 1-800-543-7040, www.arscomfg.com.

Replacing registers

Q. I have just bought an old house with a lot of charm but there is one thing that is out of character: the heat registers are cheap looking, flimsy and too modern.

Where can I get the handsome old fashioned cast-iron registers that would really fit in this house?

A. Reggio Register Co. offers registers in cast iron, porcelain enamel finishes, wood, aluminum and brass. Check www.reggioregister.com.

Removing rust from cast-iron stove

Q. How can I clean the rust off the top of our cast iron stove?

A. If the top is smooth, use fine steel wool. If it has an orange-peel texture, use one of the liquid rust removers available in hardware stores.

Chimneys

See Chapter 2—Roofs and Siding—for information on proper flashing around chimneys and related outdoor maintenance issues. Also, see the warnings about the dangers of improper chimney caps earlier in this chapter, under the heading Health and Safety.

Oil furnace filling chimney with soot

Q. Our chimney has not been cleaned for several years. It vents our oil-fired furnace. Soot blows out of the damper and is also found on top of the gas water heater. Would vacuuming or brushing be best? The clean-out at the bottom of the chimney is filled. Is it all soot or is some of it sand?

A. The only way to tell if sand is mixed with the soot is to look at it closely and feel it between your fingers. The presence of sand is possible only if the chimney is not lined.

It is very dangerous to let deposits of any kind accumulate in the bottom of a chimney as it could build up to partially or completely clog the vent pipe, forcing exhaust gases back into the house through the barometric damper of the furnace and the draft hood of the water heater.

The fact that you have soot blowing out of the barometric damper now and that it collects on top of the water heater is a good indication that there is some occlusion of the flue, either where the furnace pipe connects to the chimney or higher up within the chimney because of an accumulation of soot on its walls.

Have the chimney professionally cleaned immediately by a competent chimney sweep, preferably a member of the National or State Chimney Sweep Guild.

Fireplace smoke is sucked down furnace flue

Q. On certain days, depending on the wind direction, I smell smoke from my living-room fireplace in the basement, most noticeably around the furnace and water heater flue. This leads me to believe that the smoke from the fireplace flue is being sucked down the furnace flue. The chimneys do not have caps and they are both cleaned every year. Any suggestions?

A. Your diagnosis is correct. The easiest way for air going up one chimney to be replaced is through another chimney.

Have a directional cap installed over the fireplace flue, with the through-opening at right angle to the axis of the two flues. Or have a full cap with dividers, called a wythes, separating all flues. The clearance between the top of the flues and the bottom of the cap must be a minimum of 8 inches.

Capping chimney to prevent smoke re-circulation

Q. We have two fireplaces—one in our first-floor family room and the other in the basement. Both flues are in the same chimney and capped to keep wildlife out. When we use the first-floor fireplace, a strong smoky smell is noticed in the basement stairwell even though the basement fireplace has never been used and its damper is kept closed.

Both fireplaces have fresh-air inlets in their backs. The man who cleaned our chimney said that smoke from the first floor chimney is being drawn down the other flue. Is this likely and how do we prevent it?

A. He is right, but why hasn't he told you how to prevent it? When you say that both flues are capped, you probably mean that wire mesh has been put over them. What should be done now to stop recirculation of the smoke is to build a weather cap over the chimney, consisting of two exterior wythes, and one wythe between the two flues. They must be built of solid masonry and should be capped with two separate bluestones so one can be lifted and put over the other when the flues are being swept. Or use individual metal tunnel caps installed parallel to each other (not facing each other), to accomplish the same thing.

Learning how to sweep a chimney

Q. I am a do-it-yourselfer with a two-year-old zero-clearance fireplace with a triple-walled flue. I would like to clean it myself in the spring. Can you start a future chimney sweep in the right direction?

A. If you are interested only in your own chimney, the best resource I know of is the out-of-print book *Be Your Own Chimney Sweep* by Don Post and Chris Curtis (1979, Garden Way Publishing). It should be available from libraries, or major used booksellers. The equipment you'll need is available at hardware or home stores.

If you hope to become a professional sweep, check out the National Chimney Sweep Guild at www.ncsg.org to learn about the requirements, training, etc.

Cleaning chimney and ducts connected to oil furnace

Q. Must chimney venting an oil-fired furnace, warm-air ducts, be cleaned regularly, and, if so, how often must it be done?

A. There is no need, usually, to clean a chimney into which an oil burner is vented. The ducts that carry the warm air of a furnace to the various rooms should not need frequent professional vacuuming if you change the furnace filters regularly—every three to five years—only if there are indications of a problem. It's a good idea to occasionally remove the register covers and vacuum inside as far in as you can.

Flue liner is cracked

Q. The chimney sweep who cleaned our chimney told us that there is a crack in one of tiles. I called the fire department and a few other places and got different opinions on how correct this situation. I heat with wood and want to be sure that it is safe to use our stove. Last season, when using the stove for the first time, there was a smoky smell in the garage, which the chimney sweep said was caused by the cracked tile. How can I have this repaired, how much will it cost?

A. Cracked flue liners are indeed dangerous under any circumstances, but particularly so when venting a wood-burning stove.

There are several strategies to repair them. Some chimney sweeps are experienced in repairing certain types of cracks with refractory cement, but this may not be possible in your case. The chimney can be relined with stainless steel or concrete, and this gives you the opportunity to size the diameter of the new lining to that of the flue pipe of the stove and, at the same time, to insulate the new chimney if the size of the present flue liner permits it. This would help reduce creosote formation when burning wood in an air-tight stove.

The cost of relining is in the $700 to $1,000 range, depending on the height of the chimney and the difficulty involved.

This is third degree creosote coating a flue liner.

Creosote forms in outside chimney

Q. There is a considerable amount of creosote formation in my brick chimney that is eating the mortar joints between the bricks. The chimney is outside the house at one end and is used to vent a wood stove. How can this be stopped before further damage is done?

A. An outside chimney is cold and can never be warmed enough by the gases of an air-tight stove to prevent condensation. Moreover, most stoves require a smaller flue than fireplaces. Discharging gases from a stove into a flue that it too large reduces the buoyancy of the gases, causes turbulence, and cools them even more.

You should have the flue lined with a stainless steel liner of the proper diameter for your stove and insulation packed in between the metal chimney and the existing flue liners. Or have insulated concrete poured in around special forms.

Check in your Yellow Pages for the names of people who do this type of work under Chimney Builders & Repairers and Chimney Lining material.

Chimney cleaning in house with steep roof

Q. Our cabin in northern Wisconsin is heated entirely with wood. Its steep roof makes it very hard to get to the peak to run brushes to clean the chimney of creosote that builds up in the metal pipe. Do you have any suggestions? Are there products that allow climbing up a steep pitch roof less dangerous?

A. Chimney-sweep supply stores sell lightweight ladders that hook onto the ridge of the roof and allow for safer climbing. Another way is to disconnect the flue from inside and run the brush up, using the same flexible fiberglass rods that you would use from the roof. Be sure to run the rods through a small hole in a large plastic trash bag, fastened to the flue with a heavy-duty rubber band, so the loose creosote falls into it and not in the house.

Fireplaces

Although most fireplaces are more for aesthetics than heating, they are discussed in this chapter because the issues overlap with related subjects, such as chimneys and wood-burning stoves.

Large fireplace needs large flue

Q. The 48×24-inch fireplace in our camp is connected to a flue that is 20×14 inches almost all the way up, except that it is capped with a 10-inch round section a few feet tall. Our space heater is also connected to this flue.

Whenever the fire doors are open, the fireplace smokes so badly that we can't stay in the camp. When one door is closed it is not so bad. The space heater draws well, but is it causing the problem—or is the fire box too big?

A. The correct ratio between a fireplace opening and its chimney is generally ten to one. There are variations depending on the height of the chimney, etc.

tion of termites or carpenter ants (they both love moist conditions). It may also be wise, after the grade changes are made, to have the ground treated against termites and ants before the deck boards are screwed back on.

Attaching deck to house

Q. I am planning to build a deck in the back of my house this summer and wonder what is the best way to attach it to the house to avoid problems later.

A. The best way to attach a deck to a building, in my opinion, is to do so with Maine brackets, aluminum deck brackets that are lag-screwed to the house under the siding, and to which the deck header is fastened. If your local building-supply store does not carry them, have the store order the brackets or buy them at www. deckbracket.com.

Concrete piers under deck have shifted

Q. The concrete piers under our deck have heaved tremendously and have lifted the deck to a point that necessitates repairs. How should I go about it and what can I do to prevent this from happening again? The deck is 3 feet off the ground and there are three piers under the beam on the outside of the deck.

A. The piers may have heaved because they were not properly built or there may be water collecting under the deck, or at each pier, if there is the frequent depressions I so often find there. Another possibility is a high water table but it's rather rare and this space doesn't permit me to deal with every situation. If it is the problem, write again.

Keep in mind that the ground under any deck is not insulated by a layer of snow so frost tends to travel quite deep. All piers need to be set below the frost line unless some other means of preventing deep frost are taken. You'll probably have to replace the piers.

Place a couple of screw jacks on wide boards under the outside beam of the deck between the piers (you can rent them in any tool rental place). Remove the existing piers, which you will probably find have no footings. As a result, frost grabs the piers and yanks them right up in what I refer to as "bear hugging."

Have the three holes excavated to below the frost line. The bottoms must be firm and flat. Set plastic forms such as the Big Foot on the bottom of the excavation. Set Sonotubes or equivalent on top of the forms, plumb them and cut the tops off at the desired height, remembering that they must all three be level.

Pour the concrete and place in it whichever hardware you have chosen to attach the deck beam to the piers. Lower the jacks after the concrete has cured at least twenty four hours. Backfill around the piers with sand and top it off with native soil, making sure that the dirt slopes away to shed water.

It is also imperative that you fill any depression under the deck with native soil—not sand or other granular mix—so water cannot pool under the deck. The area under the deck should be higher than the surrounding ground to shed water.

The dirt should be tamped. You may have to remove some boards to do that; screw them back up instead of nailing them.

Free-standing deck

Q. We moved into a hillside ranch last fall. The land falls off in the rear allowing a walk-out finished basement in which there are two bedrooms and a bath facing our lovely backyard.

We would like to have a large deck built so we can enjoy the backyard and eat on the deck in season but we don't want to block the light to the downstairs bedrooms. There is a door from the kitchen to an outside wood stoop and steps on the side of the house. The detached garage is about 12 to 15 feet away from the house. We haven't been able to come up with a good solution. Do you have any suggestions?

A. What about building a free-standing deck some 10 feet away from the back of the house and connected to the house by a bridge that would tie into the stoop? If the steps are on the side of the stoop facing the garage, they may not need to be changed. You may even want to extend a walk from the base of the steps to the side garage door and have a roof built over it to be able to get from the garage to the house under cover from the elements.

Another solution is to build the deck attached to the house but not put boards on the first couple of feet from the house in order to let light in downstairs. You will need a railing for safety.

Solid floor desired for deck

Q. We plan on adding a deck to our house which we will eventually screen in. How can we avoid having spaces between the deck boards? We are considering tongue and groove cedar planking which we would seal. Would that survive snow and rain? We are also considering pressure-treated plywood. We probably will carpet the porch floor some time later. Any other recommendations?

A. Cedar boards properly treated would be fine but I would not recommend putting carpeting on them later. There are plastic composition deck systems available today that do not have spaces between boards and plastic covering system for existing deck boards that could be covered with carpeting. Pressure-treated plywood is also a practical option as substrate for carpeting but, if that is your final choice, you should consider framing the joists 12 inches on center to make the plywood stiffer; ½-inch thick plywood on 16 inches on center framing will flex. But pressure-treated plywood should only be used if the porch will be enclosed in a few years.

Special deck screws worth the price

Q. I plan on building a deck in my back yard this coming spring. What is the best way to fasten deck boards to the joists? Should I use nails or screws and which type?

A. Use special deck screws. Although they are slightly more expensive than nails, they have a number of advantages over nails—one of which is that they will not come out and will control warping much better.

Stain deck floor, don't carpet it

Q. We have had our pressure-treated deck for a number of years. Each year, it requires a good deal of time and money to keep it looking presentable. We had the thought of covering it with indoor-outdoor carpeting but wonder if this is a good idea. How would we fasten it to the floor: with staples, glue or nails?

A. I don't think the carpeting is a good idea. It would telegraph the spaces between the deck boards and need adjustment from time to time as it stretches. Thus, fastening it down permanently would be a poor idea. You'd end up hating it.

A better solution is to clean the deck with a deck cleaner/restorer such as Wolman Deck & Fence Brightener and to coat it with a sealer such as Wolman Rain-Coat Water Repellent or Wolman Deck Stains, depending on the final effect you want. Keep in mind that stains do not need to be re-applied as often as clear coatings. A stain should last for several years. There are other brands to do the same.

Don't coat deck with linseed oil

Q. The ten-year-old deck on my house needs attention. It is not built of pressure-treated wood and the deck boards have cracks and splits. Someone suggested that I coat it with linseed oil on a yearly basis to preserve it. Yes or no?

A. No way. Raw linseed oil would never dry; boiled linseed oil would, but linseed oil is gourmet fare for a variety of molds. Your deck's life may be prolonged but at the cost of your living with a dark, mottled mess.

One of this nation's authorities on wood preservation, who has done extensive research for years on a variety of products, considers Amteco TWP Roof & Deck Sealant the best way to go. They offer a line of ready-to-use products ideal for homeowners, whereas concentrates to be mixed with special oils are more suited to commercial applications that require large quantities of material at a lower cost.

Sap leaching through deck stain

Q. I have just finished staining my backyard deck. It is treated wood, approximately six years old, and this is the third application at about three-year intervals. I used Cabot brand deck stain in a dark-brown hue. The problem is that there seems to be sap leaching up through the stain in random areas; it is whitish in color, has the texture of dried glue droplets and is quite noticeable on the darkened finish. Is there a product or homemade solution that will remove the sap without affecting the stained wood? Cabot recommends one coat only. Your comments would be greatly appreciated.

A. It sounds as if a lower grade of yellow southern pine was used for the deck. Number 2 pine has knots, and sap exudes from it and will continue to do so until all the sap is gone. There is nothing you can do to stop the sap bleeding through the stain. Too bad a better grade of pressure-treated wood, such as B-select, was not used.

Different treatments for cedar and PT decking

Q. I applied Amteco TWP Cedartone over cedar decking that was treated with TWP Cedartone five years ago, and it is taking two weeks to dry in some spots. What mistakes did I make? How should I apply TWP Cedartone to a pressure-treated deck initially treated with TWP Cedartone five years ago? Should I scrub the deck with your suggested mixture of 1 cup TSP, 1 quart fresh Clorox bleach and 3 quarts of warm water?

A. Do you have two kinds of decking—cedar and pressure-treated? There is a difference between the two in the way that they react to a second application of Amteco TWP. A second coat of TWP applied over a five-year-old coat on a cedar deck should not cause the problem you have, as cedar has an open grain structure that is very absorbent unless that structure has been plugged by various pollutants. However, a second coat applied over a pressure-treated deck (southern yellow pine) that has a much harder surface, even after five years, could result in poor drying, especially if you applied the TWP too thickly.

This may be due to the fact that some years ago TWP's formula was changed to conform to federal regulations regarding the control of volatile organic compounds. Highly-refined linseed oil was added and the mildewcide and solids were doubled, making it more important to apply thinner coats, thus increasing the coverage per gallon to 600 square feet. To remove the excess that does not dry within a few days, take a clean rag dampened with mineral spirits and wipe off the excess that has not been absorbed.

In any case, before applying a second coat of TWP, even after five years, the decking should be cleaned using the solution I have recommended that you mention in your letter. The easiest way to do this is to spray the solution on with a garden sprayer and then scrub the deck with a scrub brush (a long-handled one to spare your back). Then the decking should be pressure-washed at 1,200 psi to remove all dead fibers and other pollutants loosened by the solution and the scrubbing. However, you may want to try flushing it with your garden hose equipped with a pistol-grip sprayer set to full force; this may be enough to do the cleanup.

Wood on deck is splintering

Q. I am seeking your advice regarding my wood deck. It was built with our house about four and a half years ago, and about three years ago I pressure-washed it and then treated it with Olympic WaterGuard clear wood sealant. This appeared to work nicely, but within a year or two the wood started splintering and separating and curling at the grain in many places, mostly on the flooring surfaces. I am afraid I may have held the pressure-washer nozzle too close to the surface of the wood, but my in-laws also live in the neighborhood and they have the same problem.

Last summer, I re-applied the sealant to the railing and a different brand of sealant to the flooring. It is getting slowly worse, and I would like a long-term solution. I have considered renting and using an orbital sander and then applying something different to the wood, such as marine varnish, but I'm not sure what would be best. Can the wood be salvaged? Should it be sanded first? What do you recommend? Any advice would be appreciated.

A. It sounds as if the best grade of wood was not used. You didn't mention whether the deck is made of pressure-treated wood or some other type. It may be that the wood used has a flat grain instead of being quarter-sawn; flat-grain boards have a tendency to splinter and separate along the growth layers of the wood. I doubt that your pressure-washing had anything to do with the problem you have; it's more the nature of the wood that was used. You could try sanding the deck boards, but if the wood is flat-grain it will continue to splinter, curl and separate as the seasons take their toll.

I would not recommend varnishing the wood. It is best to use a penetrating preservative.

Clear sealer for wooden deck

Q. I plan on pressure-washing my pressure-treated deck and want to seal it before the weather gets cold. What product would you recommend? I would prefer a product that does not change the natural color of the wood.

A. There are several products on the market that will accomplish what you want to do. One I have used with great success is Wolman RainCoat. Keep in mind that any clear product needs to be re-applied more frequently than those with a hue.

Plant growing through deckboards

Q. The decorative plant we have growing around our deck is now growing under it and coming through the deck boards. We realize we should have put plastic under the deck but we didn't. How can we control it now?

A. You have not mentioned how close the deck is to the ground. Can you get under it, remove the parts of the plant that have grown under it and lay heavy black plastic on the soil? The plastic should be weighted down with stones or bricks. The plant should not grow back under the deck if you block all light and keep water out with the plastic. If there isn't enough room to crawl under the deck, perhaps you can pull as much of the plant out as possible from the perimeter of the deck and, with the help of another person, slip the plastic under the deck.

Weigh its perimeter down. You may want to dig a trench on the deck side of the plantings to cut its sprawling roots and insert in the ground a plastic or metal border to prevent further root incursion.

Cleaning a Trex deck

Q. I installed a Trex deck last year. It is now spotted and dirty-looking. I washed it with a bleach and water solution but that didn't help. What can I do? Also, should the deck be coated with a sealant to prevent this from happening?

A. Trex does not need any sealant or other treatment, according to the manufacturer. The treatment for removal of the stains depends on the kind of stains. For stains caused by mildew, fruit and leaves, use a conventional deck wash (you can buy one in a hardware, paint or building supply store). For rust and grime, the recommended cleaning agent is one containing phosphoric acid (available in home centers and hardware stores). If the stains are caused by oil or grease, scrub with a degreasing agent or sand lightly with fine sandpaper. The resulting discoloration will eventually weather to the original grey.

Refinishing a concrete deck

Q. Our concrete deck needs to be painted and sealed. How should it be cleaned? What kind of paint and sealer should we use?

A. A good cleaning solution is one cup TSP-PF or other strong detergent, 1 quart fresh Clorox bleach to 3 quarts of water. Scrub with a stiff bristle brush. Rinse thoroughly. Be aware that this solution is caustic to vegetation. Soak all adjacent vegetation before treating the concrete, cover it with plastic, do not use so much of the solution that it will run off onto the vegetation and flood the entire area with water as you rinse to dilute the solution.

I would not recommend painting the concrete. Instead use a concrete stain; it gives a much better and longer-lasting job. There is no need to apply a sealer after staining.

Patios

Covering concrete patio with ceramic tiles

Q. I am interested in covering my concrete patio with ceramic tiles. I reside in the Chicago area and I am concerned about the effect of the winter weather on the tiles.

I have checked with tile representatives at two home improvement stores in the area and they both indicate that there is a tile that is appropriate for outdoor use. However, both wondered if the winter weather would be more than the tiles could tolerate. The concrete is old and has had cracking problems in the past but I have recovered it and it is, at this time, level and free of cracks. Is it possible to cover existing concrete with ceramic tiles or am I wasting my money?

A. The first question to address is the stability of the patio. If it is old and has had cracking problems in the past, there is no assurance that the topping you put on is not going to suffer the same fate. The original slab cracked because it was poured on an unstable substrate. It could be that there is poor drainage under it or that the backfill settled and caused it to crack. This is not good news for the topping you put on.

However, on a sound slab, you can install ceramic tiles; the Canadians do it all the time, but success depends on the installation. The tiles must be vitreous or labeled impervious to moisture. The slab should slope or be domed or crowned to drain effectively, or trouble is not far behind. You should use a latex thinset adhesive specially made for impervious tiles, use latex grout, and apply a sealer over the entire surface.

The most successful installations are made over slabs that have a drainage layer under them; unfortunately, it's too late for you. Are you wasting your money? Probably, with what you have told me.

Pouring new concrete over old on patio

Q. My concrete patio has sagged on one end. I would like to pour 2 to 3 inches of cement on top of it to level it. Is there a bonding material that would bond the new to the old? The patio is above ground so it does not sit in water. What is the best way of doing this job? What about reinforcing? I would appreciate your advice.

A. The surface of the existing patio would have to be cleaned thoroughly and etched with a solution of muriatic acid (1 part acid to 9 parts water) applied with a stiff brush attached to a long handle. Be very careful with muriatic acid; it is very corrosive and must be handled with great care. Use only glass or plastic containers; do not use any metal and do not get any on metal. Pour the acid slowly into the water and not the other way around. Wear heavy-duty rubber gloves and old clothes.

There are several adhesive products that are painted on the concrete before pouring the new concrete over it (buy one in a masonry supply house). Keep in mind that it is difficult to feather the new concrete to the old in the high end so you should plan to have the concrete at least 1 inch thick there.

Reinforcing is difficult to do on such a thin application. It may be better to use fiberglass-reinforced concrete, but that may leave you with fibers sticking out and a rougher surface. Chicken wire, hardware cloth, galvanized plaster lath or 2×4-inch mesh fencing are alternatives, although you may not need anything.

There are also some important steps that must be taken to ensure a successful and lasting job during the pour and the ensuing finishing phase. The main key to success is to allow the concrete to cure so it won't develop hairline cracks into which water can eventually get and cause problems in time.

This is a job best left to an experienced concrete contractor.

Concrete patio loses color

Q. We paid a contractor to install a stained (bluestone) stamped concrete patio about three years ago. The patio has now lost much of the gray color and the contractor is out of business. Do you know how we can re-stain and reseal the patio? We do not want to just paint the patio.

A. As you have discovered, exposure to the elements will bleach color out of concrete and other materials. A concrete stain should work if the surface is cleaned with any household detergent and thoroughly rinsed before application. You will have to repeat the process every few years due to continued exposure.

Brick patio subject to water damage

Q. We built a brick patio with old bricks about two years ago. The bricks are laid on a bed of crushed rock and sand, and we have swept crushed rock between the bricks. Now, we are concerned about the moss that is growing in the crushed rock fill. Although it lends some charm to the patio, I am worried that it can cause damage by moving the bricks. Can you advise us?

A. The moss should not affect the bricks by moving them, but old bricks are not pavers and are subject to water damage. The moss thrives in humid conditions and actually retains water which, in turn, can be absorbed by the bricks.

Rain water, snow melt and soil moisture are all factors which may eventually cause the bricks to disintegrate so, if you like the appearance of the moss, you might as well leave it as it is only one of the potentially destructive forces that may do the bricks in.

Moss growing on patio

Q. Is there a way to get rid of moss that is growing on my patio deck? I have red pavers, and the moss is growing between them. Is there some spray or solution that I can apply that will kill the moss but not bleach the stones?

A. Spray the area with a mixture of 3 parts white vinegar to 1 part water, but it is not likely to last for the entire season

Clearing mold and ants from brick patio

Q. I've not noticed the following question in your column and I would appreciate it if you could provide some solution to my problem. I have a 20-foot by 12-foot brick patio in my backyard. The problem is that most of it is covered with green mold that grows in between the bricks, together with small weeds and ant soil heaps! While I can control the weeds to a large extent and the ants to a small extent, I cannot find any way to get rid of the mold at all. My main goal is to keep the patio as clean as possible throughout the year.

A. The anthills can be easily controlled by pouring boiling water on them. As for controlling the green mold, try scrubbing the bricks with a mixture of 1 part fresh Clorox bleach to 3 parts water. Do not rinse.

Cleaning pine sap from patio

Q. How can I remove pine tree sap from our new brick patio? I have tried turpentine and mineral spirits without success.

A. Try Lestoil. That has worked for others.

Which patio materials will stay cool?

Q. I am planning to remove my maintenance-intensive wood deck and replace it with a patio. While I like the idea of a slate patio, I am concerned about the heat the slates will absorb. What materials would be best for a patio and stay relatively cool?

A. Any masonry material will absorb and retain more heat than wood. Slates, paver bricks, concrete would all store heat and release it slowly as the sun no longer hits them. Paver bricks would be the best, if you insist on masonry, as they are less dense (thus containing air). Placing any masonry material on sand instead of a concrete base would also help keep it less hot.

There are alternatives to masonry. Since you have a deck, and you wish to get rid of the wood decking surface, you might want to consider substitute materials such as Trex (made of recycled supermarket bags and waste wood products). There are other man-made materials based on plastic also available.

One great option we tend to forget is grass. Give it some thought.

Don't blacktop patio

Q. Our 15-year-old patio has developed long cracks that have been patched but it still looks like a road map. This summer we plan to have our driveway recoated with blacktop. Would it be advisable to have the patio blacktopped too?

A. Don't do it! On hot days the blacktop will soften and be tracked into the house, and furniture legs will sink into it.

Although more expensive, your best solution is to cover the patio with flagstones or blue stones in a cement bed—provided the patio has finished settling, the cracks are stable and you have enough clearance under the door to raise the patio's surface about two inches. Flash properly at the joint of the new surface and any wood on the house and consider having the area treated against termites. Wood hidden behind masonry is vulnerable. Remove the siding, coat the sheathing with a wood preservative and cover it with Grace Ice & Water Shield or equivalent.

Bricks around patio are flaking

Q. We have a brick wall around our patio. The bricks are flaking badly due to moisture and frost. One bricklayer suggested replacing the bad bricks for $1,000 while another would rebuild the entire wall for $9,000. I wonder about simply plastering the wall with a colored stucco but the bricklayers said that the moisture would be trapped in and flaking would continue. But I have seen houses redone with decorative cement work. Wouldn't moisture be trapped in those walls? So would it be any different for our wall?

A. Is the brick wall around the patio acting as a retaining wall? In other words, is there dirt against it on the outside of the patio? If so, you would have to moisture-proof its back and provide good drainage or the moisture would travel through the bricks and cause problems in the front.

But, if the wall is free-standing, you could try stuccoing both sides after removing all loose material. The stucco should be reinforced with a vinyl additive for better adhesion. The top will also have to be waterproofed. This can be done by covering it with flagstones or any other fitting material.

The only unknown is whether or not moisture is drawn from the ground, a process known as "rising damp." It could cause spalling of the bricks and pop out the stucco. The wall may have been built with used bricks or poor quality bricks. Paving bricks would be more resistant to moisture.

Options for renovating a concrete patio

Q. I would like some information about renovating my backyard concrete patio. The patio measures 15 by 30 feet, and was laid approximately 12 years ago. Over the last few years, several cracks have developed and the concrete has discolored to the point of being unattractive. I would like to have the concrete completely removed and replaced with a material that is easy to maintain, will withstand the elements (I live in northeastern New Jersey and get a fair amount of sun, rain and snow). My backyard faces north. Besides concrete, what other materials do you recommend, and what are the general costs associated with those materials? I have thought of outdoor tiles, composite decking and pavers, but have not looked into the costs of materials and labor. Any information you can provide is greatly appreciated.

A. If the cracks are minimal, there are several options that would save you the cost of removing the concrete. But they depend on how much space there is between the concrete patio and any door that opens onto it.

One option is to have a concrete cap poured over the existing concrete; for best results, it should be mesh-reinforced. The new concrete can be stained (not painted) after installation, or a color can be added in the mix before it is poured. This would be the least expensive solution. Another option is to have a mason lay paver bricks or flagstones in a mortar bed over the existing concrete. This will cost more than pouring a cap over the existing concrete. In either case, make sure the new surface slopes gently away from the house for drainage.

Yet another option is to remove the existing concrete, lay a crushed stone bed 4 to 6 inches deep, and lay concrete paver blocks over the crushed stone. You should be able to find some form of concrete pavers in local building supply stores; the ones I am familiar with come in such sizes as 2-feet square, 2 feet by 30 inches, etc. They usually have a pattern such as diamonds on top. If there is a slope to your land and the soil under the patio is heavy (such as clay or silt), a drainage system should be provided to drain any accumulating water from the stone bed to a point downhill.

Another way to go is to lay flagstones or paver blocks directly onto a sand bed. Any needed adjustments can easily be done if frost heaves some of the pavers or flagstones.

Garages, Carports, and Sheds

Repairing concrete garage floor

Q. The cement floor in my garage is badly pitted. Is there a way to repair it rather than tear it out and repour it? A couple of inches of new concrete could be added except at the garage door.

A. The existing concrete surface should be cleaned with TSP-PF to remove all grease, oil and other pollutants. Then, all loose cement should be removed in the process of rinsing off the detergent treatment. Steam cleaning is also very effective.

The cleaned concrete can be patched in a number of ways, depending on how badly pitted it is. You can use Thorocrete for small areas. Or a new cap can be poured over the old concrete, feathered at the door. Have a competent concrete contractor do it for you.

Removing oil and grease from concrete garage floor

Q. How can I remove oil and grease stains from my driveway and garage floor?

A. The most effective way to remove grease and oil from concrete is to spread a layer of granular TSP-PF over the stains, sprinkle hot water over them and scrub with a stiff brush. Let stand for half an hour and rinse off.

You can buy TSP-PF in hardware, paint and agricultural stores. Protect eyes and skin.

Removing paint layers from concrete garage floor

Q. How can I remove several layers of latex and oil paint from my concrete garage floor? What can I use other than ordinary paint removers, as I would need at least 5 gallons? Who sells paint removers in 5-gallon pails?

A. You can rent a concrete grinder and have its operation explained by the rental store. The bricks used to grind may clog with paint so, if available, you should blow them clean with an air compressor or you'll have to use several sets of bricks. Ask the rental shop if a floor tile stripper would not work better in your case—depending on how many coats of paint you think there are.

The alternative is a non-flammable paint stripper. Apply it at the rate of one gallon per 100 square feet and cover the coated area with plastic immediately to retard evaporation. Let it stand for an hour or more; remove the plastic and scrape. Do it in sections. Repeat, if necessary. Ventilate well and wear eye and skin protection. You should also use a paint vapor respirator.

Paint removers are available in 5-gallon pails, but on special order. Check with your paint store to see if there would be any savings.

Roots growing through a drain pipe, clogging it.

Tree roots damage garage slab

Q. A 50-foot-tall black walnut tree between my house and garage appears to have busted my garage concrete floor. It was all right until recently. Will it continue to break the floor? What can I do about it?

A. The tree may be responsible. One way to make sure is to see whether it gets worse every year without getting better seasonally. Another is to remove badly-cracked sections of the floor and dig for the roots.

You should ask yourself if it's doing the same thing to your house's foundation wall if you have a crawl space or basement.

I certainly would not feel good about recommending the destruction of such a beautiful old tree. So, if only the garage slab is affected, you could simply remove it and put crushed stones in its place. However, if the house foundation is also affected, you may have to cut any large roots pressing against it. A tree surgeon is the person to call for advice and the job.

Filling gaps under garage slab

Q. An area under our garage slab has eroded over the past several years. The foundation walls of the garage are built with concrete blocks. The garage floor is concrete reinforced with steel rebar. A construction firm says they can fill these voids with grout injected through holes in the floor. Have you had any experience with this method? Do you think it would work?

A. When done by an experienced crew, this is a very good option. Care must be taken not to blow the block walls out. Insist on a copy of the contractor's insurance on work performed and completed operations.

Half-boiled linseed oil to treat garage floor

Q. You have mentioned coating a garage floor with a mixture of half-boiled linseed oil and half mineral spirits to seal it. I am not clear on how to half-boil linseed oil and when to add the mineral spirits.

A. Interesting question. How does one "half boil" anything (my bad choice of words)?

There are two kinds of linseed oil: raw and boiled. Raw takes forever to dry, if ever. Boiled dries fairly quickly. You buy boiled linseed oil ready to use; you don't boil it yourself. You make the mixture with equal quantities of boiled linseed oil and mineral spirits. This treatment is particularly desirable in areas where the streets are salted to clear them of snow and ice in winter but it will also help protect concrete from oil and other stains.

Fibers in fiberglass garage door are showing

Q. The fibers on my fiberglass garage door are showing. Is there any kind of clear coating that can be applied to the panels?

A. Clear coating would not hide the fibers that have probably collected dirt. Clean the door, rinse it and try Gel Gloss. It may be what you want. An alternative is to prime it with Zinsser's Bull's Eye 1-2-3. and paint it with a good quality exterior latex.

Garage door needs adjustments

Q. My double garage door comes down with a bang and is very hard to lift. It binds and requires a great deal of strength to get it started. This has been a progressive situation but it seems worse since I painted it a few months ago. What can I do to make it work better?

A. Over time the torsion spring or stretch springs have weakened and need adjusting. The coat of paint you put on also added weight and thickness where the door comes in contact with the door stops.

If your door has a torsion spring (over the door and parallel to it), adjustments are not a do-it-yourself job. A special tool is required as well as training. The spring is under great tension and, if not properly handled can cause serious injury.

Stretch springs are safer and easier to handle. There is one on each side of the door and they are parallel to the tracks. To tighten them, either move the S hook to the next hole or shorten the cable by moving the cable clamp, whichever is appropriate, while the door is open and the springs not under tension.

Never grease or oil the door tracks; they will collect dirt and cause the wheels to bind and wear out. The tracks must be kept dry. You may, however, use WD-40, a dry lubricant, on the ball bearings of the rollers or a special lubricant available from garage door installers.

Rub hard yellow soap or beeswax on the door stops to reduce friction. The door stops may have to be moved after repeated paintings.

Garage-door opener fails in cold weather

Q. My garage-door opener works fine except in cold weather. The door does not go all the way up and has to be pushed up manually. We have adjusted the lifting screw on the box but this has not helped. How does cold weather affect the operation of the door and what solution is there?

A. You have given me very little information. For instance, is the door opener chain- or gear-driven? Gear-driven openers are prone to cold-weather difficulties, whereas the chain-driven types seem free of them.

But the problem may be with the door itself. Disconnect the operator mechanism from the door and try to open and close the door by hand. If the door binds in any way, this may be the reason for the incomplete operation; the door may bind more in winter as the cold affects the metal parts.

It may be time to call a service person to adjust the door anyway. This routine service involves lubrication, checking all the pulleys, the cables, and the tension on the springs.

Low-clearance garage-door openers

Q. Is there a company that makes automatic garage door openers that do not have to have space over the door when open? My door opens against the ceiling and I've been told all the openers have to have at least two inches clearance over the door.

A. There are two options that should be looked at by an experienced garage door installer. One is a quick close fixture and the other is a low headroom track.

Keeping water from seeping into garage

Q. My concrete garage floor has very wide cracks. The grade slopes toward the garage and water comes in when it rains. I plan on putting in a new floor. Is it necessary to raise the garage or should I simply put in a drain system to lead the water away from the garage

A. Can you simply pour a new concrete floor over the cracked one and have it slope towards the door, as it should?

To keep the water out, a concrete trough can be built in front of the garage door. Cover it with a steel grate; you can find one in a steel shop. Look for one in your Yellow Pages under "Steel Distributors & Warehouses."

Driveway settles lower than garage floor

Q. After letting the ground settle for one year, we paved our six-year-old driveway with asphalt. After this past, very cold winter, the driveway has dropped 2 inches below the level of the concrete garage floor and has pulled away from it about 1 inch. What should be done to prevent the cracking of the concrete floor from either water freezing in that space or from continually driving over that 2-inch drop?

A. You can get a bag of blacktop and fill the separation between the driveway and the concrete garage floor with it. If you slope it a bit, you can close the 2-inch differential in height somewhat but there should be no need to make the two even. The concrete floor may be resting on a frost wall anyway and be secure.

Garage is sinking

Q. My home is a 1921 colonial with a one-car detached garage. The garage is sinking (approximately ½ inch) on one side. This was first apparent when the garage-door opener motor burned out due to the off-balance; currently, the door is difficult to open manually. Numerous contractors have had different opinions on how to fix this, ranging from tearing down and rebuilding to just jacking up and replacing the bottom sill and the 2×4s on the side that is sinking. Please advise.

A. My advice would depend on the cause of the settling. I am not clear, from your description, if the settling is caused by a sinking foundation or by a rotting sill. If it is caused by a settling foundation, fixing it would also depend on when the settling occurred and if it has now stabilized—only time can tell you this (you didn't say when you discovered the problem, but it sounds recent).

If the foundation is settling, it was either poured or built on unstable ground. Jacking up the garage may not solve the problem in the long run unless the situation is stable and has been that way for several years. In that case, it may be best to underpin the foundation. However, if the settling is due to a rotting sill and 2×4s, they can easily be replaced with pressure-treated wood after jacking the garage up to its former position.

My guess is that the settling may be due to a rotting sill, based on the assumption that the garage is as old as the house (since it is only a one-car garage) and that foundation problems would have become apparent long ago. It sounds as if the contractor suggesting replacement of the sill may be the best one to use.

Covering steel garage with bricks

Q. More than 20 years ago, we had a steel garage built. I now wish we had it built with bricks to match our house and would like to know if you can recommend where I could purchase brick facing or sheets of fake bricks to cover our garage.

A. There are several manufacturers of thin bricks that are applied with mastic to sound substrate. They are not fake—they are real bricks but only ½ inch thick. Some of the makes I am familiar with are Endicott, www.endicott.com; Summitville Tiles Inc., www.summitville.com; Ambrico (American Brick Company), www.ambrico.com.

Water drips from underside of steel carport roof

Q. The roof of our carport is made of steel with a baked-on enamel finish. During the winter, water dripped from the underside of the carport onto our new car, leaving big blotches on it. What can we do to stop this problem?

A. Condensation formed on the underside of the carport roof because metal can get much colder than the ambient air on clear nights when radiation is strong. The air under the carport is warmer and humid and water vapor condenses on the cold metal.

A temporary solution that may work, if there is not much wind blowing in your carport, is to fasten a plastic tarpaulin on a slant under the carport and over the car. This will catch the drips and discharge them on the low side of the tarp. If you let the tarp droop at the low end, you can concentrate the water in one spot and catch it in a bucket.

A permanent solution is to install extruded polystyrene (¾- to 1-inch thick) on the underside of the car port roof. This can be done with an adhesive such as Styrobond. The metal will be insulated from contact with warm moist air, and the dripping should stop.

Leaks in combination sun deck and carport

Q. I have a combination sun deck/carport. The deck is pitched 3 inches in 10 feet and is covered with plywood. I caulk the seams between the sheets and paint them yearly, but the floor still leaks and the plywood is rotting.

You have mentioned in the past covering a porch with canvas to make it watertight. Is this a practical solution for my problem and if so, where can I get information on materials and methods?

A. It can be a practical solution to your dual problem: rotting plywood and water leaking onto the car below. Roofers used to install heavy canvas years ago and it had to be painted with several coats of porch enamel, then re-coated every few years. But you'll have to check around to find a roofer who still may do this type of work.

If not, another solution is to remove the railing and let the plywood dry, sweep it clean, and lay Grace Ice & Water Shield (I&WS) over it, overlapping each 3-foot section by 2 inches after installing metal drip edge all around. I&WS has a sticky side that is put down on the original clean and dry plywood deck. It must be covered to prevent damage from the sun. An alternative is a synthetic membrane such as EPDM or Trocal.

Since your photos show a considerable step down from the door to the deck, rip pressure-treated 2×10s, 10 feet long, to get 2 pieces from each one with one end about 3 inches and the other about 6 inches. Place them on the deck with the shallow end at the house as you would to build a new deck with headers at both ends. This will give you a level surface.

Then screw pressure-treated 1×6 deck boards to the sleepers, tight to each other (shrinkage will create spaces as the wood dries). Replace the railing by fastening it to the new deck.

Particle-board shed deteriorating fast

Q. The storage shed I bought last year is made of particle board. I was told it did not need to be painted. However, it has turned black on most of its surface and the roof is beginning to sag. How can I salvage it?

A. It should have been painted. Wash the mold, dirt, air pollution and stains off with a solution made of 1 cup of TSP-PF, 1 quart fresh Clorox bleach and 3 quarts of water. Rinse thoroughly and allow to dry. Prime with a quality oil-based primer and paint with two coats of a top-quality latex exterior house paint.

It's too late to do anything about the sagging roof. It may need to be replaced.

Fences, Walls, and Railings

Products to restore exterior wood finish

Q. You mentioned once the name, Dekswood, that can be used to restore a warm color to a red cedar fence, as well as decks and other outdoor wood structures. I have called many hardware and department stores, lumber companies and home centers. No one has ever heard of them, even people who have been in the business for years.

A. Both Dekswood and CWF®-UV5 Premium Penetrating Wood Finish are products of the Flood Company of Hudson, Ohio. Flood's products are nationally distributed and generally found in paint stores. I mention product names when it seems appropriate to do so in order to help my readers, but can't always specify where they can be bought in each location. In this case, you can go to the company's Web site, www.flood.com, to locate a store near you or purchase products on line.

Refinishing a galvanized fence

Q. Our galvanized fence has rusted badly over the years. We'd like to paint it. How should we prepare it and what kind of paint should we use?

A. You'll have to remove the scaly rust. If your fence is of the chain link type, you have a big job ahead of you. The best way to do that may be to apply a liquid rust remover with a paint roller. However, wire brushing may do a better job. Try it first. Then prime and paint with Rust-Oleum primer and finish coat.

Neighboring construction cracks cinder-block wall

Q. Thirty years ago, I built a cinder-block wall approximately 4 feet high and 100 feet long covered with a cement scratch coat. A construction company started to build new homes on the other side of the wall and the builder backed all his dirt against my wall. This has caused three ugly cracks to appear on the wall.

I have come up with the idea to cover the entire wall with ivy. Can you recommend a fast growing, bug-free type of ivy and tell me how many plants I would need.

A. The first thing that comes to mind is the responsibility of the builder. If your wall was a free-standing wall as I assume it was since the contractor piled dirt against it on the other side, he had the responsibility to make sure the wall could stand the pressure applied against it by the dirt.

You haven't given me any more details but I am assuming you built the wall with 8-inch-thick blocks. That is fine for a free wall but if the wall becomes a retaining wall, and it is in a straight run without angles, corners or buttresses to reinforce it, the builder should have known better than push dirt against it. You should have him rebuild the wall for you as a retaining wall, starting with a couple of courses 2 feet thick, the next 2 courses 16 inches thick and the top two courses 12 inches thick.

The alternative is a reinforced concrete wall 12 inches thick. In either case, there should be weep holes every 4 feet at the base of the wall on your side and the wall should be backfilled with stones covered with filter fabric, followed by coarse material and native soil.

Make sure the structural issues are taken care of, then consult a local nursery on what to plant.

Mildew keeps returning to white metal railing

Q. At the start of the warm season and once more during the summer, I clean the white metal railing of our wrap-around porch with a solution of bleach and water to remove mildew that forms on it. It's quite a chore as there are many slats and curlicues. Is there a product I could use that is mildew retardant so I only have to do this chore once a season?

Also, last year, I noticed that some of the railings are chipping exposing a silver metal (aluminum?). How can I repair this? Is the solution I use too harsh, causing the coating to chip off?

A. You could try adding a mildewcide to the solution you use. You should be able to find one in paint and hardware stores.

I think that the solution you use is not responsible for the chipping; it's more likely that these areas were hit by something. Repairing the chips of the railing is more difficult. You are not likely to be able to match the paint (white is the most difficult shade to match) and it certainly would not be of the same consistency. However, if you can't live with the chips, you could attempt to touch the affected areas with an epoxy paint.

Or you could consider repainting the entire railing. If that is your eventual choice, use an epoxy or 100% acrylic gloss latex and add a mildewcide to the paint.

Rust-stained railing

Q. There are unsightly rust stains around the bases of the wrought iron railing on our concrete front porch. Is there a way to remove them and to prevent them from coming back?

A. The success of the treatment will depend on how deep the rust stains are. If they are recent and superficial, they may be removed with a solution of oxalic acid (1 ounce of acid to 1 cup of water). Swab the solution on with an old paint brush. Oxalic acid is caustic! Use caution, wear heavy rubber gloves and other skin and eye protection. Mix the solution in a plastic container (do not use metal containers or tools with it). Let the solution stand for two to three hours after which scrub the treated areas with a stiff bristle brush while rinsing them with clear water.

Deep stains are not in the province of do-it-yourselfers; they require professional attention with poultices of very strong chemicals.

To prevent recurrence, be sure that the railing and posts are kept painted with a rust-inhibiting paint.

Outdoor Stoops and Stairs

Painting steps to make them less slippery

Q. I would like to repaint my wooden porch steps but make them less slippery. Someone told me to put sand in the paint. Is this on the level?

A. Coarse sand mixed with deck paint has been used for years as an anti-slip coating for steps but it must be constantly stirred. It is an option, but there is another one. Your paint store probably has SKID-TEX; if not, buy in a pool supply company. I am told it remains in suspension in the paint, to which it is added and well mixed, much better than plain sand.

Outdoor carpeting on steps

Q. I want to put outdoor carpeting on my front stoop but want to be able to remove it later. I have read of the problems people have had removing it and the glue.

A. If you want to remove it later, I would urge you not to do it. Moreover, I am not in favor of painting or carpeting exterior concrete; the problems down the line are too difficult to solve. You can improve the looks of concrete stoops or steps by putting clay flower pots along their edges. Fill them with flowers that will bloom all summer and fall.

Removing carpeting from front steps

Q. Our concrete steps are covered with a dark green indoor/outdoor carpeting, the kind that first came out and has a flat, almost velvet-like surface. It is impossible to remove and we were told that removing it would damage the steps. Can we brush over it the type of paint that's made for concrete?

A. The carpeting should be removable with boiling water. Wear heavy rubber gloves, start in a comer, and pour boiling water on an area about two square feet. Wait a minute to let the water dissolve the adhesive and pull the carpet up. Continue doing this to a small area at a time. Use a broad blade putty knife to scrape off remaining adhesive as you pull off the carpeting. This should not damage the concrete, but there might be some residue left that you may have to sand off when it is dry, or use a adhesive remover.

Porous bricks develop mildew

Q. A couple of years ago I had my two front steps and a wall that is also a planter replaced. The brick I originally chose became unavailable so I picked a different one which is a light pink/orange color. The color is okay but the brick is very porous. After the plants have been watered or after it has rained, the wet always shows on the wall, seems to stay for a long time and always develops mildew. I think they look old and shabby.

Could you please tell me the best way to deal with mildew and green on an outside wall, and is there any way that I can treat the bricks to stop them from being so porous. Also, is it possible to paint bricks one by one, leave the grout how it is and still have it look natural?

A. For the front steps, and any flat surface, it would have been better to choose paver bricks which are more resistant to moisture penetration. Painting is unlikely to be successful; it would not give you a lasting surface on the steps and is very likely to peel off the planter wall, pushed out by the moisture from inside the planter.

You can clean the bricks with a solution made with 1 cup TSP-PF, 1 quart fresh Clorox and 3 quarts water using a stiff bristle brush. Rinse thoroughly. Be aware that TSP-PF is lethal to plants so use carefully and avoid contact with them.

Unless the inside of the planter wall was waterproofed, moisture will work its way through the bricks as you water plants and repeat the cycle of mildew and green growth. You could remove the soil from the planter and line its walls with 6-mil black plastic before refilling it. Be sure all seams are folded over to keep water from creeping through them.

Bricks on steps deteriorating

Q. Several bricks on my three-year-old front steps have cracked or are deteriorating. They are all at the end of brick rows or where the iron railings were installed. The place where I bought the bricks tells me they are good and the problem is water getting between the concrete and the bricks and freezing.

What can I paint on the bricks to eliminate this problem? Should the mason be responsible for re-doing the job at no cost to me? Some of the bricks are discolored from leaves, etc. How can I clean them?

A. Bricks used on outside flat surfaces like walks, steps and patios should be pavers—bricks manufactured for that type of heavy duty. Perhaps yours are not and, if so, the merchant should not have sold them to you if he or she were made aware of the intended use. The mason should also know that regular bricks are not satisfactory for these purposes.

Workmanship has a lot to do with success. The mortar joints should be tooled in a concave manner and be tight to resist water penetration. The joints of railings and bricks must be waterproofed. The bricks must have a certain moisture content at the time they are laid so they have a limited water suction capacity or there will not be a proper bond between them and the mortar. The ratio of sand and cement is also important.

Try removing the stains with a solution of equal parts of fresh Clorox bleach and water.

Railroad ties used as steps are slippery

Q. The railroad ties that make up my front and rear steps are slippery when wet and have caused people to fall. What can I do about them?

A. Scrub the ties regularly with a solution of ½ water, ½ fresh household bleach to kill off and remove the mold that grows on them. You can also try to roughen the surfaces with a steel brush attachment on a drill or stick strips of gritty fabric on the parts that are stepped on. Buy them in hardware stores and apply them to thoroughly clean and dry surfaces.

Nails on porch steps rusting

Q. The nails used when my new porch steps were built several years ago are rusting. The steps look like they have the measles. What can I do besides taking all the nails out to stop this? As it is, I have to paint the steps every spring.

A. The contractor should have used double hot-dipped galvanized, stainless steel or ring-shanked aluminum nails. If there aren't too many steps, you may want to have the nails removed and replace them with deck screws or one of the above type nails.

If this is not practical, you'll have to remove the rust by sanding it off the nail heads (although that's not going to remove the deeper rust that formed on the shanks), wire brushing it off, or by applying a liquid rust remover. Then prime the nail heads with a rust-inhibiting primer (apply at least two coats), using a small artist's brush. Paint them with two coats of an exterior latex deck enamel, working it all around as much as you can. Finally, paint the steps to blend the whole thing in.

Outdoor Furniture and Equipment

Table wobbles on bluestone patio

Q. My patio is made of bluestone and its surface is somewhat irregular, causing my table to be wobbly. I have tried moving it around but cannot find a spot where it won't rock. This is very annoying. Is there a simple way to steady the table besides using cardboard that gets wet?

A. You can settle your table once and for all by using plastic "Wobble Wedges" from Focus 12, Inc. Wobble Wedges can be purchased at The Container Stores wherever they are located. Their Web site is www.containerstore.com where you can locate the nearest store. Other stores and on-line sources are listed on the manufacturer's site at www.wobblewedge.com.

Half barrels for flowers

Q. I recently purchased two half barrels made of cedar for planting flowers. They will be outdoors in all kinds of weather. I am wondering if it's necessary to put any type of water proofing or sealer on them to preserve them.

A. Are you sure they are made of cedar? The half barrels available in all garden and nursery stores I am familiar with are made of oak from whiskey barrels cut in half. Their interior is burned which contribute to their durability. These barrels do not need any treatment. Mine have been out for 20 years and are still in good shape. If yours are really made of cedar, liberally coat them inside and out with a wood preservative and line the inside with 6-mil black plastic.

Cleaning plastic lawn furniture

Q. How do you treat the white plastic resin lawn chairs which have developed gray mold stains? I've tried Purex and Soft-Scrub but neither removed much.

A. I have had success wiping these chairs with a solution made of 1 part fresh Clorox bleach and 3 parts water to which is added a small amount of detergent. The mildew stains should be gone quickly after which you should rinse thoroughly. Once dry, apply a coat of Gel-Gloss.

Half barrel that has been sitting outside for over 25 years

Building a bird bath with waterfall

Over the years, I have received letters from readers who have built birdbaths with waterfalls, with helpful comments and leads for pumps for such waterfalls. They write:

• Six or 12-volt pumps are much better than 110 volts, as the wiring is simpler and less dangerous. Buy them at Fleet Farm Stores or through boat supply stores or catalogs which sell them as bilge pumps.

• You'll need a deep-cycle marine battery and a charger to recharge the battery when it's down and out. One reader says he runs his pump at 6 volts as, at 12 volts, the water jet is too strong. He also says that it will not hurt the pump to run it at 6 volts.

• One pump recommended by several readers is the Little Giant Pump from the Little Giant Pump Co. of Oklahoma City, Oklahoma (www.lgpc.com). There are plenty of others on the market available through garden centers.

Go to it. The birds need open water in winter when all is frozen. The pleasure of watching the variety of birds that flock to fountains is unmatchable.

Spiders plug up gas grill

Q. I have an outside gas grill that uses natural gas. It gets a lot of spider webs that cut off the gas. I used to be able to clean the grill myself but as I am getting on in years, I cannot do it any longer. The gas company charges me between $50 and $60 to do it. I was told to put moth balls in and around the grill but that did not work. I was also told to switch to propane gas. I would appreciate any information you can give me to eliminate this problem.

A. Spiders can really plug up the venturi holes that are essential for the proper and safe performance of gas grills. Spiders will plug these holes just as much with propane gas as with natural gas.

I do not know of a way to prevent spiders from plugging the venturi holes. I would advise you to budget the amount necessary for a gas technician to prepare your grill for safe operation. It's a small price to pay to ensure you won't blow yourself up or burn your house down.

Cleaning a bronze and brass sun dial

Q. My bronze/brass pedestal sun dial, thought to be about 100 years old, has badly weathered over time. Although I don't want a bright finish, I would like to clean some of the scale and oxidation that has built up in its highly-ornate pedestal portion. What products and procedure would you recommend?

A. Try Wright's Brass Cream first. If this is not enough to achieve the results you want, try Wright's Copper Cream, which is stronger. Both bronze and brass are alloys of copper with other metals. If you cannot find these products locally, call My Brands at 888-281-6400 for the name of the nearest source or visit their Web site www.mybrands.com or at Wright's Web site at www.jawright.com.

Clear sealer for wooden mailbox

Q. I have made a wooden mailbox and painted it pure white with flowers on the lid and a bird on the front. Because the mailbox will be outside, I want to use a sealer on it. However, varnish will leave an amber shade and all polyurethane sealers are for interior use. Please tell me if there is any sealer I can use that won't turn my white mailbox amber.

A. Your mailbox sounds beautiful, and I understand how proud you are of it and why you would want it unaltered by the sealer.

Rejoice! You can use an exterior acrylic polyurethane varnish (they do exist); it won't alter the color of the mailbox and will last a long time.

Loud noise from neighbor's AC

Q. Our new neighbors have installed an air conditioning and heat pump unit. It stands on a concrete slab outside, between their home and ours. The noise is overwhelming and, when the unit is running on high, our concrete floor vibrates. Is there a buffer that can be installed to eliminate this noise? We appreciate any help you can give.

A. There is something you can do to reduce both the noise and the vibration of your slab, but you need your neighbor's cooperation, as it has to be done from their side—and, hopefully, at their expense if they are good neighbors.

I once successfully solved this problem for someone by building a two-faced brick wall with each brick set at an angle (instead of the bricks laid in a running bond, as is usually done). This made for a sawtooth pattern that is very effective in deadening sound. Because of the configuration of the bricks there is also a space between the two faces, and the sound bounces on the staggered bricks of the outer wall.

The wall should be built on the edges of the concrete pad that the air conditioning unit is on, facing your house and with side wings around the unit, but should still allow access for servicing. The wall should be about 1 foot higher than the unit. To reduce the vibrations, the unit should be set on heavy-duty rubber blocks.

Lawns

Re-grading a lawn

Q. In reading your columns, I have always been aware of your emphasis on making sure soil is graded properly for drainage. Very fortunately, I have never had a problem with water in my basement. Now, though, I am afraid I may have created a situation where there is a potential for a water problem.

I am living in a home built in 1955, with very sandy soil. However, there were massive shrubs (some sort of evergreen) growing all along the front of the house that I'm sure were put in when the house was first built. They spread 8 to 10 feet into the yard and had never been taken care of. You know what happens next. I hired my teenage boys to chop, haul and dig! The yard is ever so much bigger now, but after the removal of roots and stumps, the ground is about 6 inches shallower than it used to be! I immediately realized that this calls for "correct grading," but I am unsure of how to go about it.

In order for me to act preventively and do it correctly the first time around, I hope you can give me specific pointers. I am not sure if I should merely bring in a huge load of topsoil to fill in the "trench." Should I fill a couple of inches with gravel and then top off with dirt to increase drainage? How far up the foundation wall should the top be? The topsoil along the front of my house (next year I will attack the back) is about 6 inches lower than the rest of my front yard. This shallow area extends from the foundation wall about 10 feet toward the street and about 40 feet along the foundation. The street-side edge of my property has a curb. My soil is very sandy and drains well. How should I repair the trench so that I can best grade the front yard and keep water from finding the low point of my yard and seeping into my basement?

A. You are wise to think about doing the work now. The fact that you have had no water problem so far is no guarantee that you won't have any in the late winter or early spring, when the snow melts—and even this fall under some special weather circumstances. Once the sand gets wet and freezes, it will no longer absorb water and the possibility is strong that water collecting in the "trench" will run down the side of the walls and leak into your basement. A worse scenario is that, if your foundation wall is made of cinder blocks, the frost could cause the walls to crack.

You do not need gravel at the bottom of the trench. Have a load of good topsoil delivered and fill in the depression; from the measurements you gave me, it looks like you may need a minimum of 7 yards of topsoil. Remember to keep a clearance of 4 to 6 inches between the topsoil and any wood or other type of siding. Slope the ground gently away from the foundation for as far as possible. If there is not enough slope between your house and the street curb to allow for a smooth and gentle grade slope, carry the slope as far as possible and count on the sandy soil to absorb the water away from the foundation.

Removing ivy from yard

Q. We just bought a home and it has a large patch of ivy growing on the ground on the side of the house. We would like to get rid of the ivy and possibly grow grass in that area. However, I heard that it is almost impossible to completely remove ivy without it growing back.

A. Ivy is, indeed, very difficult to remove. However, it can be done. You have to dig out as much of the root system as you can with a small, curved fork tool (like a forked hoe) and your hands. Any small pieces of root left will grow back. In that case, you can spray a contact herbicide such as Pronto Fast-Acting Brush Killer or Ortho Brush-B-Gon on the new, green growth, but such products should be used sparingly. You will have to use a sprayer that will never be used for anything other than an herbicide, as any residue on the sprayer parts will kill any leafy plant.

Raising a section of a sodded lawn

Q. We have been in our house 14 years now; it was built on an old cornfield. The yard was sodded. In one small section of the yard, the soil (sod) has sunk a couple of inches, in an approximately 10-foot by 10-foot area. I would like to raise this back up to the rest of the grass. Can I just lay another layer of sod right on top of the old, existing grass? Or do I have to remove the old grass? Sod is about the right thickness to bring things back up to normal. Any information will be appreciated.

A. No, you shouldn't lay new sod over the old. Doing so will cause the old sod to rot and develop mold that will kill the new sod. Moreover, the old sod prevents the new sod from getting nutrients from the soil itself.

You should remove the old sod with a spade by cutting it in squares that are manageable (this is known as "scarfing") and laying the squares aside on a plastic sheet. You do not need to go deep; a couple of inches is fine, and that is why a spade is the best tool—used horizontally, its flat blade allows you to cut the roots cleanly. Renting a sod cutter is an option for a very large area, but it is hardly worthwhile for an area that's just 10 feet by 10 feet.

Spread new topsoil in the sunken area to bring it back to the level of the adjacent sod and lay the sod squares back. Tamp the sod firmly and water it thoroughly. If you do this at this time of the year one good soaking may be enough, but if you do it next spring, water the area at least once a week if not more depending on the amount of rain you get. The main thing is to keep the soil moist until the sod has taken root, and this will take several weeks.

Mushrooms growing in new lawn

Q. Last spring, I had a new lawn put in. It looked lush and beautiful until about the end of summer. At that time, mushrooms began to sprout everywhere. I plucked them daily in hopes that they would not spread (I wish I could have sold them as there were so many!). I am hoping that you might know of a solution to my lawn problem. Is there a spray or application of some sort that I can apply that will kill these ugly plants?

A. Mushrooms are fungi that grow in moist soil with decaying vegetation. This means that there is some buried wood decomposing in your soil. It could be tree stumps, other parts of trees such as buried branches, construction lumber or wood chips mixed with the soil. The growth of mushrooms will stop if you remove the offending material, or when the decay process is complete. There is no need to use chemicals.

You may also want to have your soil analyzed to find out what nutrients it may need. Contact the extension service of your state university for instructions in taking soil samples to be sent to them for analysis and recommendations.

Ridding lawn of small saplings

Q. My lawn is covered with small oak saplings that grow faster than the lawn. What can I do to get rid of them? There are too many of them to think of pulling them out.

A. Can you hire a local high school student to pull them out for you? If not, keep mowing them with the lawn; they'll eventually die.

Underground cable installation causes weed problems

Q. The area between the curb and my sidewalk is covered with marble stone. Recently, the telephone and cable TV people installed underground cable with a machine to dig a trench. In doing so, they tore up the plastic barrier that had been put there to keep the weeds out. Now I have all kinds of weeds growing through the stones. I use Roundup; it kills the weeds, but I have to get down to pull the dead plants out. I am in my 80s and would like to avoid all this work every couple of months. Is there a weed killer that does the job permanently?

A. Ortho Season-Long Grass & Weed Killer is a ready-to-use, pre-emergent liquid herbicide that kills weeds and grass within three to five days of application, and poisons the soil within two weeks. Ortho claims that its effects last for months.

Round-up also makes Round-Up Extended Control. You should be able to find either in hardware stores or garden centers.

However, if the destroyed weed barrier was on your property and you put it there, you should contact the responsible telephone and cable companies and have them come back and re-install it. They disturbed the weed-control system that was in place, and should return it to its previous state. If the weed barrier was on city property and was installed by city employees, call the city office and see what they can do about getting it repaired; they may have more pull with the telephone and cable television companies than you do, or they may get their own crews to fix it.

Landscaping Issues

Landscaping timbers

Q. I would like to use oak wood for landscaping. Is this a good idea and how can I preserve the wood?

A. Why don't you simply buy pressure-treated landscape ties? Any brush-applied treatment is of short duration and most of these products are quite expensive. Hardly worth the trouble when there is a reasonably permanent alternative.

Moss grows on lava rock

Q. I purchased eight pieces of lava rock about five years ago. The pieces that are out in the open have developed green moss whereas the ones under the house overhang have not. We purchased them at a nursery but they didn't know how we could clean them.

My husband wants to get rid of them but I don't. Any suggestions?

A. The reason the uncovered rocks have developed an algae is that they are exposed to rain and absorb it. Algae develops through photosynthesis when sunlight reacts with water and carbon dioxide in the rock. You can remove it with an algaecide spray called Fountec that you can purchase from Kinetic Fountains through their Web site www.kineticfountains.com or by calling their toll-free number 877-271-1112. Wear safety glasses, spray Fountec, brush with a stiff bristle fiber brush, rinse. To retard the formation of new algae, spray Fountec again.

Artillery fungus grows in mulch

Q. We live in a townhouse development, and in the parking lot and around the grounds we have the artillery fungus. Is there any way to remove it from the cars without doing damage to the paint job? Any suggestions would be greatly appreciated.

A. Artillery fungus grows in decaying mulch, and is expelled with great force when maturing and when the temperature and humidity are right; it is especially attracted to light surfaces. This occurs in spring and fall. I don't believe you can remove it from cars. It is impossible to remove it from siding, so it would follow that the same applies to any other finishes. Don't you wish they would make glue like this?

The only thing I can think to suggest is that you have new mulch put over the old early every spring, or replace the organic mulch with Rubber Mulch (see Resources). Or park your cars away from the mulched areas.

Protecting rose bushes from winter weather

Q. I put foam covers on my rose bushes to protect them from winter's cold and laid stones on the four corner tabs to hold them in place. However, the wind ripped the stones off, breaking the foot pads. Is there a better way to secure them in place than piling dirt around their bases (difficult to do when the ground freezes before the covers should be put on and unsatisfactory if grass will be smothered by the dirt)?

A. Place an old auto tire around each cone.

Bricks used as tree border shed paint

Q. I painted the brick border around my trees with white Rust-Oleum last year. Now, after the winter months, half the paint has come off.

What can I use on them to insure they'll stay white longer than a year? And how can I remove the rest of the paint? I'm afraid to use an acid wash for fear it will burn a hole in my clothes and burn my skin.

A. No oil- or water-based paint is going to stick under the set-up you have. The bricks will absorb moisture from the ground and the paint will peel.

Remove the remaining paint by dipping them in a bath of hot water and TSP-PF. Use rubber gloves and old clothes to protect skin and wear glasses for your eyes. Then paint the bricks with a cement-based paint.

Mortar cracks in stone pillars

Q. The mortar on the fieldstone pillars on each corner of my 70-year-old house appears in good shape although there are some cracks between the stones at the base. Would painting the pillars with a clear water sealer help prevent further damage?

A. You should fill the cracks with a cement slurry rubbed in by hand (wear heavy duty rubber gloves). Let it dry. If you want to coat the joints, although that should not be necessary, apply boiled linseed oil with a small brush but only to the joints. The stones need no treatment.

Septic and Drainage

Septic system maintenance

Q. We recently saw a spate of ads on commercial television recommending adding the product advertised to a septic system to keep it from having problems. The gist of the ad is that if you don't add their product to your septic system, it will develop problems and have to be dug up at great expense. What is your recommendation? Is this hype or true?

A. This question comes up quite frequently and my answer has not changed. All the research I keep up with reinforces the fact that additives can actually be harmful to the proper functioning of a septic system. Some research suggests that adding bacteria can increase biological activity that stimulates the formation of methane gas. This, in turn, pushes non-digested, solid particles in the sludge into the liquid where it can be carried away into the leaching field, contributing to its eventual clogging.

Additives can also be harmful to the scum layer that builds up at the top of the effluent in the tank. This scum layer holds fats, grease and other detrimental substances that float up. Enzyme additives can cause this layer to break up and be carried into the leach field with potentially harmful effects.

There is no need, according to studies performed in various labs and universities, to add any product advertised as helping proper functioning of a septic system; all the bacteria needed for the process are contained in human feces.

But of great importance to the proper functioning of any septic system is to avoid flushing into it harmful product such as sizeable quantities of bleach, Lysol and other caustic products such as drain cleaners. Toilet cleaners and deodorizers that are installed in the toilet tank or strapped to the rim of the bowl should also be avoided even though they may claim to be safe. Also to be avoided are non-dissolving tissue, sanitary napkins, colored toilet paper and other foreign objects.

It is also essential to have a septic tank pumped out every three to five years depending on the number of occupants in the house and certain other individual considerations dependent on their own digestive systems.

I hope this will help convince those reading this that nothing need be added to a septic system for it to work properly in spite of the claims to the contrary made by manufacturers of the so-called essential enzymes.

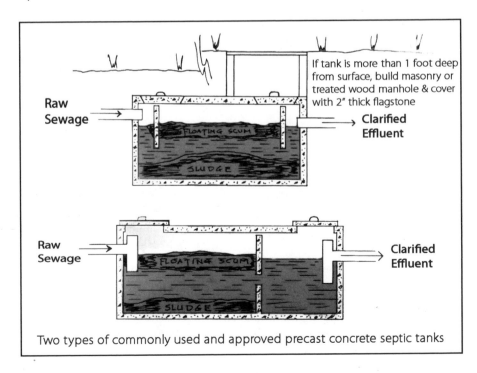

Two types of commonly used and approved precast concrete septic tanks

Dry wells fail because of silting

Q. The dry well receiving the discharge from my gutters stopped working three years ago; the gutters got full of leaves as I have many large trees on my property. Roto-Rooter could not open it as it was so packed. As it has been three years, do you think that the leaves and other matters have disintegrated? Or is there a liquid I could pour that would speed up decomposition?

A. If you are saying the dry well itself is packed solid, I have bad news for you; it's unlikely that this is due only to leaves. More than likely, the dry well has silted and that would explain why the Roto-Rooter mechanic could not open it unless there is a clog in the line that is so tight that the cutter could not dislodge it.

Dry wells have a limited life span for that very reason; they eventually fill up with silt. This is why I have not been in favor of them for years, having seen too many of them fail. In my opinion, it is best to discharge gutters on the ground onto a splashblock and have the grade sloping away so water does not linger against the foundation.

Pools and Ponds

Removing stains from apron around pool

Q. The cement apron around our pool has turned black in spots where water is apt to stand. Washing with TSP-PF hasn't helped. How can these spots be removed?

A. A loyal Canadian reader who has had the same problem solved it after many attempts with a variety of other products by pouring liquid pool chlorine on the stains, brushing them, and then rinsing. Use a stiff, long-handled, fiber scrub brush (buy in hardware stores), wear old clothes, and be sure to protect your eyes and skin.

Rust spot on pool

Q. We have a vinyl-lined pool. Upon removing the winter cover, we discovered a metal pin, which had lodged in a crevice. We removed it but it left an ugly rust spot about 3 to 4 inches long and 5 feet deep.

All attempts at removing this stain have failed. Stain removers quickly dissolve before reaching the spot. We have even tried an SOS pad at the end of a pole. We are assuming this rust spot will eventually eat away at the liner. Could you suggest how to remove it?

A. I doubt the rust spot will eat away at the lining; the source of the rust is no longer there. You may want to check with your pool maintenance company or the installer to make sure. If it needs to be removed—or you insist on doing so—you would have to lower the level of the water in the pool to be able to reach it. Buy product such as BioGuard Stain Remover or equivalent from a company that sells and installs pools.

Removing carpeting from around pool

Q. We purchased a home with an in-ground pool that has indoor/outdoor carpeting around the pool area. The carpeting is beyond cleaning and also has moss growing in various spots. We've had it pressure washed several times but the moss keeps coming back.

We would eventually like to put ceramic tiles or have textured concrete poured in place of the carpet. Meanwhile, we want to rip the carpet up and remove the glue from the deck. What is the best way to tackle this phase?

A. After you have torn the carpet out, the adhesive can be removed with boiling water. Work an area of about two square feet at a time, pouring boiling water over it and, as the adhesive softens, scrape it off with a broad-blade putty knife. Be sure you use heavy rubber gloves. Dispose of the dregs environmentally in a heavy-duty plastic bag and ask your local authorities whether it can be disposed of in the trash or if it needs to be dealt with as a hazardous substance.

Retiring a pool by filling it in

Q. I hope you can help me. Now that I am living alone, I cannot maintain a 32-foot by 16-foot in-ground, vinyl-lined swimming pool, and I would like to have it filled in. I don't want the job to be done incorrectly, so I would feel much more secure dealing with contractors if I have some background information.

Who should I call to do the job? What should I look up in the Yellow Pages? What should be done with the lining, diving board and slide? What should the pool be filled with? There is a wooden deck around the pool and a concrete section to anchor the diving board, as well as a 10-foot by 8-foot poured-concrete pad for the shed and the pump. What should be done with these? The gas has been turned off, but should anything special be done with the gas pipes in the ground? How about the electrical box in the shed in which the pump is plugged? Do you have any idea of the cost of such a project?

A. I assume you plan on staying in the house for quite a while, but you should still consider other options with the pool. You may want to consult with a local Realtor you trust to determine whether or not the existence of the pool adds a lot to the value of the house, if and when you decide to sell it.

But if you are firm in your decision to get rid of the pool, considering the several factors of the removal you are aware of, your best solution is to hire a general contractor. He or she will handle the securing of the gas line with a gas service company; the removal of the electric service with a licensed electrician; and the removal of the wooden deck, shed and concrete structures. He or she will also handle the removal or slashing of the bottom of the vinyl lining (to allow for drainage) and the filling of the pool with the appropriate local material—probably sand or bank run gravel, or excess material from an excavation job nearby (in this latter case, the material should cost you nothing).

The best way to find a reliable general contractor is to ask several neighbors and friends for the names of contractors they have used, and inquire about their experiences with these contractors; also be sure to ask for and check references. Get two or three bids and take the one you feel best about—not necessarily the lowest. Let your intuition guide you; nothing beats it.

Sorry, but I can't give you any idea of the costs involved, as much depends on local conditions, access to the site, and disposal costs.

Controlling algae on small pond

Q. A few years ago, I had a small pond built in the back of our house to enjoy watching wildlife come to drink or play in it. We also put fish in it. The pond is fed by underground springs which were obvious before construction as the selected area was quite marshy. It has been a source of great pleasure but there is a new problem. During the hot weather, some growth is developing and getting worse every year. It causes the water to become turbid and unappealing.

Do you know what this growth is and is there anything we can do to control it?

A. The unwelcome growth is probably some form of algae. It is dormant over the winter but grows back as the water temperature rises.

There is an effective control measure that is biologically safe: barley straw—but to be effective, it must be put in place very early in the spring before the algae has a chance to grow. Once the algae has bloomed enough to affect the quality of the water, the straw is nowhere as effective.

You can buy pre-packaged barley straw packed in mesh nets that include a float and an anchoring loop. They should be placed as close to the center of the pond since your pond is spring-fed but away from the outlet. They should be just below the surface but anchored to the bottom of the pond with a nylon rope and a weight such as a brick (select one with holes) or other kind of suitable weight. If your pond has water lilies, place the barley bags under a leaf.

The way it works is through the slow decomposition of the barley which releases chemicals that interfere with the growth of algae while encouraging the growth of other desirable aquatic plants. Isn't nature wonderful if we know how to nurture her?

You should be able to get these pre-packaged small bags of barley straw in stores selling plastic ponds, liners and pond supplies. You may also find barley straw in some garden centers. Check the Web site www.barleystraw.com for more information such as quantity needed, how it works and why. You can also call the manufacturer: Scrypton Systems Inc. The toll-free number is 800-229-5454.

Resources

1 Foundations

Masonry Lusta: Silpro Corporation, 978-772-4444, 800-343-1501, www.silpro.com

Thoroseal products: Thoro Consumer Products, 440-786-2100, www.chargar.com

2 Roofs & Siding

Drip Edge Vent, Flash FilterVent, Shingle-Vent II: Air Vent, Inc., 800-AIR-VENT, www.airvent.com

SV-10 Starter Vent: Lomanco, Inc., 800-643-5596, www.lomanco.com

Vented Drip Edge: Lamb & Ritchie, 888-802-8015, www.lambritchie.com,

Xtractor Vent X18: Benjamin Obdyke, www.benjaminobdyke.com

3 Windows & Doors

Insulated window shades: Gordon Window Decor, Colchester, VT, 877-966-3678 www.cellularwindowshades.com

Replacement parts: Blaine Window Hardware, Inc., 1919 Blaine Drive, Hagerstown, MD 21740, 800-678-1919 www.blainewindow.com

Sliding glass storm doors: Mon-Ray, www.monray.com, 800-544-3646

Strike plates: Door-Tite Inc., 3219 Creston CT, Dublin, OH 43017, 513-891-0210. Also available online through www.joneakes.com.

4 HVAC

Cast iron replacement parts: JHL Foundry, PO Box 1084, Mt Pleasant, PA 15666-1084, 724-547-8210

Clark/clock set-back thermostats: Clark Co., Inc., Underhill VT 05489, 802-899-2871.

Floor registers: Reggio Register Co., 24 Central Ave., Ayer, MA 01432-0511, 508-772-3493, www.reggioregister.com

FreezeAlarm: Control Products, Inc., 1724 Lake Drive West, Chanhassen, MN 55317, 800-947-9098, www.protectedhome.com

Freez-Warn: Freez-Warn, PO Box 325, 40 N Main St, Sharon, CT 06069, 860-364-0332, www.freez-warn.com

Gordon Wrench: The Gordon Tool Co., Inc., 14851 Jeffrey Rd. #22, Irvine, CA 92618-8022, 949-552-7613, www.gordonwrench.com

Radiator covers: ARSCO Manufacturing Co. 3330 East Kemper Road, Cincinnati, OH 45241, 800-543-7040, www.arscomfg.com

System 2000 Boiler: Energy Kinetics, 103 Molasses Hill Rd., Lebanon, NJ 08833. 908-735-2066, www.energykinetics.com

5 Kitchens & Baths

Broken part repairs: Don McElwain, 16 North Street, Bristol, VT 05443, 802-453-2648

Kampel SeamFil: Kampel Enterprises, Inc., PO Box 157, 8930 Carlisle Rd., Wellsville, PA 17365-0157, 717-432-9688, 800-837-4971, www.kampelent.com/seamfil.htm

Marble Hand Polishing Powder: Gawet Marble & Granite, Inc., Route 4, Center Rutland, VT 05736, 800-323-6398, www.vermontel.net/~gawet/

Metal cabinet replacement parts: Blum, Inc., 7733 Old Plank Road, Stanley, NC 28164, 800-438-6788, www.blum.us

Nok-Out: Osburn Distributors, LLC, 888-600-6673, www.nokout.com

See Free (mirror defogger): Clear Products, Toronto, Canada, 866-256-8161, www.clearproducts.com

6 Interior Surfaces

Flexi-Wall: Flexi-Wall Systems, 800-843-5394, www.flexiwall.com

GCFR Grout & Concrete Film Remover: Miracle Sealants Co., 800-350-1901, www.miraclesealants.com

Grout colorant: Aqua Mix, Inc., 800-366-6877, www.aquamix.com

Hillyard's Super Shine-All: Hillyard, Inc., 800-365-1555, www.hillyard.com

Host Dry Carpet Cleaner: HOST/Racine Industries, 800-558-9439, www.hostdry.com

Hotsy pressure-washer: Hotsy, 800-525-1976, www.hotsy.com

Squeak-Ender: E&E Engineering, 800-854-3577, www.squeakender.com

Squeeeeek No More, Counter Snap: O'Berry Enterprises, 800-459-8428, www.squeaknomore.com

7 Insulation

Drip Edge Vent, Flash FilterVent, Shingle-Vent II: Air Vent, Inc., 800-AIR-VENT, www.airvent.com

Xtractor Vent X18: Benjamin Obdyke, www.benjaminobdyke.com

8 Critters

Bat information: Bat Conservation International, Inc., www.batcon.org, 800-538-2287

Bat Zone at Cranbrook Institute of Science, 248-645-3232, obcbats@aol.com, www.batconservation.org

Bird-X YardGuard pest animal repellers: Bird-X, 800-662-5021, www.bird-x.com

Gnatrol: Valent Corporation, 800-89-VALENT (898-2536), www.valent.com

Lavender sachets: The Store, Waitsfield, VT, 800-639-8031, www.vermontstore.com

National Pest Management Association (NPMA): National Pest Management Association, 703-352-6762, www.pestworld.org

Controlling birds and animals humanely: Nixalite of America, Inc., 800-624-1189 or 309-755-8771, www.nixalite.com,

Revenge Pantry Bug Traps: Gardener's Supply Company, Burlington, VT, 800-427-3363, 888-833-1412, www.gardeners.com

Rubber mulch: Rubber Mulch, 888-436-6846, www.rubbermulch.com

Squirrel Away: Scrypton Systems, Inc., 800-229-5454, www.squirrelaway.com

Stuf-Fit: Allen Specialty Products, 800-848-6805. Also available through www.absolutebirdcontrol.com

Victor M702 Sonic Pest Chaser: Woodstream, 800-800-1819, www.woodstream.com

9 Outside the House

Barley straw: Scrypton Systems, Inc., 800-229-5454, www.barleystraw.com

Fountec: Kinetic Fountains, 877-271-1112, www.kineticfountains.com

Little Giant Pump: Little Giant Pump Co., Oklahoma City, OK, 888-956-0000, www.lgpc.com

Maine Brackets: The Maine Deck Bracket Company, Minot, ME 04258, 207-212-0888, www.deckbracket.com

Wobble Wedges: Focus 12, Inc., 800-635-4494, www.wobblewedge.com. Also available at The Container Stores, www.containerstore.com

Index

C

About the Author

Henri de Marne is among America's best-known and most-trusted experts on residential housing. For more than 32 years, homeowners through the U.S. and Canada have relied on his weekly syndicated column for advice and information to maintain, repair, upgrade, and enjoy their houses.

He began his construction career in the mid 1950s, concentrating on all aspects of residential construction, repair, and remodeling. As a skilled researcher, holding a master's degree in arts and sciences and with an avid curiosity, he accumulated a vast store of knowledge in order to solve the myriad problems besetting the average homeowner.

In addition to his column, de Marne has contributed the first chapter of the Consumer Reports book *Preventive Home Maintenance*, written by members of the American Society of Home Inspectors (ASHI) and was senior consulting editor of a previous edition of the Readers Digest book *New Complete Do-It-Yourself Manual*.

He serves as an expert witness in construction cases, and as a consultant for homeowners, architects, engineers, builders, and condominium associations. As a member of ASHI (American Society of Home Inspectors) he inspected homes for prospective buyers until his retirement from the profession. He has taught courses on home inspection to the real-estate and appraisal industries, arbitrated construction disputes, lectured construction-industry groups on building techniques, and has written numerous articles for builders as a contributing editor of the *Journal of Light Construction*.

His column, "About the House," began in early 1974 in the late *Washington Evening Star*, which was at that time a large-circulation afternoon daily in Washington, D.C. The column was syndicated nationally in 1982 by United Feature Syndicate, and has appeared ever since in newspapers throughout the U.S. and Canada, under the title "First Aid for the Ailing House."

In that time, he has provided thoughtful answers to countless thousands of questions posed by his readers. It is hard to imagine a single question about houses that hasn't been raised and responded to, in plain language that the average homeowner can understand.

For this book, he has sorted through the extensive archives to choose the material that will be most useful. He has edited the answers whenever appropriate, for the organization of the book and to bring all information up to date. The result is a valuable resource for homeowners, enjoyable for browsing through, yet organized to make it easy to find information whenever it is needed.